Praise for *My Life in a Cat House*

"Cooper, who charmed readers with the best-selling memoir of her intrepid blind cat, *Homer's Odyssey*, returns with escapades of other past and present felines. Cooper's witty, breezy writing, her unabashed love of felines, and her admission that her spoiled cats have trained her will delight and resonate with cat people."

—**LIBRARY JOURNAL**

"Fans of *Homer's Odyssey* will rejoice upon hearing that Homer's owner, Cooper, has returned with more true cat stories...both hilarious and deeply moving. Readers...will delight in these anecdotes of cats who seemingly have something to say about everything. Fans of Vicky Myron and Brett Witter's *Dewey* and James Bowen's *A Street Cat Named Bob* will be highly satisfied."

—**BOOKLIST**

"If you've ever lived with a cat, then this book is for you ... In *My Life in a Cat House*, Cooper lovingly and humorously depicts the ups and downs of a life with cats and the ways in which they mimic human behavior and feelings. A fun read for all animal lovers."

—**NEW YORK JOURNAL OF BOOKS**

"A literary fur fix for Homer fans!"

—**CATSTER MAGAZINE**

"As Gwen shares the joys, sorrows, laughter and tears of sharing her life with her cats, both past and present, you will find yourself nodding in recognition and perhaps remember the antics of a cat long gone. You may even gain a deeper understanding of your own feline companions... Gwen is a brilliant writer who can evoke emotion like no other. Her writing goes straight for the reader's heart. *My Life in a Cat House* is a treat for the cat lover's soul."

—**THE CONSCIOUS CAT**

"Gwen has the uncanny ability to touch our hearts with her gift of conveying thought-provoking and heart-stirring emotions...Gwen's writing is unpretentious, it's authentic, it's REAL. Whether like me you have nearly all of Gwen's books, or if this one is your first, you will delight in her descriptive, often hilarious and loving stories about her cats."

—CAT CHAT WITH CAREN AND CODY

"There's something about Gwen Cooper's cat books that touch my heart like few others, and *My Life in a Cat House* is no exception. Whether you›ve enjoyed every one of Gwen›s cat books or this is your first, snuggle up with a cat or two while you›re reading. I guarantee with each turn of the page you›ll pull them just a little bit closer as you realize just how empty your life would be without their unconditional love."

—MELISSA'S MOCHAS, Mysteries and Meows

"This book perfectly encapsulates the unique and amazing experience of being owned by cats and the joy they bring into our lives. That alone is reason enough to read it."

—JAMES BOWEN, international bestselling author of *A Street Cat Named Bob*

"Gwen Cooper is the Queen of Cat Love—and in these fun and frisky stories, she perfectly captures all the reasons felines rule our hearts and our homes. No cat lover should be without this book, but more important, give it to the folks who haven't yet seen the light. At least they'll understand us better!"

—SY MONTGOMERY, bestselling author of *How to Be a Good Creature: A Memoir in Thirteen Animals*

"What a pleasure to read [Gwen Cooper's] beautiful stories, brimming with her cat-love and even more important her ability to get you to actually see her cats . . . You will want to see more and more. She can become your next obsession, as she has become mine!"

—JEFFREY MOUSSAIEFF MASSON, international bestselling author of *The Nine Emotional Lives of Cats*

"An elegant, incisive account of love, laughter, and the deep meaning and magic cats add to our lives."

—BRITT COLLINS, author of *Strays: A Lost Cat, a Homeless Man, and Their Journey Across America*

Praise for *Homer's Odyssey*

"Touching...one not to miss."

—*USA Today*

"This memoir about adopting a special-needs kitten teaches that sometimes in life, you have to take a blind leap."

—*People*

"Cooper is a genial writer with both a sense of humor and a gift for conveying the inner essence of an animal."

—*The Christian Science Monitor*

"Delightful...This lovely human-feline memoir, following in the footsteps of Vicki Myron's bestselling *Dewey: The Small-Town Library Cat Who Touched the World*, is sure to warm the hearts of all pet lovers."

—*Library Journal*

"A poignant story, well written with...tenderness and realism...Your life will be richer for having taken this journey with [Gwen and Homer]."

—*I Love Cats magazine*

Praise for *Love Saves the Day*

"Prudence [is a] sassy but sensitive feline heroine."

—*Time*

"Cooper brings readers a...tale that cat lovers will treasure...This book will make most readers laugh and cry, and probably lead them to wonder more often what, exactly, their pet is thinking."

—*Fredericksburg Free Lance-Star*

"Once again Gwen Cooper shines her light on the territory that defines the human/animal bond. In *Love Saves the Day*, she creates an emotional landscape so beautifully complete that we can't help but share in the heartbreaks and triumphs of her characters, regardless of their species. That, in itself, is a reason to stand up and cheer."

—**Jackson Galaxy,** star of *My Cat From Hell* and *New York Times* bestselling author of *Total Cat Mojo*

"*Love Saves the Day* eloquently explains why so many of us would do anything at all for our pets."

—**BARBARA DELINSKY,** *New York Times* bestselling author of *Escape*

What readers are saying...

"Gwen Cooper is the Nora Ephron of cat writers!"

—TERESA PESCE, Idaho Falls, ID

"I cannot get enough of Gwen Cooper's cat stories! They're a respite from this crazy world, and Gwen's vivid descriptions of caring individuals and courageous, inventive, funny, loving cats fill me with hope and an appreciation for the softer, kinder side of life."

—LISA SCHOELLES, Newbury, MA

"Gwen's new stories about her cats really connected on a personal level for me as a cat dad. I laughed, I cried, and I cheered at their adventures."

—MICHAEL MACIAS, Fort Worth, TX

"Gwen's stories showcase her wicked sense of humor and keen eye for detail. She nails both feline and human quirks. To top it off, she is an excellent writer, period. I start each story with the sense of anticipation that I usually reserve for dessert!"

—CAROLE LOFTIN, Atlanta, GA

"There is nothing more relaxing than reading one of Gwen's stories. They are full of energy, laughter, tears, and excitement. I never know what to expect as each story is so different and heartwarming."

—SHERRI SMITH, Jacksonville, FL

"Being a huge fan of Gwen's books, I greatly anticipated reading her new cat stories. I have not been disappointed! Gwen's writing is so visual and her thoughts and emotions so vividly described that it is easy to get drawn into each story and feel as if you are there watching as everything unfolds. These wonderful stories will make you smile, laugh out loud, even cry a little, and definitely leave you wanting more."

—DEBORAH CAPPA-KOTULSKI, Newington, CT

"Gwen Cooper has an incredible talent for bringing the reality of cat ownership to life on paper. From the desperate desire to gain the love and affection of a standoffish cat, to the pure bliss of a kitty nursing you back to health, Gwen shares these memories in a way that makes you remember every cat you've ever loved."

—AMANDA BROOKS-KASSAK, Alton, IL

"With a laugh and a tear, every story, every page truly touches your heart and soul."

—ALEXANDRA CAMPS, Panningen, the Netherlands

"What I truly love about Gwen's writing is she has that ability to paint such a vivid picture in my mind. As she tells these tales with clear description and fun wit I can actually visualize the cats while their story unfolds. I have enjoyed all of her books over the years and feel she is the author of what I consider the absolute best cat story ever written. Homer made such an impression on me when I read it that to this day when I see it in the bookstore, I take every copy and spread them out to be in front so some other lucky cat lover will pick it up and become lost in Homer's story. Now I may need two shelves to do the same with this, her latest book!"

—VICKI FARRETTA, Lynnwood, WA

"Gwen has an astounding caring and patience with all these furry characters! Cat owners will totally connect with Gwen's writing about a subject she knows and loves so well. I want to read any book she writes. You will, too. Thank you, Gwen, for these little treasures!"

—RONALD HOLMES, Clovis, California

"Every time I read Gwen's cat stories I forget everything around. They are full of emotions and make me laugh a lot. I'm always a bit sad when the tale is finished."

—TOMI TOMEK, Noiraigue, Switzerland

"I LOVE the short stories from Gwen Cooper about her cats, they are definite "feel good" reads! Each heartfelt and amusing story is something that any animal lover can relate to! After each of her stories, I look at my own cats a little more closely to see their fun quirks!"

—STACI CALLAHAN, Philadelphia, PA

Other Cat Stories by Gwen Cooper

Homer's Odyssey:
A Fearless Feline Tale, or How I Learned
About Love and Life with a Blind Wonder Cat

Homer: The Ninth Life of a Blind Wonder Cat

Love Saves the Day

Homer and the Holiday Miracle

The Curl Up with a Cat Tale series

My Life *in*
a Cat House

True Tales of Love, Laughter, and Living with Five Felines

GWEN COOPER

BenBella Books, Inc.
Dallas, TX

BenBella Books, Inc.
10440 N. Central Expressway, Suite 800
Dallas, TX 75231
www.benbellabooks.com
Send feedback to feedback@benbellabooks.com

Printed in the United States of America
10 9 8 7 6 5 4 3 2 1

Library of Congress Cataloging-in-Publication Data for the hardcover edition is available upon request.
978-1-948836-6-09 (trade paper)
978-1-946885-5-48 (e-book)

Editing by Leah Wilson
Copyediting by Karen Wise
Proofreading by Michael Fedison and Amy Zarkos
Text design and composition by Silver Feather Design
Cover design by Emily Weigel
Cover photos © Stocksy, Carles Rodrigo Monzo and iStock, Hein Nouwens
Printed by Lake Book Manufacturing

Distributed to the trade by Two Rivers Distribution, an Ingram brand
www.tworiversdistribution.com

Special discounts for bulk sales are available.
Please contact bulkorders@benbellabooks.com.

For the five fab felines who put the "cat" in Cat House:
Scarlett, Vashti, Homer, Clayton, and Fanny

*For my father, who taught me to love animals—
especially rescue animals*

And for Laurence, always

Contents

Author's Preface

Cat lovers love cat stories. We love seeing them on the news, finding and sharing them on social media, and exchanging them in real time with our fellow ailurophiles.

With the publication of my first cat book, the memoir *Homer's Odyssey: A Fearless Feline Tale, or How I Learned About Love and Life with a Blind Wonder Cat*, Homer and I found ourselves part of a vibrant online community that spanned social-media platforms and engaged us daily with cat lovers and their stories—tales that were always unique, because every cat is a one-of-a-kind original, but also allowed their readers to find common cause in the joys and challenges (*Why won't you eat this food??? YOU LOVED IT LAST WEEK!*) that all cat lovers share.

While a YouTuber can upload two or three new videos a week, however, and an Instagrammer might post two or three new photos a day, it takes at least a year to write and publish a book (and by book publishing standards, a year is lightning fast; most books take two years or longer). I wanted to try to find a way, through my work, to maintain the feeling of everyday immediacy that had flourished in Homer's and my online community, without relying too heavily on photos and videos as stand-ins for the deeper stories that had brought us all together in the first place.

Thus Curl Up with a Cat Tale was born, a story series that would deliver one all-new, all-*true* tale about our feline family—Homer, Scarlett, Vashti, Clayton, and Fanny—at the beginning of each month. The stories would be substantially deeper than a blog or social media post could be, while also being significantly shorter than an entire book.

My Life in a Cat House grew out of the Curl Up with a Cat Tale series. Some of the monthly stories haven't made it into this book, and some of the stories in the book won't ever be published as part of the monthly series. And, hopefully, by the time *My Life in a Cat House 2* rolls out in late 2020, there will be even less overlap between the two.

The book and the series may be different things, but they were born together and share the same DNA: candid snapshots of a life with cats lived in full, with all its everyday joys, sorrows, messiness, laughter, and imperfect *purr*-fection. The stories in this book don't follow any particular chronological order. Some focus on my "first generation" cats (Scarlett, Vashti, and Homer) during our years together in Miami and New York City, and some are about my husband's and my current owners—Clayton and Fanny—in our Jersey City row house. A few of these adventures have taken place within the last few months (or are still ongoing), while others stretch all the way back to my earliest memories of my very first kitten.

Perhaps you've been keeping up with Homer and the gang for a while, or maybe this is the first you've heard of any of us. But whether you're a new reader or an old one, in every story you'll find—along with the laughter and tears—a deep and abiding love for these entertaining, frustrating, and utterly captivating creatures who somehow always manage to steal our hearts.

I Choo-Choo-Choose You!

Pandora ("Pandy" for short) was a purebred Siamese and could only be described—although this phrase wasn't in common use twenty years ago—as a hot mess.

Some of her problems were obvious even to a casual observer. For one thing, Pandy was morbidly obese. She had all of a Siamese cat's fine-boned delicacy of frame from the shoulders up and the hips down. But her midsection carried an excess seventeen pounds of pure lard. The tiny, porcelain-doll perfection of her head and neck made for a jarring contrast with the enormous belly—ballooning out on each side of her body—that swayed ponderously as she walked. Watching Pandy stroll about the house always made me think of a song popular on Miami dance radio at the time, which admonished, *Shake it . . . don't break it . . .*

I loved Pandy dearly, but I was probably the only one who did, aside from Maggie, my boyfriend Jorge's mother. She didn't do a very good job of keeping her hindquarters clean, bless her heart. (Pandy, that is—not Jorge's mother.) Whether this was because her girth hampered her ability to reach around and *get in there*, or because Pandy had given up in some fundamental way, was unclear. But every upward flick of her tail revealed an incriminating brown ring, as permanently fixed as if it were tattooed to her fur, no matter how often or assiduously Maggie tackled Pandy with the Baby Wipes.

Pandy would unerringly zero in on the visitors and house-guests who were the least interested in cats, and when—after she'd repeatedly pawed at their legs for attention—the hapless visitors would finally relent and try to pet her, she would lash out violently, leaving confusion, claw marks, and little tufts of yellow Siamese fur in her wake as she fled for refuge under Jorge's parents' bed. And woe betide the unsuspecting cat lover who attempted a friendly scritch behind Pandy's ears and ended up pulling back a bloodied hand for their trouble.

At seven years old, Pandy still suckled daily at the long-dry teats of her mother, Persephone (aka "Persy"), from whom she'd never been separated a day in her life. This, according to Maggie, was the true source of what was alternately referred to as "Pandy's quirks," "Pandy's problems," or, perhaps most accurately, "Pandy's neuroses."

"Cats aren't supposed to live with their mothers their whole lives," Maggie would say. And then she'd add, "Nobody is, really."

In human years, Pandy would have been somewhere in her mid-forties. I thought about *Grey Gardens* and *The Glass Menagerie*, and the entire literary pantheon of bitter or dotty middle-aged spinsters who'd never left their parents' homes—and then I tried to imagine what I might be like if I were still living with my own mother when I was in my forties.

"Definitely not," I'd agree, with a shudder.

I was twenty-three and had just moved in with Jorge, my first serious relationship post-college. We were living in a small one-bedroom apartment in a two-story low-rise owned by one of Jorge's uncles, nestled deep in the warren-like side streets of Miami's Little Havana. The people living all around us had emigrated from the mountains of Cuba, and they kept chickens in the postage-stamp backyards of their tiny, ranch-style homes. It was an odd (and often irritating) thing to be living in Miami in the 1990s—among bustling traffic and construction and silvery skyscrapers gleaming on the horizon—yet wake up at five thirty every morning to the sound of roosters crowing twenty yards away.

My own family were also "animal people." My father liked to spend time at the stables where Miami's mounted police kept their horses, and the puppies we adopted came from these animal-loving officers, inevitably with some heartrending backstory: Misty, a petite German shepherd/whippet cross, had been thrown from a moving car on I-95; Casey, a yellow pit bull/Lab mutt, had been used as bait in a dog-fighting ring. And so on.

We made much of these dogs, conspicuous even in a neighborhood of pampered, pedigreed pooches as a family who "spoiled their dogs rotten." Often we came home to find that one or another of our neighbors' dogs had escaped from his own yard and was camped out on our front porch. We would joke that the neighborhood dogs must have some kind of communications network, a way of telling each other that while they all might be treated well, at the Coopers' a dog lived like a king! We laughed about it, but I do think we were always trying—

with years of love and slavish attention—to make up for those early traumas our dogs had suffered.

I'd always imagined that I would get a dog of my own when I finally moved into my first "grown-up" apartment. But the place Jorge and I shared was very small, without so much as a proper patch of grass for a dog to run and play on—and, as young adults striving to build our careers, the hours Jorge and I worked were long. I was running a youth outreach program that promoted community volunteering among middle- and high-school students. Jorge was a production assistant on commercial video shoots. When we weren't working, we were often at after-hours networking functions, trying to make the connections that would give us the next leg up. Nothing in our lifestyles seemed conducive to canine guardianship.

Still, as far as I was concerned, a home wasn't a home at all if there weren't any animals living in it.

The highlight of my week was always Sunday, when we'd go out to brunch with Jorge's parents and then back to their house to while away the afternoon until Sunday dinner. It was a joy to spend time with Pandy and Persy and Olympia—a slender, auburn-hued Abyssinian—along with the family dog, a coal-black pit bull named Targa. Targa was more utterly gaga over humans than any dog I've known before or since. In fact, Jorge's parents' house had been robbed three times (such was Miami in the '80s and early '90s) while Targa was in it—and, according to the one intruder the police had eventually caught, Targa had done little to foil the burglars beyond licking them ecstatically and bringing over her toys.

Targa may have loved people, but she hated all three cats with a deep and murderous hatred. I never witnessed any of it firsthand, but I heard stories of close calls and surprise attacks that very nearly ended in bloodshed. Jorge's parents never left Targa and the cats together unsupervised when they were out, and even when they were home they always kept Targa's muzzle close at hand.

The feeling was more than mutual. The cats delighted in finding little ways to goad Targa when they thought no one was looking. Pandy, in particular, would take malicious glee in peeing on Targa's dog bed the moment Targa left it unattended to play in the backyard.

As I said, many of Pandy's problems in life were apparent at a first glance. That Pandy was a menace to new people, however—or even to people she already knew; Jorge, his father, and his sisters bore their share of Pandy-inflicted war wounds—was something I didn't know initially. I didn't find out for months, until Maggie confided it to me one afternoon in a kind of shocked undertone, upon finding a blissed-out Pandy, purring and unconscious, draped across my legs. By that point, Pandy and I were already deep into the early stages of our four-year love affair.

Pandy and I fell for each other instantly, from the first day we met.

Jorge's family were a bookish clan, and I was a reader myself. Many a Sunday would find me lounging in one of the comfy chairs in his parents' living room, nose buried in a novel while Pandy sprawled on my lap or my chest, belly fat oozing out and around until her body was an enormous perfect circle atop which perched a teeny-tiny cat's head.

Her weight should have made her an unwieldy lap cat; the body heat generated by her bulk should have made her a sweaty, uncomfortable burden on a humid Miami day. But something about us just meshed, and neither of those things ever bothered me. Pandy's rumbling purr was a deep, intensely happy vibrato that sank into my chest and radiated through my entire body as I absentmindedly stroked her back or rubbed her chin in between turning book pages. If I got too immersed in my novel and neglected to pet her for more than a few minutes, Pandy would bonk her head against my hand or paw gently at my shoulder until petting was resumed. My fingers seemed to know instinctively how to find just the right scratching spots that would make her purr deepen, her half-closed eyes turned to my own in a gaze of such melting adoration that it could break your heart.

As for me, I sometimes felt that I hadn't known true serenity until those Sundays with Jorge's parents, when the late-afternoon sunlight would slant through the windows and transform the fur of Pandy's rising and falling chest, lying across my own, into a gleaming mound of golden flax.

Pandy's instant affection for me—unprecedented in the annals of Jorge's family lore—became something of a tall tale among them, the story about The One Person Pandy Liked. It was heady stuff for a budding, inexperienced ailurophile.

You heard all the time about people who one day discovered some latent talent or ability they'd never known they had. Maybe *I* was one of those people. Maybe I had this previously untapped, deeply instinctive understanding of cats. Maybe I intuitively "got" cats in a way that other people didn't.

Maybe I was secretly a cat *genius*.

And so, when one of Jorge's sisters announced one Sunday that her mechanic had found a litter of four-week-old kittens, and did any of us know somebody who might want them, I didn't hesitate before claiming one for myself.

It was another two days before Jorge's sister could drive out to her mechanic's garage to pick up the kitten, and I was in a fever pitch of excitement the entire time. For two nights, I tossed in bed with the restlessness of a ten-year-old on Christmas Eve. *A KITTEN is coming! I'm getting a KITTEN!*

I went to the pet store for a litter box and kitten food, and came home with a toy-filled shopping bag so large that I struggled to carry everything up the stairs to our apartment. I'd been an easy mark for the enthusiastic store owner, who'd probably closed up shop and gone home for the day after I left. (I imagined her calling her husband and saying, *Good news, Herb! We can go back to imported wine!*) I'd bought miniature mice by the dozen: some made from felt, some from plastic or sisal rope, some that rattled or squeaked when shaken, some with hidden compartments you could stuff with catnip. I'd gotten a toy that consisted of a circular sisal-rope base with a large metal spring jutting up from it vertically, at the end of which was attached a belled cluster of feathers. There was another circular toy, this one a plastic wheel with a ball trapped inside and slats through which a cat could shove a paw to push the ball around and around in an endless loop. And I'd bought balls in every color of the rainbow: some made of cloth and plush with stuffing, some that whirred and sparkled when pushed, others made from candy-colored plastic. Last but not least, I'd bought a toy worm made from three puffs of cottony material with a little bell attached to one end.

I spent the hour before the kitten arrived arranging this bounty strategically around the apartment as Jorge looked on, until our home resembled a kitty day-care center through which a dozen or so cats might troop at any moment, demanding entertainment.

"They always end up being more interested in the bag the toys came in than the toys themselves, you know," Jorge told me.

I knew that Jorge had far more experience with kittens than I did (I having no experience at all). Still, I silently pooh-poohed him. I knew the kitten would be delighted with this avalanche of playthings—would love the toys not only for their own sakes, but also because of all the love for her and excitement at her arrival that they represented. And we would be so much more than cat and owner, this kitten and I. From the very first look—from the very first *moment*—she and I would form an instant, unbreakable bond and be the best and closest of friends forever. These toys were merely the first step in that process.

At the very least, they certainly brightened up the place. Jorge and I didn't have much in the way of décor in those early days of living together—just a futon, battered coffee table, and highly weathered entertainment center in the living room; a hand-me-down circular plastic table and three chairs in the kitchen area; and another futon along with an ancient dresser in the bedroom. I didn't want the kitten to look around and wonder if maybe her luckier littermates had gone to better, fancier homes, while she'd drawn the losing ticket in the lottery of life.

Cats, I'd been given to understand, could be very judgmental creatures.

I'd barely finished arranging everything just so when the doorbell rang and Jorge's sister entered. She toted a kitten-sized lavender plastic carrier, across the top of which a piece of masking tape with SCARLETT written in black marker had been affixed.

One of the things I'd been looking forward to most was getting to name the kitten. I'd never been the one to name a pet before—with our dogs, that privilege had always fallen to my parents—and I'd seen naming rights as one of the adult prerogatives I would now assume with a cat of my very own.

"She was so dehydrated when the mechanic found her that she kept fainting," Jorge's sister explained. "So he named her Scarlett."

Any disappointment I may have felt upon learning that someone else had already named my kitten dissolved, along with my heart, upon hearing this. *The poor little thing!* I knew I could easily rename her. Young as she was, she wouldn't know the difference. But this name was so closely tied to her origins in life—and the hardships she'd endured before being rescued—that it seemed as if changing it would also erase something important and essential about her.

Scarlett, then, she would be.

Jorge's sister had placed the carrier on the floor at my feet, and I knelt before it, fumbling with the clasp until it sprang open. A tiny black nose poked its way out, quickly followed by the head and body of what was probably the smallest living creature I'd ever been close to.

She was a gray-and-black tiger-striped tabby, with a white belly and chest, white chin, and white "socks" on her lower legs and feet. I marveled at her miniature perfection—the little pink pads of her paws; the tiny, nearly imperceptible tufts of fur sprouting from the tips of her ears; the wee, feathery whiskers on each side of her nose, as if an adult cat's features had been rendered into something small enough to fit in a dollhouse. The next time I went to Jorge's parents' house, only a few days later, their cats would seem to me almost monstrous in size.

Fully emerged from the carrier, the kitten looked at me with wide blue eyes (which would turn a yellowish green in only a few weeks' time). "Hey, Scarlett," I said. I knew I must look like a giantess to her, so I made my voice soft. "Come to your new mama."

This was the moment I'd been waiting for. My mind soared off on flights of quasi-poetic fancy that even now, some twenty years later, I'm embarrassed to remember. This would be a moment of epiphany—a moment when the workings of Destiny (with a capital *D*) would be revealed. That I was about to publicly assume my previously secret identity as "Gwen Cooper, Cat Genius" was a given. Jorge and his sister—and even I, myself—would see that my immediate rapport with Pandy hadn't been a fluke. But it would be more than that, this happening of an instant that was fated to change all our lives. Our eyes would meet, Scarlett's and mine, and that meeting would strike a gong that would resound down through all our remaining years together.

For the merest fraction of a second, Scarlett's blue eyes rested squarely on my own. "Come here, baby," I said encouragingly.

I held my breath, waiting for Scarlett to leap rapturously into my outstretched arms, until my arms began to tire from being extended for so long. But still they remained empty of kitten flesh, rapturous or otherwise.

Scarlett's eyes seemed to glaze over—was I imagining it?—into a look of indifference. She looked at me, and then she looked through me, and then she kitten-waddled *around* me as if I were no more than an inconveniently placed traffic cone.

"Awwwww . . . look at her go!" exclaimed Jorge's sister.

When Scarlett had gotten about five feet away, she flipped suddenly in a kind of half-turn so that she was facing me again. She lifted one of her front paws slightly off the ground as her back arched and her tiny comma of a tail puffed up, and she did a funny little sideways crab walk.

She wants me to play with her, I thought, feeling the beginnings of a smile. Rising to my feet, I hurried over to where she was now standing and hunkered down again, stretching out one hand toward her. "Hi, baby girl!"

For a second time, the kitten turned a blank, wide-eyed gaze in my direction. Then she spun around and scurried off into the bedroom.

Jorge and his sister were watching, and I was painfully aware that the kitten had now rejected me not just once, but twice. But that was silly, I told myself. Of course she hadn't *rejected* me. She was in an entirely new and foreign place, after all—naturally she was a little thrown off. You didn't have to be any kind of a cat expert, secret *or* public, to know that much. So, trying to shift the tenor of my thoughts to more practical matters, I asked Jorge's sister, "Will I need to train her to use the litter box?"

"She'll probably figure it out if you just show her where it is," Jorge's sister replied. She leaned down to pick up her purse, then walked over to give Jorge and me each a peck on the cheek. "I should be getting home," she said. "I still have a half-hour drive ahead of me. Good luck with your new kitten!" she added, aiming a warm smile in my direction, as Jorge walked her downstairs to the parking lot.

We didn't have any big plans for that evening, having set aside the whole night to help our new kitten acclimate. Scarlett reappeared from the bedroom a few minutes later, and I watched as she ran around for a while, keeping an eagle-eyed lookout for any signs of distress or potential hazards that might have gone overlooked when I'd kitten-proofed the apartment. But Scarlett seemed fine in her new home—more than fine. She skittered around for a while, chasing shadows across the floor and invisible bugs up the walls, pausing every so often to impatiently knock one of the cat toys I'd bought out of her way. I crouched down a few more times—trying to get her attention by tapping my fingernails on the tiled floor or tossing a tiny toy ball in her direction—but Scarlett seemed to find my presence as extraneous as she found the toys themselves. Finally, right in the middle of hopping repeatedly into and then out of the shopping bag the toys had come in (thus fulfilling Jorge's prediction), she fell into a deep sleep while still sitting up.

I was pretty tired myself, not having slept much the two nights before. Whenever my family had brought a new puppy into our home, it was always an unspoken rule that the puppy would spend her first night in bed with one of us—born out of a feeling that nobody should spend her first night in a strange place all alone.

And so, as Jorge and I headed into the bedroom, I knelt and gently lifted the sleeping kitten in one hand, marveling at how easily she fit into my palm. It was the first time I'd touched Scarlett. My heart dissolved again at feeling her soft fluff, at seeing up close the little whiskers that swayed gently with her breath, the rise and fall of her tiny, perfect chest.

I carried her into the bedroom and deposited her gently on the bed, lying down next to her once Jorge and I had changed into our pajamas and turned out the lights. I'd thought her likely to sleep all the way through the night, so exhausted did she seem. But, at feeling us settle down next to her, Scarlett awakened, stood up, and bent into a deep, languorous stretch. Then, without so much as a backward glance, she clambered down from the bed and toddled back into the living room. When I checked a few minutes later, I found her asleep in a ball on the couch, her tail wrapped snugly around her nose and forehead.

I couldn't help feeling that the two of us hadn't exactly gotten off to a roaring start. Still, we were in the early stages of our relationship. It had been unrealistic to expect everything to happen all at once. There would be plenty of time for Scarlett and me to bond, I assured myself, and for that bond to blossom into everything I'd imagined it could be.

After all, tomorrow was another day.

ONE OF THE GREAT CHARMS OF LIVING WITH A DOG IS THAT A dog has a way of making you feel as if—unbeknownst to anyone else—you might actually be the greatest person in the world. And not just the greatest, but also the most fascinating. A dog might not understand anything you say beyond her name— from a dog's perspective, your monologues may sound like nothing more than, *Blah blah blah blah,* Casey, *blah blah blah*— but she'll still hang enraptured on your every word like ancient scholars trying to unravel the mysteries of the gods. Even Pandy the cat, in singling me out so decisively, had made me feel as if I just might be special and interesting in ways that I, myself, had never suspected.

Scarlett, however, had none of that particular brand of charm. Scarlett's great power was her ability to make me feel as if I might actually be the *least* interesting person that the entirety of human civilization had ever produced.

I would never have said that Scarlett was charm*less*. She was a kitten—she was charming by definition. Everything she did, every gesture she made, every time she chased some microscopic ball of fluff, or raised one miniature paw to her face in a grooming ritual (she was immaculately clean, my Scarlett was), or rubbed a fuzzy cheek against a table leg or doorframe to mark it with her scent, I was charmed. I was enthralled. Seeing her play and gambol about was an endless source of fascination.

I may have been fascinated by all things Scarlett, but Scarlett couldn't have been less fascinated by me. Watching her scamper around—as happy and healthy as any kitten, despite the ordeal of her earliest life—I wanted nothing more than to cuddle and play with her, to entertain her and find new ways of increasing her joy.

But if I walked into a room, Scarlett would either walk out of it or continue whatever she'd been doing with barely a glance in my direction. If she was asleep on the bed at night when I got into it, she'd wake up just long enough to hop down and head off to sleep on the living room couch. Or, if she was asleep on the couch and I sat down next to her—even if I sat all the way at the other end, as far from her as possible so as to avoid disturbing her catnap—she'd promptly decamp for the bedroom and snooze in there.

"Seriously—what the hell?" I said to Jorge one day, as we watched Scarlett unceremoniously exit a room we'd just entered and I fought the sudden impulse to sniff under my arms for offensive body odor.

Her kitten fluff, which refused to lie flat no matter how strenuously she tried to lick it into place, was a sore temptation for my fingers. How I longed to feel the warmth and softness of her fuzzy little body! Scarlett didn't shrink from my touch, exactly, when I tried to pet her, nor did she violently lash out. Rather, she took no visible notice of my caresses one way or the other. She'd just kind of slide out from under my hand, like someone absentmindedly brushing lint from their shoulder, and trot off to do something else.

That she took no interest in the treasure trove of toys I'd bought her probably goes without saying. I'd dangle a little felt mouse enticingly by its tail over her head, and she wouldn't even muster a half-hearted swipe at it. I'd bend the vertical spring attached to the sisal-rope base until its feathered and-belled crest touched the floor, then let it spring back to make the feathers flutter and the bell tinkle merrily. "Look, Scarlett!" I'd say in my best talking-to-a-kitten voice. (It was very similar to my sing-songy talking-to-a-dog voice.) Widening my eyes to feign great astonishment, I'd say, "What's *this*, Scarlett? What's *this*?"

That voice had never failed to rouse even the sleepiest dog to near frenzies of tail-wagging, hand-licking, and playful crouching. Even Pandy always responded to it with louder purrs and spirited Siamese mews of acknowledgment.

Scarlett, however, would merely level a bored gaze in my direction. *It's a bunch of feathers, stupid.* And that was all the response I'd get.

"At least *somebody's* playing with them," Jorge observed, coming home one day to find me flat on my belly in front of Scarlett, a cat toy in each hand, absorbed in yet another fruitless attempt to engage her attentions.

"Don't you dare say *I told you so*," I warned him.

Naturally Scarlett liked to play—she was a kitten, after all. When she wasn't sleeping or eating, playing was all she did. She chased her tiny tail in dizzying circles until she appeared little more than a gray-and-white blur. She would frequently do that sideways flip and crab-walk that I'd come to call "Ninja kitty." She found bits of dust or tufts of her own shed fur and chased them furiously from one end of the apartment to the other, or sat up on her hind legs like a prairie dog and tried to catch the dust motes that appeared like flecks of gold in the sunbeams that fell through the windows.

Scarlett's favorite game of all was to chase a crumpled-up ball of paper around the room, batting it furiously between her front paws and then knocking it just far enough out of reach that she'd have to run after it. It was her favorite game, that is, if she happened to find the wadded paper ball on her own. If, however, I obligingly crumpled up a new piece and tossed it over to her, she'd watch the paper ball as it rolled to a stop at her feet and then stare at me, as if wondering why an apparently sane person would throw garbage around her own home.

Scarlett had, at a minimum, caught on to the fact that it was I, and not Jorge, who was her primary caregiver. As the weeks passed and her kittenish cheeps matured into more adult-sounding tones, she developed what Jorge and I called "Scarlett's mother-in-law voice," a harsh, guttural, and distinctly unloving meow that sounded like *MRAAAAAAA* and was deployed only when Scarlett felt she had something to complain about. And I was the only one she ever complained to.

When her food bowl was empty, for example, or her litter box was dirty—even as a kitten, Scarlett had exacting standards when it came to litter box maintenance—I was the one who heard about it. "*MRAAAAAAA,*" Scarlett would say, sitting on her haunches on the floor directly in front of me if I was on the couch watching TV. If I didn't jump up immediately to attend to her, she'd advance to the coffee table, making sure to position herself directly between me and my view of the TV screen. "*MRAAAAAAA,*" she'd repeat. "*MRAAAAAAA!*" If I was reading a book with my legs stretched out, she'd sit on my knees until the pressure of her weight made the joints ache and demand, "*MRAAAAAAA.*" And if I didn't look up from my book quickly enough, she would put one paw directly onto the page I was reading, insisting at the top of her voice, "*MRAAAAAAA!!!*"

"All *right!*" I'd finally say, getting up and scurrying off to attend to whatever it was that was bothering her. "You know," I suggested once, looking back at her over my shoulder, "it wouldn't kill you to say something *nice* every once in a while."

To Jorge, Scarlett paid literally no attention at all—and he, after a few attempts at petting her or tossing her paper balls, was content to let her go her own way without any further interference. "Some cats just don't like people," he said.

He was right, of course. There were cats who flat-out didn't like humans. Nevertheless, it struck me as a premature judgment in Scarlett's case. She was still so little! She'd been only four weeks old when we'd gotten her—and she was barely twelve weeks old now. Surely, a kitten rescued at such a young age, and adopted immediately into a loving home, should be capable of forming an emotional bond with *someone*.

I felt vindicated a few days later when, sitting on the couch, I felt a tickling at the back of my head. Twisting my neck just a fraction so I could see her from the corner of my eye, I observed Scarlett sitting behind me on the futon's arm, her face buried deep in my hair as she nuzzled gently and insistently. I remembered my mother telling stories like this about Tippi, a little beagle/terrier mix she and my father had adopted before I was born. Tippi had been so attached to my mother as a puppy that she'd insisted on sleeping each night on my mother's pillow, nestled in her hair.

Awwww, I thought, and my heart began to puddle—what could this new behavior of Scarlett's be if not, at long last, an affectionate gesture? *I knew I was right!* I thought, and decided not to say anything to Jorge—not right away, at least. I'd let him discover the two of us like this on his own one day. I tried reaching my hand slowly back and around to stroke Scarlett's fur as she pressed her nose and whiskers all the way into my scalp. But she wriggled out impatiently from under my touch, and—not wanting to push her too far, too quickly—I left her to it, murmuring, *Good Scarlett . . . sweet kitty . . .*

This went on for some days, and I began to cast a complacent eye over Scarlett as she tore around the apartment, absorbed in her play. I still longed to rub beneath her little white chin and hear her purr of contentment, to watch her stir and sigh as she fell asleep in my lap or curled up next to my leg. She wasn't yet what anyone might call demonstrative, aside from those moments she spent buried in my hair. But a good time was coming—I could feel it. We were finally starting to bond, my kitten and I, and the rest would happen in its own time.

All that newfound complacency was shattered a couple of weeks later, however, when I happened to catch a glimpse of Scarlett in my peripheral vision, sitting behind me with a thick lock of my hair—*which she'd gnawed off my head*—hanging from her jaws.

"What the—" I sat bolt upright, the book in my hands tumbling to the floor. "Is *that* what you've been doing this whole time?!"

I'd been blessed (or cursed, depending on Miami's up-and-down humidity) with an extraordinarily full head of hair—enough that I hadn't noticed from one day to the next as bits of it had begun to disappear. But now, disbelieving at first, I reached around and felt what I realized was a decidedly thinning patch on the back of my head.

I told myself to stay calm. After all, was it even *possible* for one smallish kitten to chew a bald spot right into a person's scalp?

With mounting horror—as I clutched at a limp clump of wispy strands that had, only recently, been a thick tangle of curls—I decided that, yes . . . yes, it was.

"*Oye!*" I cried. "*No se hace!*" (Jorge and his family disciplined their own cats in Spanish, and I'd fallen into the habit myself.) "*Malo gato!*" I shouted. "*MALO GATO!*"

Startled, Scarlett leapt from the couch and I chased her, trying to wrest the lock of my hair from her mouth. Obviously I didn't think I could stick it back on, but at least I could stop her from swallowing it, if that was indeed her plan. After about three minutes of pursuit—she nimbly evading my grasp, I feeling more than a little ridiculous to be lumbering so ineffectually after a *kitten*, for crying out loud—she darted under the bed and out of my reach.

She emerged a little while later but ignored me for the rest of the day, not even bothering with the litany of complaints she usually took up around twenty minutes before her dinnertime. The small pot of cat grass I bought the next day—as a more suitable source of fiber, as well as a gesture of reconciliation (*like an erring husband coming home with flowers*, I thought wryly)—remained untouched.

STRICT HONESTY COMPELS ME TO SAY THAT THERE ACTUALLY *WAS* one game Scarlett enjoyed playing with me—although describing it that way requires loose definitions of the words *game*, *play*, and *with*. The "game," such as it was, consisted of Scarlett hiding behind a table leg, or underneath the couch or bed, and leaping out at me as I walked past. She'd hurl herself at my ankles, latching on with her teeth and front claws while her back claws kicked at me furiously, "bunny feet" style, until she drew blood, or I tripped and fell, or both.

I wore heels to work every day. I didn't have the greatest balance in them, and I was always terrified when Scarlett jumped at me that a pointy heel might inadvertently puncture her head or vulnerable belly. In the process of trying to quickly shuffle my feet away from Scarlett and remain upright at the same time, it wasn't at all unusual for me to end up tumbling to the ground, falling heavily against whatever piece of furniture Scarlett had just jumped out at me from. I bruised rather easily, and my arms, shoulders, and chest were soon spotted with incriminating black-and-blue marks.

It couldn't really be said that Scarlett played this game of hers "with" me, because if I made any attempt to touch or even look at her, the game was immediately over, and off she'd run. And even describing it as "play" seems inapt, because Scarlett's surprise attacks didn't feel playful so much as . . . mean-spirited. How else could I describe it? Whenever I hit the tiled floor of our apartment with a loud "Oof!" I always sensed that Scarlett was enjoying a silent kitten laugh at my expense. *It's funny when humans fall down!*

Still, I was pathetically pleased at receiving even this much attention from my otherwise aloof feline. Like her complaining, this was something else Scarlett did only with me—never with Jorge. Maybe it was true, I reflected (trying not to notice how desperately I was grasping at straws), that you only hurt the ones you love.

Things came to a head one day at work. The school-based community service program I ran was considered a crime prevention initiative, and our administrative space—located in a small office park in southwest Miami—had been donated by the Miami police department. Our next-door neighbor was the bomb squad, and I spent many a happy work break in our shared parking lot, watching as the puppies who were being trained to sniff out explosives bonded with their handlers.

On this particular day, I'd taken off my blazer in the heat of a broiling afternoon, and the sleeveless silk top I wore underneath left my battered arms bared. I didn't really think about it until one of the bomb-squad officers I was friendly with—a six-foot-two wall of muscle named Eddie del Toro—followed me through reception and into my private office as I returned from lunch, closing the door behind him. Startled at this unprecedented behavior, I turned to face him with a question mark clearly written in my raised eyebrows. Eddie took one of my hands gently in his own, looked earnestly into my eyes, and said in a soft, reassuring voice:

"Just tell me his name and where I can find him."

This has gone far enough, I told myself a few minutes later, as I stalked out to my car to retrieve my discarded blazer. Naturally I'd understood the conclusions Eddie had reached upon seeing my bruises—and why his first thought had been *abusive boyfriend* and not *evil kitten*. I'd explained to him about Scarlett, but I'd still had to show off the corroborating itty-bitty claw marks on my ankles, and then exaggeratedly mime tripping over a small cat a few times, before I'd finally been able to send Officer Eddie— laughing and shaking his head—back over to the bomb squad.

Things were getting ridiculous. I didn't intend to start going around in turtlenecks and wigs to cover up bruises and bald patches inflicted upon me *by a kitten*, as if I were the hapless heroine in a Lifetime movie. Something about an abusive, emotionally unavailable cat and the woman who couldn't help loving her anyway. *Seduced by a Feline*, I thought. *A Kitten to Die For: The Scarlett Cooper Story.*

I headed to Barnes & Noble after work that evening and bought an advice book about kittens. Once I was home, I turned immediately to the chapter on how to deal with early signs of aggression. The book advised that, should your kitten show a tendency to attack you in overly aggressive play, you should say

No! in a firm voice, and then provide the kitten with an appropriate toy as a substitute for your own flesh.

"No!" I said to Scarlett the next time she leapt out at me from under the coffee table. Reaching down carefully to remove her, claw by claw, from around my ankle, I held out one of the neglected toy mice that had been gathering dust in the corners of our apartment these past three months. *"Here,"* I told her firmly, "is your appropriate toy."

Scarlett looked at the felt mouse in my hand with an air of disdain. Then, with all the offended dignity of a society matron in a state of high dudgeon, she turned her little rump to me and strode away, swishing her tail twice to emphasize her displeasure. This silent treatment lasted until Scarlett's next surprise attack—which happened about fifteen minutes later.

It was a pattern we repeated four or five times over the course of the night, always with the same results. The book advised that, if all else failed, the best way to break a cat of aggressive habits was simply to ignore her. When she wrapped herself around one of my ankles, I should detach her and then disregard her. I wasn't to talk to her, pet her, try to engage her in play, or even so much as look at her. There was no worse punishment for a playful young kitten, the book assured me, than being denied interactive play time with her human.

"HA!" I exclaimed when I read this. The next day, I dropped the book off at the Salvation Army donation bin.

I TOLD MYSELF THAT SCARLETT WAS JUST INDEPENDENT—AND, moreover, that being independent was a good thing. I was a little fuzzy as to why, exactly, independence was a desirable quality in a companion animal. (It wasn't as if I were preparing Scarlett to pursue an equitable marriage or high-powered career someday.) Still, "independent" was one of those generically positive descriptors—like "attractive" or "has good taste"—that most people were pleased to have applied to themselves. Why wouldn't I want it applied to my cat?

I also told myself—and actually knew, deep down at the bottom of things—that it wasn't Scarlett's job in life to interact with me in any specific manner, or to make me feel a certain way about myself. Our relationship was based on what *my* job was—and it was my job to keep her healthy and safe, to love her no matter what her personality turned out to be, and to give her everything she needed to live a happy life on her own terms.

But what if, I sometimes wondered, I simply wasn't able to give her that happy life? What if Scarlett and I had been mismatched—what if the reason she hadn't yet "chosen" me was because she'd been meant for somebody else, and I'd interfered somehow in her destiny? Maybe Scarlett's true human soulmate—a person who could make her happier than I ever could—was still out there, forever to remain undiscovered.

It would be a gross mischaracterization of our relationship to say that it was all bad, that I didn't love her, or even that I wished I'd gotten another kitten instead. The truth was, I'd fallen irretrievably in love with this bossy, snooty, semi-sadistic little imp who—when she wasn't tormenting me or demanding something from me—seemed otherwise uninterested in my existence.

I didn't love her just because she was mine (although that— as with any other parent, cat or otherwise—would have been enough to raise Scarlett above all other kittens in my eyes).

I loved the little freckle of black fur, which I called "Scarlett's beauty mark," resting on the left side of her upper lip. I loved the way she cocked her head thoughtfully to one side before leaping at a paper ball. I loved the serious, evaluating expression she wore as she sniffed at some new variety of food I put before her when she outgrew her kitten food. I loved the little sway of her backside as she walked away from me in a huff.

When she developed a large sore on her lower lip—the result of a feline herpes virus she'd inherited at birth from her mother, which would plague her on and off for the rest of her life—I fussed and fretted and dragged her to the vet (which didn't exactly raise me in Scarlett's esteem), and mixed the icky pink antibiotic formula the doctor prescribed with some water from a can of tuna, trying to make it more palatable. I'd give her some of the tuna itself afterward to get the yucky-medicine taste out of her mouth, as miserable over her obvious discomfort as if it were my own.

Sometimes, watching Scarlett nap peacefully on a pillow in a patch of sunlight, surrounded by toys she didn't seem to care about representing a love she didn't seem interested in—I thought about what might have become of her if she hadn't been rescued or found a home. I often took my teenage volunteers to local animal shelters, and had spoken with their staffers enough to know the kinds of things that happened to very small kittens left to fend for themselves on the streets. That Scarlett had been saved against all the odds—that she now had the privilege of being indifferent, if she chose, to a human who provided her with food and shelter and love—seemed like a kind of miracle. My cat was daily proof, in my own home, of goodness in the world. How could I not have loved her?

There are two sides to every story, and I'm sure that Scarlett would have had her own list of complaints about me if she'd been able to talk. She tries too hard, Scarlett might have said. She intrudes on the games I like to play by myself. I can't even stretch out comfortably on my back without her trying to rub the white fur of my belly—as if I were a *dog*! She disappears for hours from the apartment every day, and then turns up again whenever she feels like it. And she expects me to *cheer* about it like it's a big deal! She hogs the pillows on the bed. She'll open a can of tuna and, sure, she'll give me a *little*—but she still keeps most of it for herself.

One night Jorge and I were watching a rerun of *The Simpsons* on TV. It was a Valentine's Day episode, and Lisa Simpson had, as an act of pity, given a Valentine's card to a slow-witted boy named Ralph, whom nobody else in the second-grade class had even acknowledged. "I choo-choo-*choose* you!" Ralph read ecstatically from Lisa's card, which was decorated with a drawing of a smiley-faced train engine.

Crazy as it sounds, I was envious of that slow-witted little boy. He'd been chosen, and I had not.

It had been May when we first adopted Scarlett, and it was November when my boss sent me to attend a three-day national conference for youth outreach programs like ours. Although the conference was being held in Miami, the downtown hotel where I'd be staying was far enough away to make it impractical for me to get home to feed Scarlett twice a day. Jorge traveled frequently for work and was scheduled to be away himself that entire week. We couldn't find a pet-sitter willing to come all the way out to our neighborhood for what we could afford to pay, so Jorge's parents offered to take Scarlett for a couple of nights.

I arrived at their house early on the morning of the first day of the conference to get Scarlett and her gear—her litter box and extra litter, cans of food, her water and food bowls, her scratching post, her brush, her antibiotic medication in case her herpes flared up in my absence, and a few toys—set up in the guest bedroom. With its adjoining bathroom, Scarlett would have free run of a space nearly as large as our apartment. Keeping her separated from the other three cats—and especially from Targa—meant she would spend most of her time shut in by herself, except when Maggie could slip in for feedings and visits. Given how much Scarlett seemed to crave solitude, however, I didn't think she'd mind a few days of extra alone time. She'd probably see it as a vacation.

Scarlett sprang from her carrier as soon as I opened it. I'd spent half an hour that morning chasing her around the apartment to get her *into* it, and the fresh claw mark on my hand attested to just how reluctant to travel Scarlett had been. I tried to give her a conciliatory scratch behind the ears with that same hand now, but the decidedly cool manner in which Scarlett shook me off let me know that I hadn't been forgiven. Exploring the room with her little black nose to the ground, she seemed reassured to find so many things with her own familiar scent on them.

The window in Scarlett's room overlooked the driveway, and as I headed out to my car I saw her sitting on the sill, watching me. I crept over and, with one finger, lightly rubbed the glass over the bridge of Scarlett's nose. "It's only a few days," I told her. "I'll be back for you soon."

Scarlett opened her mouth wide in a mighty yawn, then hopped down from the windowsill and disappeared from sight.

I thought about her in between conference sessions during those three days and called Maggie both nights to see how Scarlett was doing. I'd be lying, though, if I said I worried about her much. Scarlett's independence—her apparent indifference to me, specifically, and humanity in general—had become an accepted fact. There would be someone to feed her while I was gone and to clean up after her, and she'd have her little paper balls and the stuffed worm—the only store-bought toy in which Scarlett had shown even the remotest interest—to play with. What more had she ever really needed?

This assessment seemed borne out by Maggie's reports when I called to check in. "I haven't heard a peep out of her," Maggie told me. "If I didn't already know she was here, I'd never guess there was another cat in the house." She added that Scarlett would retreat under the bed whenever Maggie entered the room, or else head for the bathroom where she could watch from an untouchable distance as Maggie put down food and cleaned out used litter.

"Don't take it personally," I told her. "Scarlett doesn't like people all that much." I realized, as I said it, that I'd been secretly angry at Jorge for saying something not very different, not so very long ago.

I'd dropped Scarlett off at Jorge's parents' house on a Wednesday morning, and it was around five o'clock on Friday afternoon when I arrived to pick her up. Jorge's parents had their own architectural firm and often worked long hours, and the house was empty as I let myself in with the key Maggie had lent me. Jorge's sister had been by earlier to release Targa into the backyard, and I poked my head out to say hi to her—and, of course, I stopped to give Pandy an affectionate hello as well.

"Hey, *Scarlettsita bonita!*" (Spanish for "pretty little Scarlett") I called cheerfully as I opened the door to the guest room. Scarlett leapt from the bed and ran over to where I stood, stopping a few inches away to sit on her haunches and look up into my face with bright-eyed anticipation. Scarlett had never once greeted me at the door like this—preferring, as always, to evacuate any room as I entered—although at the time I didn't register how unusual her behavior was. My mind was too occupied trying to figure out the most efficient way to get Scarlett and all her things loaded into the car and a route home that would avoid the worst of Friday rush-hour traffic. There was too much for me to carry out in one trip, so I decided to load Scarlett's gear into the car's trunk and back seat first, and then I'd return to the house to put Scarlett herself in her carrier and bring her out.

I had just slammed the lid of the trunk shut over the litter box when I heard it. The wild howling of an animal in great distress rose—sudden and sharp—to cut like a band saw through the peaceful tweeting of birds and humming of insects in the glowing, late-afternoon air.

Jorge's parents lived at the end of a quiet cul-de-sac, just beyond which lay a wooded copse. There were a few feral cats who lived among the trees who Maggie had arranged to have spayed and neutered some time back, and who she still continued to feed. They reminded me of Scarlett, with their tiger stripes and yellow-green eyes, and their persistent wariness of any human contact. Every so often they would emerge to sunbathe on the hot asphalt of the driveway, and I was always careful when I drove up to the house to make sure the coast was clear before pulling in.

My first, awful thought now was that, despite my precautions, I might have run one of them over. My stomach rose into my throat as I knelt on hands and knees to look beneath my car. Thankfully, there was nothing there.

Loud as they were, the howls had a curiously muffled sound. Maybe a stowaway had crept unnoticed into the trunk or backseat as I'd packed in Scarlett's things? But a thorough check of both revealed nothing. I also examined the wheel wells of all four tires and popped the hood to see if a cat, or some other small animal, might have crawled in to doze on the warmth of the engine and gotten trapped.

Nothing.

The howls sounded close by, but I couldn't find anything in or around my car to account for them. As I slammed the hood and doors shut, however, they escalated in both urgency and pitch. Thoroughly mystified, I stood in the middle of the driveway and turned in a slow circle, nerving myself to venture into the darkening woods for further investigation if I didn't spot anything immediately obvious.

The glare of the setting sun off the guest bedroom window, which had previously obscured my view inside, receded a little. And that's when I saw her.

Scarlett was on the windowsill. She stood high on her back legs, her front paws clawing desperately at the glass. She was looking directly at me; when our eyes met, she threw back her head and opened her mouth wide, yowling at the top of her lungs.

"Scarlett!" I cried. "Scarlett, I'm coming!"

For the second time, I felt my throat tighten and my stomach clench. I had no idea what was wrong with Scarlett—my only thought was that some unknown, terrible thing was happening to her. My hands shook, and I nearly dropped my keys as I fumbled with the lock to the front door of the house. I raced down the hall toward the guest room, nearly tripping over the purse I'd set down upon entering, and flung the bedroom door open.

Scarlett broke off mid-yowl when I came in, and the abrupt silence was as piercing as her cries had been. She leapt from the windowsill to land at my feet, whirling and dipping in frantic figure eights in front of me. At the head of each loop, she paused to rub furiously against my ankles from her cheek to her hip before resuming her spins once again.

I saw no blood, no swelling, no limping or hobbling, nothing to indicate any kind of injury or illness. I hadn't seen any sign of the other three cats when I came into the house, and I guessed they'd gone into deep hiding when the howling started. At any rate, they hadn't gotten into Scarlett's room to attack or upset her. Targa remained securely in the yard; I'd caught a glimpse of her sitting at attention just outside the glass door that led out back, looking anxiously into the house as a low whine rose in her throat. Clearly, Scarlett's cries had disturbed her, too.

"Hey," I said, gently. "Hey, Scarlett." I crouched down and reached out to her. I wanted to pet her, to try to calm her with the touch of my hand. But I hesitated. When had the touch of my hand ever meant anything to Scarlett?

To my surprise, Scarlett half-rose on her hind legs so that her head met my hand in midair. I tentatively scratched along the side of her neck and lower jaw, and she turned to press her whole face into my palm.

I lowered my body further until I sat cross-legged on the floor, facing Scarlett with my back against the bedroom door I'd closed behind me. She sat down on her haunches facing me, and as I continued to scratch gently along her neck and jaw, her eyelids drooped, and the low, rumbling sound of her purr rose to fill the room.

It was the first time Scarlett had ever purred when I touched her.

"Did you think I was leaving without you?" I asked softly. And I realized, as I said it, that that was exactly what Scarlett had thought. She'd seen me walk out with all her things, and then she'd heard the slam of the car door, and she'd assumed that the next sound she would hear was the car engine as I drove away and left her behind.

My fingers paused in their scratching, and I cupped Scarlett's face in my hand. She regarded me solemnly with her luminous, inscrutable yellow-green eyes.

I leaned forward slightly, to make my own eyes level with hers. "I will *never* leave you," I told her. "Not ever. You and I are stuck with each other. Okay?"

I didn't expect a reply, of course, and I didn't get one. Instead, Scarlett stretched out her front legs and her neck, until her belly rested on the floor and her chin rested on my ankle. Then she closed her eyes. The vibrations of her purr soon gave way to the steadier rhythms of her breath as she fell asleep.

The room grew dim in the gathering dusk, and I reached up to flip the wall light switch that would turn on the bedside lamp. The fur of Scarlett's neck was soft on my ankle, and I lowered my arm to stroke her back.

I waited for my legs to stiffen, to feel my arm growing tired or the weight of Scarlett's head becoming uncomfortable on my ankle. But that never happened. The warmth and drowsiness of Scarlett's sleeping body seemed to seep into my own, and all I felt was a sense of balm. Balm and ease. The feeling that a tiny, twinging knot, which I'd lived with long enough to have stopped noticing it, had finally begun to loosen.

"Good Scarlett," I murmured. "Good, good girl."

We sat together like that, in the amber circle of lamplight, for a long time.

THINGS CHANGED BETWEEN US AFTER THAT, ALTHOUGH NOT dramatically, and not right away. Scarlett most certainly did not become a lap cat. She didn't start running over whenever I called her. There was never a moment when Jorge looked at the two of us together and said, *Look how affectionate Scarlett's become! You're a miracle worker!*

In May of the following year, when Scarlett was a year old, we adopted another kitten—a tiny white fluff-ball only five weeks old, who'd been found wandering the streets of Little Haiti alone, near where my mother taught elementary school. My mother called me in tears over this half-starved, mite-ridden creature, who she couldn't bring home with her but couldn't bear to leave. So the kitten came to live with us, and I named her Vashti. Vashti was an affectionate cuddle-bug right from the start—and while Scarlett was initially a reluctant big sister, it wasn't long before Vashti's gentle sweetness won her over. Having a kitten to boss around put an end, once and for all, to Scarlett's game of "let's trip Mom and make her fall down!"

I don't know when exactly it happened, although I do know that it was well before a month-old, permanently blind kitten named Homer, adopted more than a year after Vashti, came to complete our little family. Maybe it was seeing Vashti so frequently snuggled into my lap or curled up with me in bed that gave Scarlett the idea. But I began to notice how sometimes, waking up in the morning, I'd find Scarlett on our bed, fast asleep between my ankles. Or I'd be reading a book on the couch and Scarlett would come to stretch out across the top of the sofa behind my head—mercifully leaving my hair alone, but resting one small white paw on my shoulder and purring as she nodded off. Before Homer came to rewrite all the old rules, it was Scarlett who was the first to greet me at the door every day when I came home from work—even if she didn't do much more than quickly brush her head against my ankles and then run off before I could pet her.

And it was Scarlett, when Jorge and I finally broke up for good after nearly four years together, who followed me as I got into bed that first, agonizing night, curling up on the empty pillow next to mine as I cried myself to sleep. When I awakened in the morning, feeling somehow warm and calm even as I remembered what had happened the day before, I realized that Scarlett was lying across my chest. Her heart beat against my own, and her head nuzzled into the crook of my neck as she purred gently into my ear. It was as if she'd known that the hardest thing about that first morning would be waking up by myself, and she was telling me that even without Jorge, I wasn't alone.

Insofar as Scarlett became affectionate at all, it was only ever with me. Her disdain for humanity as a general concept would remain with her for the rest of her life. Scarlett was always the cat who immediately left the room when people came over, who would reject—with claws and teeth, if necessary—anybody else's attempts to pet her. She would always be the cat who required an explanation. *You shouldn't touch Scarlett. You definitely shouldn't try to pet Scarlett. Maybe it's best if you don't even look at Scarlett.* After Jorge and I had ended things, when I lived for a few years on South Beach—and unexpectedly found myself part of a tightly knit, somewhat snobbish nightlife scene, whose glittering VIP rooms were closely guarded against any incursion by the "hoi polloi"—I would warn visiting friends, with a certain mock hauteur, "Scarlett is *very* exclusive." And they would eye her with respect, grasping something fundamental—and, in its way, endearing—about Scarlett's nature in far less time than it had taken me. It was, after all, undeniably flattering to be the one and only human permitted into a highly selective cat's inner life.

All that's jumping ahead, though. What did change immediately—right then on that November day when I picked up Scarlett at Jorge's parents' house—was my realization that Scarlett knew who I was, beyond just a hand that dispensed food or scooped out a litter box. She knew who I was *to her*. It mattered—more than either of us had known—that the hand feeding or cleaning up after her was *my* hand and nobody else's.

Maybe Scarlett and I hadn't "chosen" each other, exactly. There never was that one magical moment, the meeting of eyes, the resounding gong of two souls' instant recognition of each other. What Scarlett and I had was, as it turned out, something far more elusive and enduring than that. It wasn't the sort of thing that sprang up in a flash; it had to develop quietly, through months and years of love, patience, and growing trust.

The world may have been filled with other cats who would have come when I called or cuddled in my lap or slept every night next to me in bed. And it may also have been filled with other humans who could empty a can of food into Scarlett's dish and then leave her alone, just as easily as I could.

At the rock-solid core of things, however, there was only one me for Scarlett, and there was only one Scarlett for me.

And that was enough. It was more than enough. It was everything.

Stop Trying to Make Fetch Happen

Even as I sit to type these words, I hear it. It's the sound that's come to define my waking hours and haunt my dreams, the first thing I hear when my eyes open in the morning and the last thing I hear at night before I fall asleep. Whether I'm writing, cooking, reading a book, cleaning the bathroom sink, talking with my husband, blow drying my hair, or lying in bed, it's always with me, like the beating of my own heart.

Rattle. Rattle. THUMP. Rattlerattlerattlerattlerattle.

It's the sound of a tiny, felt-covered plastic mouse—adorned at its tail with rainbow-colored feathers and filled with something or other that produces a rattling noise—being picked up and shaken vigorously by a cat, then dropped at increasingly closer intervals to my desk chair before being picked up and shaken again. Sure enough, when I swivel in my chair to look behind me, Clayton sits on his haunches about a foot away, his black fur groomed to a high gloss in the sunlight that streams through the window next to us. His golden eyes are impossibly round and hopeful as he stares at me without blinking.

"*MEEEEEEE!*" Clayton's meow has no "ow" at the end, so he lives perpetually in the insistent first person. His voice is comically high-pitched and squeaky for such a stocky cat, and under different circumstances I'd probably laugh as he repeats "*MEEEEEEE!*" picking up and rattling the toy mouse once more for good measure. Its tail feathers curl to form a jaunty rainbow moustache beneath his little black nose.

But it's already later than I had intended to begin my writing for the day, the precious morning hours of peak mental clarity slipping into the creative doldrums of early afternoon. My arm is sore from having spent the better part of two hours hurling that plastic mouse: pitching it down the stairs as I yawned my way out of bed, throwing it from the bathroom to the living room as I brushed my teeth, tossing it from one end of the kitchen to the other as I poured myself some orange juice, and spiking it from my office nook in the back of our little house all the way to the bay window at its front—then throwing the mouse *again* and *again* each time Clayton retrieved it.

Enough is enough.

"Clayton, I'm *working*," I tell him, in a voice that's meant to be stern but comes out sounding like a plea. "How can I afford to keep buying you toys if you won't let me *work*?"

Human logic so rarely prevails with actual humans that I shouldn't be surprised when it fails to move my cat. Still, for the first time all morning, he sounds uncertain. "*Meeeeeee?*" He lets the mouse drop from his mouth and noses it a few inches closer to me, reaching out to paw at my leg with gentle persistence. "*Meeeeeee?*"

His dip in confidence helps me find my own. "*No*," I say firmly. "Playtime is over. I have to work now." I make a show of turning away from Clayton and toward the computer keyboard, randomly hitting the keys to type nothing in particular as I watch him from the corner of my eye, trying to gauge if, indeed, he's ready to let me move on with my day.

Perhaps my exaggerated determination has done the trick. More likely, however, is that the effort required to propel a three-legged cat up and down the stairs of a three-story house for two hours has finally sapped even Clayton of his energy.

Whatever the cause, I exhale a small sigh of relief as Clayton uses his powerful upper body to haul himself up to the windowsill next to my desk, stretching out his forelegs with the toy mouse balanced carefully between his front paws.

"Good boy." I reach over to scritch him affectionately behind the ears, and he responds with a sleepy, subdued, "*meeeeeee.*" His yellow eyes are still fixed on mine, but the lids droop as he nods off into the first of today's catnaps.

I turn back to my computer screen and start typing again — actual words, this time—while birds chirp outside the window and, from his perch beside me, Clayton begins to snore lightly. Serenity reigns in my sunlit writing nook. Finally, the game of fetch is over.

Well, maybe not *over*. But at least my demanding feline overlord seems willing to allow me a small window of time in which to get some actual work done.

For now. Until the next round of fetch begins.

Cat lovers are fond of referring to themselves as their cats' "slaves" or "adoring servants." *Dogs have owners, cats have staff,* the saying goes. I've repeated it myself often enough for humorous effect, but privately I never used to think of myself as being the servant of any dog or cat I've lived with. I've always *indulged* them, of course. I legitimately don't know what the point of adopting an animal—especially a rescue animal—even is if not, at least in part, to allow yourself the fun of spoiling them silly.

I'll freely admit, however, that nowadays I'm wholeheartedly and downright euphorically enslaved to my three-legged cat, Clayton, in a way I've never been with any other cat before— not even my blind cat, Homer, who burrowed so deeply into my heart that I felt as if he were literally my flesh and blood. Clayton hates to be alone, and if he awakens from a nap to find himself in an empty room, he'll let out an anguished howl— and I always come running, no matter where I am or what I'm in the middle of doing. He pushes me like a slave driver, nipping at my ankles with his teeth when it's his feeding time and I'm not walking to the kitchen quickly enough, or at my calves if I'm standing and talking to my husband, Laurence, or doing any- thing that doesn't involve paying attention to Clayton. He has a habit, when I'm sitting at my desk and working on the com- puter, of hopping in semi-circles behind the desk chair, rising up on his one hind leg, every other hop, to nip at whatever parts of me he can reach through the chair's lower back—usually my hips and rear end.

"Silly boy!" I'll say with a smile, as I reach down to rub beneath Clayton's chin and Laurence looks on in amazement at my cheerful benevolence.

If I'm reading a book, a throw pillow in my lap to prop it up on, Clayton will often pull himself up onto the couch and unceremoniously head-butt the book out of his way, installing himself in its place. Not only don't I get angry at this, I don't even get irritated. "Who da fuzzy wizzle man?" I'll croon, my book forgotten. As I scratch Clayton's back, he lifts his head at a regal angle and sprawls out to his full length atop the cushion on my lap. "Who got da mushy wizzle belly? Who such a good boy? *Gooooooood* boy . . ."

"It's unbelievable how much better the cat's treated than I am," Laurence likes to grumble. He's not wrong. There's nothing more irksome to a bookworm like me than being pulled abruptly out of an engrossing read. If *Laurence* were to slap a book out of my hands and shout, "Pay attention to me right NOW!" he'd be treated to an earful of obscenities rather than a back scratch. I can state with near certainty that no affectionate rubs of his "fuzzy wizzle belly" would be in the offing.

Clayton, without question, fares much better.

Eventually, Clayton will flip onto his back and nestle in the crook of my arm, his nose wedged into my armpit (Clayton being something of an armpit fetishist) and his chin resting on my breast, which he kneads ecstatically with his front paws. If there's one thing I've learned from watching *My Cat From Hell*, it's that cats emphatically do *not* like being cradled on their backs like babies. But Clayton is the exception to this rule. Not only does he like it, he insists on it. At least once a day, while I'm working at the computer, he'll crawl into my lap, flop onto his back, and snuggle himself in the bend of my elbow. I've learned to type with one hand so that the other is free to balance Clayton's supine body against my chest—as if my arm were a baby sling—as he drifts into sleep.

"You did this to him," Laurence says whenever he comes upon us in this Madonna-and-child pose. (Laurence likes to think that he's much more measured and "reasonable" in his affections for the cats than I am, but when he thinks he's out of earshot upstairs, I hear him with them. *How's my little man?* he'll say. Or, *You're a sweet kitty . . . yes, you are! Yes, you are!*) "You made him this way."

"*Un*true!" I reply. "Clayton's just *naturally* a very attention-seeking cat, and I'm just naturally the kind of person who pays attention to attention-seeking cats."

There's some truth to the idea that Clayton is far more people-oriented than even the friendliest feline. It's one thing for a cat to leap immediately into the lap of every visiting guest, without so much as first giving a preliminary sniff or receiving a cursory pat on the head. But how many cats fling themselves—purring and rapturous—into the arms of a veterinarian who's just given them a shot? *You stuck a needle in me!* I imagine Clayton saying. *That means you're paying attention to me! You're my new favorite human!!!*

Whatever natural, attention-seeking inclinations Clayton might have started out with have certainly been amplified by the sheer volume of time my cats and I now spend together. I adopted my first generation of cats—Scarlett, Vashti, and Homer—twenty years ago. Back then I was young and single, working long hours in an office all day and going out with friends or on dates at night.

STOP TRYING TO MAKE FETCH HAPPEN

But I adopted Clayton and his littermate, Fanny, in 2012. By then, I was already a full-time writer working from home, as was (and is) my husband. I used to be out of the house ten to fifteen hours on a typical weekday. Nowadays, Laurence and I will make a point of going somewhere, even if only out to lunch or to run errands, at least once every day. Some days we play hooky in Manhattan, taking in a movie or going to a museum for the bulk of the afternoon. We'll go out a couple of nights a week to the theater, or to meet friends for dinner. Still, it's not at all unusual for us to be home and with our cats for a good twenty-two hours in any given day. When I meet people at functions and they ask me what I do, I'm as apt to quip, *I'm a stay-at-home cat mom* as I am to go with the more serious-sounding *I'm a writer.* Both feel like equally accurate descriptions of my life.

Clayton and Fanny, in other words, are used to having near-constant access to their humans—and to human attention. Clayton spends his entire day in close proximity to me. If I go upstairs to talk to Laurence in his office—even if Clayton is in a deep slumber, and I'm only up there for a couple of minutes—Clayton will follow, eyes half-closed and dazed with sleep. If I head to the bedroom for a brief afternoon siesta, Fanny inevitably crawls out to join me from whatever hiding/sleeping spot she's designated for the day—and a room that contains both Fanny *and* me is a room that Clayton absolutely must be in. Any foray into our first-floor kitchen—even a quick one to get a glass of water—automatically becomes a group excursion.

If I run out to the corner bodega, a mere half-block away, to get a can of soda, Clayton and Fanny race to greet me at the door upon my return as if I were coming home from the wars after a years-long absence. I can't even describe how overwrought they are when Laurence and I get back from an overnight vacation, or a trip to do a book reading at an out-of-state animal shelter. Clayton and Fanny cling to us like two little black burrs—refusing even to let us go to the bathroom or take a shower unattended—and it takes days for things to return to normal. *We thought you'd be gone forever!* they seem to be saying. *We thought you might* never *come home!*

So we've become quite the codependent little foursome, Fanny, Clayton, my husband, and I. I often think that if cats could talk to each other, and if Clayton were to hear tales from other cats about humans who leave their homes for work *every single day*, and stay away for up to *ten hours* at a time, he would react with the same mingling of pity and horror I used to feel as a small child in Miami when my grandmother would tell stories about Life In The Olden Days—before there was air-conditioning, television, or Cheez Doodles. "But what did you *do*?" I'd demand, fighting back tears at the thought of my beloved grandmother enduring such hardships. "How did you *live*?"

This is all by way of saying that when Clayton first taught himself to play fetch, and then decided that he really liked playing fetch—and then further decided that he wanted me to play fetch with him *all the time*—the stage had already been set for casual interest to develop into full-blown obsession.

LIKE SO MANY GREAT INNOVATIONS, CLAYTON'S INITIAL DISCOVERY of fetch was a happy accident. He'd always been fond of throwing games, particularly when they involved the crinkle balls and miniature plastic springs that were, not so very long ago, his favorite toys. I'd find one lying about, toss it a few feet away, and Clayton would run after it, batting it around for a while before finally losing interest and looking for something else to do.

That was more or less what I expected to happen one morning a few months ago when I spotted, lying next to my desk chair, one of the two little toy mice with rainbow tail feathers that I'd spontaneously bought for Clayton and Fanny the day before. When Clayton saw me lift it from the floor, his ears immediately pricked up and he sat at attention.

"You want this?" I said. "You want this, little boy?"

My tiny office nook sits off of our living room, and it was in that direction that I threw the mouse, watching as Clayton chased after it. When he caught up with it, he picked the mouse up in his mouth and shook it vigorously a few times, an instinctive "predator" reaction as much as a delighted response to the rattling sound the toy mouse made.

Something about Clayton sitting there on his haunches with that little gray-and-white mouse between his teeth—its merrily colored tail feathers curving upward toward his ear, as if he were an old-timey gentleman wearing a feathered cap—struck me as particularly adorable. "What a good boy you are!" I cried. "You're a good, good boy, Clayton!"

My delight with him in that moment was obvious, and he responded to it by running back toward me, the mouse still clutched in his mouth only because, in his excitement to reach me, he'd forgotten it was there. There's very little in this life that I find more endearing than Clayton's hippity-hoppity three-legged run, his gait resembling a cross between a bunny hop and a drunken sailor trying to find his shore footing. And so, when he dropped the mouse and lifted his head toward my hand for a petting, I picked it up and threw it again.

Clayton's second pursuit of the mouse was, if anything, even cuter than the first one had been. He ran for a bit, then slid the last few inches in dramatic fashion on his legless rear haunch, like a baseball player stealing home.

"Awwwwww!" I called after him. "You're a good, *good* boy, Clayton!"

By now, Clayton was as happy with me as I was with him. Once again, he galloped back with the mouse still hanging from his jaw, eager for more praise and petting. I was lavish with both.

Technically, I was supposed to be working. I was on a deadline and had more than enough writing ahead of me to occupy the next several days and then some. But, like most writers, a good 50 percent of my "work" time is spent procrastinating. (And at least half of the other 50 percent is spent thinking up new ways to procrastinate.) Watching my cat frolic with his toys was certainly a more appealing prospect than getting down to business. And so, once again, the little felt-covered mouse went airborne.

I think it was this third toss of the toy mouse that started the gears turning in Clayton's mind. This time, he didn't wait for me to praise him or tell him what a good boy he was before promptly running back to deposit the mouse at my feet. Instead of craning his neck to angle his head closer to the touch of my hand, he sat on his haunches and looked eagerly from my face above him to the toy on the ground, and then back again.

"Aha! So it's a game of fetch you want, is it?" Before I knew it, an hour of toss-retrieve-repeat had flown by—at which point, Clayton, seemingly spent, pulled himself up the side of my desk, stepped down from the top of the desk into my lap, and flipped onto his back for belly rubs and a snooze.

Engaging as that hour of fetch was, I'd more or less forgotten about it by the time I sat down to dinner that night. Laurence had a story to tell that took precedence. A magazine-writer friend of ours, who'd been on the receiving end of months of verbal abuse from his new editor but had yet to stand up for himself, had finally brought matters to a head in the worst possible way: He'd meant to send Laurence a text complaining *about* his editor. Instead, he'd sent the text *to* the editor himself.

"He'd just gotten out of a meeting with the guy, and it was the usual barrage of sarcasm and insults. He meant to send the text to *me*, but two seconds later he realizes he's actually sent it to his editor, whose name also begins with an *L*. And it says—"

"OW!" Looking down, I saw Clayton at my feet with the toy mouse on the ground between his front paws. I'd been engrossed enough in Laurence's story not to have noticed Clayton's soft pawing at my leg for attention—so he'd decided to step things up a notch and unsheathe his claws. "Don't do that again," I told him sternly, picking up the mouse and throwing it all the way across the kitchen. Clayton immediately tore after it. "Continue," I said to Laurence.

"So the text says, 'I can't believe—'"

"*MEEEEEEE!*" Clayton was beneath my chair again. Dropping the mouse in front of me, he nudged it hopefully in my direction.

"Just one more time—okay?" I turned from Clayton back to Laurence. "I'm so sorry. Please go on."

"'I can't believe I have to—'"

"*MEEEEEEE!*" This time, Clayton had chosen to bypass sitting at my feet and waiting for me to notice him. He'd pulled himself up onto an empty chair, hopped from there onto the kitchen table, and dropped the mouse into the middle of my dinner plate.

"*Clay*ton!" I picked up the mouse, now covered in pasta sauce, and wiped it with my napkin. "Stop it already!" But of course, having cleaned the mouse off, I threw it across the kitchen for him to scamper after.

"What's *with* him?" Laurence asked, watching as Clayton did his baseball slide across the kitchen floor, caught the mouse up between his jaws, and brought it back over.

"He taught himself to play fetch today." Without even thinking about it, I reached down as I spoke to pick up and then toss the mouse. "Anyway, *please* finish the story."

"It-said-I-can't-believe-I-have-to-sit-in-meetings-taking-abuse-from-a-cretin-who-probably-can't-even-spell-cretin," Laurence said in one long rush, trying to get the full sentence out before Clayton could interrupt again.

"Yikes!" It was probably unclear to Laurence—because it was unclear even to me—whether I was reacting to the painful implications of that text or to the fact that Clayton was standing *yet again* on the kitchen table next to my plate. "Do you think it was really an accident, or do you think he was finally trying to break a bad pattern? Here you go," I added as an aside to Clayton, and lobbed his mouse in the direction of the pantry.

"Bad patterns can be tough to break." Laurence looked at me and rolled his eyes pointedly.

"Ain't it the truth." I sighed and shook my head sadly. And then I bent forward to pick up Clayton's mouse, which he'd already retrieved, and threw it for him again.

THE OBVIOUS QUESTION IS, WHY DID I CAPITULATE SO EASILY? When it was so very clear right from the start that Clayton's new hobby, left unchecked, stood to play such a large and intrusive role in our day-to-day lives, why didn't I try to stop it—or, at the very least, limit it?

Hindsight, as they say, is always 20/20—but, in my own (partial) defense, I'll say this: When Clayton taught himself to play fetch, it was far and away the smartest thing he'd ever done.

We live in a 150-year-old row house in a leafy bedroom community just two train stops outside of Manhattan. Living in an old house has its charms (marble fireplaces! crown moldings!), but central air conditioning isn't one of them. At the height of summer heat, we rely on a small window unit in our bedroom. In an effort to retain as much of the cold air as possible—while still giving the cats free access in and out—I'll leave the bedroom door just ajar enough that it's nearly closed but still easy for a cat to manage.

Fanny has no problem with this—and why would she? When she wants to come in, she simply nudges the door with her nose until it swings wide enough to allow her to pass. When she wants to go out, she slips her paw into the two inches of space between the door and the floor and pulls it toward her until there's a large-enough crack for her to fit through.

I'll admit that Fanny is particularly adept when it comes to doors. She's figured out how to sit atop the railing of the third-floor balcony, which puts her right at the level of the knob on the upstairs bathroom door, and twist the doorknob with her front paws until it opens (something she does to startling effect if Laurence or I happen to be in there).

Still, it's hard to claim that pushing open an already slightly open door requires much in the way of special skills or intelligence—especially for a cat.

And yet, for the first four years we lived in this house, Clayton couldn't figure it out—despite having watched Fanny nose open the bedroom door when it was ajar a million times. Fanny didn't have to watch anybody push on the door before *she* figured it out. Nevertheless, the mechanics of this process were beyond Clayton's grasp. He'd sit outside that slightly open bedroom door, and cry and cry, until I got up to let him in.

To reiterate: Clayton, a *cat* (creatures universally acknowledged for their cleverness, even by their detractors), could not figure out how to walk through an open door unassisted.

I'd probably shred anyone who suggested in my hearing that Clayton isn't as smart as other cats. Whenever Laurence says something to that effect—when he tells me, quoting an old *Carol Burnett Show* episode, that "Clayton's got splinters in the windmills of his mind," or, more succinctly, "Clayton's a little doofus"—I deny it vehemently. "You're just saying that because he's so affectionate and outgoing," I argue. "Only a cynic thinks that being friendly and trusting is the same as being unintelligent."

But even I—privately, in my deepest, innermost heart—sometimes have to acknowledge that maybe . . . just *possibly* . . . Clayton is . . . well . . . perhaps not quite as bright as he could be.

Like many cats, Clayton likes to knock things off ledges or tables and watch them fall. Sometimes the thing he knocks over is, say, a drinking glass from the kitchen table, which then shatters on the ground. That's an irritation, although arguably I have no one but myself to blame for leaving an unattended glass within reach. And, again, it's something lots of cats do. But how often does a cat then proceed to *walk around*, blithely unconcerned, in the broken shards? Thank goodness that Clayton, docile as a stuffed animal, is patient enough to let me tend to his paws with tweezers and peroxide as I pull the glass splinters out.

There's an old truism that a cat might touch a hot stove once, but after that he'll never touch any stove again. That truism doesn't apply to Clayton. If I'm boiling a pot of water, I have to sit next to it and guard it the entire time, because Clayton—despite having singed his fur once or twice—will insist on walking on the stove whenever one of the burners is on, seemingly mesmerized by the pretty blue flame. I've considered the possibility that maybe Clayton doesn't feel pain—that his nerve endings might not reach all the way to his skin, or something of that nature—but he yelps when the vet gives him a shot, or when I pull the glass from his feet, or when he gets close enough to a hot stove to burn himself. He just appears to forget immediately afterward. He doesn't seem to *learn*.

Most cats have two canine teeth. Clayton has one and a half. He lost the other half chewing the ear off a cat-shaped wooden footstool that I found at a flea market one day—and ended up having to put out with the trash that night. Clayton gets a high-quality moist food, daily Dental Greenies for healthy teeth (although it's tough to see the point in vigilant dental care if Clayton's just going to *chew his own teeth off*), and plenty of fresh potted cat grass and raw catnip—so it's not as if he lacks for fiber in his diet. Still, he'll insist on chewing on wood (I've

seen him go after the very doorframes on occasion), on plastic, on the metal base of a slender desk lamp while it's lit and hot to the touch. He'll eat—or try to eat—fluff and dust that he finds on the ground, feathers that have shaken free of pillows, long pieces of string, serrated metal bottle caps, Popsicle sticks, bits of plastic shrink-wrap torn from newly opened DVDs, peanut shells, staples, paper clips, the cloth husks of toys he's chewed to pieces, small thumbtacks I didn't even know were there and that have spontaneously dislodged themselves from the undersides of furniture . . . I've become vigilant as a hawk in surveying the floors of our home, scouring the terrain for any random detritus that might find its way from the ground into Clayton's mouth. Still, on a semi-regular basis, Laurence will rush to the top of the stairs upon hearing me yell, "*No*, Clayton! Drop it! DROP IT RIGHT NOW!" and find me wrestling with Clayton, my fingers down his throat, as I pull the latest hazard from his gullet before he can finish swallowing it.

I've seen cats through late-stage cancer, chronic renal failure, liver disease, blindness, diabetes, high blood pressure, hyperthyroidism, a heart murmur, colitis, sprained limbs, infected wounds, major and minor surgeries, and mysterious colds and fevers that took their appetites and required me to force-feed them through a syringe.

I can honestly say that I've never had to work this hard to keep a cat alive.

We have friends from Tennessee who visit us a few times a year—fellow animal lovers who live on a large hobby farm with ten rescue cats of their own. There are far more interesting things to do during a long weekend in New York than pass time at our house, hanging out with our cats. Still, they insist on spending a full day in our home whenever they travel north. Clearly, it's because they adore Clayton, lovingly tolerant as he intrusively head-butts and nose-burrows his way into their armpits or wraps his whole body around their feet (Clayton being a foot fetishist as well as an armpit aficionado), enraptured by the exotic cornucopia of smells they bring with them. Sometimes, I suspect that Clayton is the real reason they head up this way as frequently as they do. And even they—perhaps after the third time that visit when Clayton has tried unsuccessfully to bring the heavy, well-secured andirons next to the fireplace crashing down onto his own head (WHY?! FOR WHAT POSSIBLE REASON?!!??!)—will eventually look at him with a kind of affectionate pity and murmur, "Bless his heart." Which, for those not conversant in Southern-speak, is about as damning an accusation of unintelligence as a well-bred Southern lady will allow herself to express.

These days, I fret constantly whenever Laurence and I go out—whether it's for a few days or only a few hours—about what would happen if someone were to break into our home and the cats got out. Break-ins, of course, have always been a hypothetical possibility wherever I've lived—and, on one memorable occasion many years ago, my South Beach apartment actually was broken into. But I've never worried as much about what might happen to my cats if they got out—not even my blind cat, Homer (and I worried about him a *lot*)—as I do now about Clayton. He's microchipped and, thanks to my cat books, I have a large-enough reach among cat rescuers online that he stands a better-than-average chance of being found and returned to me. Plus, knowing Clayton, he'd probably throw himself at the first human who walked by—and hopefully that human wouldn't be inhumane enough to leave a desperately affectionate, three-legged cat to fend for himself. Still, my deepest fear is that Clayton couldn't take care of himself for even a day if he suddenly ended up alone on the streets.

Which is why, when Clayton taught himself—*taught himself!*—to play fetch, it wasn't just that it was cute at first. Or even cute-but-also-maybe-sometimes-a-little-annoying. It was a revelation. It was a game changer. And he'd taught himself so quickly! Could even the cleverest cat have picked up the rudiments of fetch any faster than Clayton did?

I felt relieved—and also more than a little vindicated. *See!* I wanted to shout to any and all naysayers. *Clayton is smart! He's VERY smart! I always knew it! I knew it all along.*

HAVING ACCOMPLISHED THIS ONE FEAT OF LEARNING—TEACHING himself to play fetch—Clayton quickly followed it up by mastering an entire brand-new set of associated skills. There was no particular challenge in getting me to take on a round of fetch when I was already alert and paying attention to him. Clayton, however, soon became an expert at getting me to play fetch even when I was dead-set against it, and at the least-convenient times.

You can always tell which of Clayton's toys is his favorite at any given moment, because the more Clayton loves something, the more gleefully he abuses it. A few years ago, someone sent us gifts for the cats—two versions of a toy rodent called Rosie the Rat, made from real fur. There was a black-furred Rosie and a tan-furred Rosie. Truthfully, I didn't love that they were made from real fur, and was tempted to either toss them or donate them to our local cat shelter. But Clayton and Fanny went absolutely wild the second I pulled the Rosies from the envelope they'd been mailed in, which settled the matter; I couldn't bear taking away anything that made them so happy.

Clayton immediately appropriated Black Rosie as his own special property, while Fanny laid claim to Tan Rosie. But even if you'd never seen Clayton hopping around with Black Rosie in his mouth, you still would have known that she, and not Tan Rosie, was his. I would find Black Rosie drowning in the toilet, peeking forlornly from beneath a heap of leftover moist cat food in Clayton's dish, or buried in the litter box. Just about every day, I had to boil a pot of water so I could disinfect her before returning her to Clayton's custody. Over the course of a few weeks, Black Rosie dwindled down to a few tattered wisps of patchy black fuzz clinging to a cloth skeleton. Eventually, the sad day came when I had to give Black Rosie a mercy burial in the trash can. Whereas Tan Rosie (Fanny's Rosie) is still, three years later, in showroom-new condition—even though Fanny "kills" her every day and leaves her as a "gift" for Laurence and me every night.

Once Clayton discovered fetch, it seemed as if the plastic rattling mouse, his new favorite toy, was fated to suffer the same abuse. It was only a couple of days later when I was forced to fish it out of the litter box—pulling it gingerly by its colorful tail feathers—before disposing of it in the trash as Clayton bounced around me in desperate circles, pleading for me to toss it across the room for him. I replaced it the next day (they only cost ninety-nine cents apiece at our local pet-supply store). But, still, once Clayton had seen me pick the toy out of his litter box—with a heartfelt "Ugh!" of disgust—and then throw it *away* rather than throwing it *for him to fetch*, it was like a lightbulb went on over his head. After that, I noticed how careful Clayton was to maintain his new little feathered mouse in immaculate condition. Not only did he refrain from burying or drowning it, I've actually seen him groom that mouse with his tongue until it's spotless before carrying it over to lay at my feet. *You can't refuse to throw* this *one for me!* he seems to be saying. *This one's clean as a whistle!*

In sales, they call this overcoming a client's objections. In Clayton, I'll call it nothing short of genius.

As I mentioned, Fanny likes to leave little "gifts" for Laurence and me—one of her toys, if we're lucky, or a palmetto bug or some other large bug that's gotten into the house, if we're not. She tends to leave them on our pillows, or sometimes on the bath mat directly in front of the shower, where we're sure to see them as soon as we get out. That we notice her presents is very important to Fanny—she'll cry anxiously until we find them and then pat her on the head, saying, "Thank you, Fanny!" (which is difficult to do with much sincerity when the gift in question is a giant headless cockroach).

Clayton, in contrast, has never been one for gift giving. Lately, though, I find that wherever I go in the house, Clayton's rattling toy mouse has already beaten me there. It's on my pillow at bedtime and on the rug in front of the sink when I go to brush my teeth. It's atop the closed lid of the laptop computer on my desk when I sit down to work, on the kitchen counter when I go downstairs to make my lunch, and has beaten me to my favorite sofa cushion when I've finished work for the day and am ready to relax with Laurence.

The genius of this is that Clayton opts to place his mouse strategically where I'll have no choice but to pick it up in order to get it out of my way. Once I've picked it up, I have to do *something* with it. Lobbing it across the room doesn't require much more effort than just dropping it to the floor. So why wouldn't I throw it? It would seem almost churlish not to—as Clayton's wide, woebegone eyes are at pains to inform me: *Are you really not going to throw it for me? Don't you love me anymore?*

I thought for a while that throwing the mouse up or down the stairs might solve some of my problems—that maybe Clayton would exhaust himself with all that up-and-down running, or that he might even decide to just play with it on his own once I was no longer in his sight line. That was a grave tactical error on my part. Clayton now loves racing up and down the stairs after the mouse more than anything else. When he walks, he slow-hops along as if he had a limp. When he trots, it's with that hippity-hoppity/drunken-sailor gait that I love so much. But when Clayton *tears* up or down the stairs, he doesn't just run—he flies. You'd never know, as he flashes past in a black blur, that he's any different from a "normal" cat.

Now Clayton wants me to throw the mouse up or down the stairs for him all the time. If I'm in bed, it's not enough to simply hurl the mouse toward a far corner of the bedroom. I have to sit up in bed, lean forward, and curve my body around so that I can angle the toy through the bedroom door and down the stairs. Clayton, who once couldn't figure out how to pass through a slightly open door, mastered that skill with ease once he was sufficiently motivated. I'll hear his paw-steps coming up the stairs and know that within seconds the wedge of light from the hallway will grow as Clayton swings the bedroom door open wide—and then I'll see Clayton himself, standing next to my side of the bed, the beloved toy mouse clutched between his teeth as its colorful feathers glow in the half-light against the blackness of his fur.

Whether I'm awake or asleep makes no difference. If I'm there lying down, Clayton hauls himself onto the bed, walk-hops right onto my chest, and drops the mouse under my chin. I'll fight to keep my eyes closed, thinking that if I can feign sleep convincingly enough, he might buy my act and relent.

It never works. Eventually, Clayton will bring his nose directly level with mine and proclaim, "*MEEEEEEE!*"

Roughly translated, this means, *Oh, please. Even I can tell you're faking.*

ALL CATS HAVE THEIR HABITS AND ROUTINES, THEIR LITTLE RITUALS that they perform so repetitively, and in so precisely identical a manner each time, that it seems to border on the compulsive. Some of these rituals become permanent; some are temporary but intense. And while there are some habits it's nearly impossible to break a cat of, the truth is that I probably could have nipped Clayton's fetch obsession in the bud if I'd really wanted to. If I'd said no often enough, he would have gotten the point eventually and left me alone. Even now, when it's become such an integral part of his daily routine, if I could muster the willpower to be firm for a few days, I could probably cure him of his addiction—or at least tamp it down enough that I'd have more of a say as to the specific times and locations in which our game would take place.

And yet, despite his persistence and the hassle and the inter-ruption of my sleep schedule and the frequent disruptions to my work, I'll admit that I find myself reluctant to do anything to stop him.

Maybe it's because I'm no longer the same person I was twenty years ago, when I adopted my first three cats—those early years of cat-ladyhood when I proudly distinguished between myself, an indulgent but still in-control caretaker, and those who referred to themselves as their cats' slaves. These days, I'm more apt to appreciate the fleeting nature of a cat's obsessions—of a cat's life. Clayton is still young, but time moves much faster than it used to. Just yesterday, Clayton was a kitten. Today he's five. Tomorrow he'll be a little old man struggling to lug himself around on his three legs. His days of flying up and down the stairs like greased lightning in pursuit of a toy mouse will be a distant, cherished memory. Much sooner than I'm ready for it, I know, a time will come when I'll think, *What wouldn't I give to play fetch with Clayton just once more!*

No matter how irritated I may get at being interrupted while I'm working or sleeping (or paying my bills, or making a sandwich, or canoodling with my husband), how can I not smile when I see how a humble game of fetch makes Clayton so happy? *So happy!* His thick club of a tail points straight up and vibrates with his joy. When he does that theatrical, high-speed, baseball-player slide of his, I always, *always* laugh.

Every single time.

The joy of spoiling our cats is that, in giving them simple pleasures, we get them right back. And they remind us that, no matter how complicated our lives, or how complex our relationships, or how sophisticated our desires and goals may become with the passage of years, those simple pleasures are still the ones most worth having. Even as they become harder to find and hold onto.

I'll confess, though, that I can't help missing the old days sometimes. The days when, sure, maybe *some* people thought Clayton was just a lovable dolt—but at least I got eight hours of uninterrupted, fetch-free sleep every night.

It's not in the nature of masters to pity their slaves. Clayton, as much as I know he loves me, is no exception. "Clayton," I'll plead to no avail, "I'm trying to write!" Or, "Clayton, I need to sleep!" or, "Clayton, Laurence and I want some 'alone time' right now."

Alas! My pleas fall on deaf, fuzzy ears.

Awakened from a sound sleep at five in the morning to a piercing "*MEEEEEEE!*" two inches from my head, I'll put on the best *I mean business!* voice I can muster in the pre-dawn hours. "Clayton," I'll tell him, "stop trying to make fetch happen. It's *not* going to happen."

But that's a lie, and we both know it. Of course it will. It always does.

The Picasso
of Pee

There's a common belief that beauty and brains don't go hand in hand, and maybe that's why it took me so long to recognize Vashti's brilliance for what it was—because Vashti, without question, was the most beautiful cat that any of us who knew her had ever seen. Her enormous eyes were emerald green and set at just enough of a tilt to make them archetypally catlike and mysterious. The heart-shaped delicacy of her face was punctuated winningly by her little pink pearl of a nose—its powdery shade echoed in the deeper rose of her perfectly sculpted ears (not one millimeter too big or too small), which were framed by feathery wisps of scrumptious snow-white fur. That same long, lustrous fur, silky-soft as an angel's sigh, covered her entire body, exploding riotously into a gorgeous white plume of a tail that would have broken the heart of any high-end furrier, and that had led my boyfriend Jorge's father—perhaps the first man to fall in love with Vashti—to refer to her as "The Arctic Fox."

In pictures, Vashti seemed to glow—literally, to *glow*—not as if she was reflecting the light in the room, but rather as if light itself was emanating from her. Even in photos taken of the two of us together during the final weeks of her life—when illness had reduced her from nine pounds to five, and she was so weak that she couldn't so much as jump up to the bed unassisted—Vashti looks as radiant as if some silvery moon goddess had descended to earth in cat form and deigned, with exquisite grace, to drape herself across my chest.

Despite being greatly admired by everyone, very few of us gave Vashti any real consideration beyond the simple joy inspired by looking at such a stunning creature. Yet Vashti deserved to be taken at far more than face value. She may, in fact, have been the most emotionally complex of all my cats. She was almost certainly the smartest.

Looking back with hindsight's clarity, I can see the earliest signs of an above-average brain, hard at work. As a kitten, for example, Vashti enjoyed playing fetch with crumpled-up balls of paper sprinkled with a smidge of catnip. In and of itself, this wasn't unheard of. But one day Vashti started bringing over *un*crumpled sheets of paper—confiscated from the tray next to the computer printer—and dropping them into my lap for me to ball up and throw for her. She'd also helpfully retrieve the little baggie of catnip from wherever I'd last left it and place that in my lap, as well.

It wasn't something I gave much thought to at the time. Mostly, I'd just crumple the paper into an aerodynamic wad, dust it with 'nip, and toss it across the room for Vashti's amusement. When I consider it now, though, it strikes me as a bit extraordinary.

Cats aren't supposed to be capable of abstract thought. Yet what, other than abstract thought, could it be called when a cat—a kitten, actually—could look at a smooth piece of paper, and from that imagine a possible future in which that same piece of paper would take on a completely different form and appearance than its current one—a form and appearance that didn't exist in the physical here and now, and that she could see only in her mind's eye? And while I've spent a lot of time with a *lot* of cats in the years since then—cats who've brought over any number of favored playthings for me to toss or dangle or otherwise entertain them with—I've still never seen any other cat place into my hands the raw materials from which I could *build* a toy to their preferred specifications.

All that, however, was mere prelude to the revelation of Vashti's true gifts—as when an opera singer warms up with scales before delivering the big aria. The comparison is an apt one, because Vashti, I would eventually come to believe, was more than merely smart. If artistic talent is the ability to communicate, with power and immediacy, abstract thoughts and feelings through some unrelated medium—words for a writer, for example, or marble for a sculptor—then Vashti was an artist. A consummate creative spirit trapped in the body of a nine-pound white cat. Her preferred creative method involved the application of yellow liquid to cloth and paint and solid surfaces—something a museum curator might refer to as *non-traditional mixed media*.

That is, Vashti worked almost exclusively with and through her own urine. She was the Monet of micturition. The Titian of tinkling. A veritable Picasso of pee.

I can already hear the protests against such lofty claims: *Lots of cats pee in inappropriate places to express anger or anxiety.* But with most cats, it can take weeks, months, even years to figure out the precise source of their irritation—and, often, you never do get to the ultimate root cause. Vashti, however, was able to communicate far more than rudimentary basics like *I'm annoyed* or *I feel nervous.* With the specificity, timing, and sheer ingenuity of her outside-the-litter-box thinking, Vashti could convey complex thoughts and problems, and even propose remedies, as surely as if she went around with thought bubbles over her head. *Here's the exact person who's bothering me,* she seemed to say. *Here's the exact bothersome thing they're doing. And here is what I suggest that you, my mother, do to make things more agreeable for me.*

In other words, Vashti could make you understand and *feel* her feelings as if they were your own. And if there's a better definition of artistry, I can't think of one.

IN COLLEGE, I LEARNED THAT WHEN AN ARTIST INCORPORATES some everyday object into a piece—like a tree branch or a bottle cap—it's called "found art." The first thing to find its way into one of Vashti's works of found art was Jorge's favorite sofa cushion—although for a long time it was my elder cat, Scarlett, a two-year-old gray-and-white tabby, who was either given the credit or hung with the blame, depending upon your perspective. As the designated "mean one," the one who'd take a swipe at anybody (other than me) who so much as tried to pat her head, she appeared to Jorge as the likeliest culprit.

"She's a hostile cat, and she's never liked me," he insisted, a prosecutor presenting an airtight case, the evening we came home to find Jorge's preferred spot on the couch soaking wet and reeking of cat urine. *Means, motive, opportunity.* As the clincher, he added, "Scarlett *knows* that's the exact place where I always sit."

In fairness to Scarlett, it wasn't that she disliked Jorge per se. It was more that she found human beings as a category to be a sort of general nuisance—one whose reason for existence (beyond the sole human who fed and loved her) she could never quite understand.

Jorge may have found his own logic convincing, but I was skeptical. It struck me as unlikely that my haughty, fastidious Scarlett—with her exacting litter box standards, and her insistence on letting me know (loudly) whenever those standards weren't met to the letter—would ever condescend to go *outside* her litter box, on the living room sofa, in the manner of what Scarlett herself, if she'd been able to talk, might have scornfully referred to as *some common street cat.*

Privately, I was convinced that it had to be Vashti. Vashti also had means, motive (although Jorge didn't realize it), and opportunity. Her only alibi was her pretty face—but (as with so many men!) that pretty face was more than enough to convince Jorge of her innocence. With Vashti's angelic beauty on full display before him, Jorge couldn't bring himself to believe that she might have done anything as vindictive or flat-out meanspirited as ruining his favorite resting spot on purpose.

But Vashti hadn't always been so beautiful. And Jorge hadn't always been such a big fan of hers.

It was an early-summer morning in 1996, Scarlett still only a year old, when my mother called me at work from the elementary school in Miami's Little Haiti where she taught first grade. One of her students had found a tiny kitten wandering the school's playground, a kitten in such profoundly bad shape that my mother, in attempting to describe it, nearly dissolved into tears. Someone from the school's staff had temporarily locked the kitten in the janitor's tool shed to keep it from escaping, while my mother (a longtime dog owner who had no experience with cats) did the only thing she could think to do for a kitten: She called me.

I drove down to my mother's school on my lunch break, and the sight that greeted me when the janitor opened up his tool shed was a piteous one indeed. It looked as if the kitten—a wee thing, no more than four or five weeks old—was probably supposed to be white-furred, but what wisps of fur she had were a soiled brown and difficult to distinguish among the bald patches where fur ought to be. It would be weeks before I'd see that the kitten's nose was pink and not black, so encrusted with dirt it was. Her ears were also blackened, swollen from ear mites until they'd nearly closed up altogether. She pawed weakly at the hem of my pants, looking up into my face from mottled, miserable green eyes. When I knelt to lift her, I caught a sour smell that mingled grime with long-standing hunger. Nevertheless, the kitten purred feebly and attempted to climb up to my shoulder so she could nestle in the warmth of my hair.

Jorge had proudly remarked, on more than one occasion, about how well Scarlett was doing as an "only child." For her part, Scarlett would probably have been content to remain our household's sole cat forever. I knew that neither of them—and especially not Jorge—would be enthusiastic at the prospect of welcoming another feline family member.

But Jorge and his potential objections were, in that moment, hypothetical—whereas right here in front of me were the concrete realities of my mother's tears and a pitiful kitten's obvious, desperate need.

Better to ask for forgiveness than permission, I reasoned. And so, after giving her some of the kitten food I'd picked up on the way over, I took the kitten back to my office for the time being, to our family vet when my workday ended, and home with me for good the following morning, once the doctor had released her— startlingly yellow and reeking of rotten eggs from a mite-killing sulfur dip. I named her Vashti for the proud, beautiful queen from the story of Purim, who'd been exiled from ancient Persia after refusing to dance naked for the king and his drunken friends. I never suspected that *my* Vashti would grow up to be a beauty in her own right. But I'd always admired Queen Vashti for her courage and spirit, and I thought that my own little foundling needed all the help she could get.

Scarlett had been an independent kitten, wanting little from me in the way of attention or physical affection. Vashti proved to be her exact opposite. She followed me from room to room of the small house Jorge and I had recently moved into after our two years together in a one-bedroom apartment. Every night, for the first few months after I brought her home, she slept on my pillow, curling up in my hair, and when she eventually outgrew the space between my shoulder and my ear, she began instead to mold herself around the top of my head like a crown before falling asleep.

When she was still very small, she could usually be found on my lap, in my arms, or curled up under my chin. During the first few weeks she was with us, before her beauty and affectionate ways captured Jorge's reluctant heart, upon seeing us together he would invariably say something like, "Now that Vashti's getting stronger, we should think about finding a permanent home for her."

An understanding that we would "foster" Vashti temporarily had been the only way I'd gotten Jorge to agree to taking her in. It seemed impossible that Vashti could have actually understood what Jorge was saying—and yet, whenever he would make some comment like this, I'd swear I could feel a shudder go through her small body.

Most nights, I'd get home from work a couple of hours before Jorge did. I'd read a book or watch TV on the couch with Vashti snoozing contentedly on the sofa cushion by my side—the same cushion that was also Jorge's favorite spot, from which he'd unceremoniously evict her within minutes of walking through the front door.

It was, in fact, the selfsame cushion upon which—when Vashti was about nine months old—Jorge and I would come home to find that "someone" had thrown an impromptu pee party.

Of the five rescue cats I've adopted over the years, even though they were all very young when they first came to me, four of them were actually rescued by others. Other people had found them alone on the streets, taken them someplace warm and safe, put desperately needed food into their tiny kitten mouths, and provided care for their mites, worms, and other ailments. Only when they'd been deemed healthy enough to move on to a forever home were they sent my way.

Vashti was the one cat I'd directly rescued myself. My hands were the first to feed and care for her, the first to lovingly stroke her back and gently clean the gunk from her eyes and ears. The first to show her any kindness after weeks alone in what had been a cold and friendless world for an abandoned kitten.

I think that, in a way that was different from any of my other cats, Vashti thought of me as her actual mother. At the very least, as later events would prove, the idea that *my* love and *my* care were essential preconditions for her very survival had etched itself firmly into Vashti's young mind. Anything that threatened our bond was, to Vashti's way of thinking, a threat to life itself.

And also, just like any other cat, she found it profoundly irritating not to get her own way.

Which was why, even as Jorge loudly proclaimed Scarlett's guilt and then abandoned the living room with its overwhelming stench of cat pee, I had my doubts. Those doubts were validated when I returned from the kitchen—having dug out a scrub brush, the spritzy bottle of Nature's Miracle, some baking soda, and a cup of water—to find that Vashti had dragged her favorite cat-sized blankie onto the peed-on sofa cushion and was now resting comfortably atop it with an air of unmistakable triumph.

I thought fleetingly of a story I'd heard at the Miami non-profit organization where I worked. There'd once been an admin, the story went, who had intensely disliked the woman who'd held my job before I did. The admin had procured some "go-away powder" from her local Santeria priestess and sprin-kled it liberally on my predecessor's office chair, which was supposed to have the effect—through some esoteric magical process—of causing my predecessor to leave her job. (The mystical powder may have over-succeeded, insofar as now neither of them worked there.)

Vashti's eyes were positively gleeful as she gazed at me. *Now that* he's *gone,* she seemed to be saying, *howsabout we watch TV together?*

Much to Vashti's consternation, I shooed her from the couch and removed her blankie from sofa to laundry hamper. "This stays between the two of us," I told her, as I tackled the soiled cushion with the scrub brush and baking soda. Beautiful or no, Vashti was always on thinner ice than Scarlett where Jorge was concerned.

A disappointed squeak was Vashti's only response.

VASHTI'S DELICATE PRETTINESS WASN'T THE ONLY THING WORKING in her favor when it came to deflecting blame. She was a thoroughly sweet and gentle soul who I never once saw hiss at anyone, or unsheathe her claws either in play or in anger. Her voice rarely rose above the level of a squeak or the soft coos she greeted me with whenever I approached. Far more amiable than her big sister, Scarlett, Vashti was at her best whenever Jorge's guy friends would come over, as Vashti loved attention from men more than just about anything. (When it came to women other than me, her attitude was distinctly take-it-or-leave-it.) She was cuddly and affectionate even with Jorge, and it was impossible for him to imagine—when she brushed his shins with her extravagant tail and looked up at him with apparent adoration in her big green eyes—that she was at all capable of carrying grudges or formulating revenge plots.

Jorge and I broke up a few months after that first peeing incident (perhaps Vashti's homemade version of "go-away powder" had worked after all), and I moved with my two cats into the spare bedroom of a girlfriend's South Beach home. Vashti and Jorge had grown close enough by then—or so it seemed—that I worried about the effect the separation would have on her.

But Vashti appeared unruffled by the sudden, dramatic change in our lives. We stayed with my friend for six months and, while there, I ended up adopting a blind black kitten named Homer, who'd stood in danger of being euthanized because nobody else would take him in. I worried that Vashti—who still insisted on receiving so much of my attention—might find any perceived competition too much to bear, but she tolerated our new addition with perfect patience. Even when the kitten attacked her in playful frenzies—leaping wildly onto her back and attempting to pin her down—Vashti merely turned her head to lick his muzzle and then waited, the very picture of serenity, for him to exhaust himself. (Scarlett, on the other hand, was decidedly unamused by Homer's kittenish ambushes.)

After a few months in my friend's spare room, I decided to make a career transition from nonprofit work to the private sector in the hopes that I would eventually be able to afford a decent home of my own for the four of us. In the interim, I planned to move back in with my parents so I could save on expenses. My parents had two dogs, and setting up a system of baby gates in the hallways—to allow all five animals a certain amount of run-and-play space—and getting the dogs acclimated to their new "permitted" and "forbidden" zones, would be a process. So I called Jorge, who I still spoke with from time to time, and who I knew still missed Scarlett and Vashti, and asked if he'd be willing to host the three cats for a couple of weeks at our old house. He agreed immediately.

This arrangement seemed to work out initially. When I stopped by at the end of the first week, to drop off supplies and spend some time with the cats, I got a more-or-less glowing report from Jorge. Scarlett primarily went her own way and ignored Jorge altogether—but that was to be expected. This was a home that Scarlett remembered having lived in with me, and she likely assumed that I would return soon to be with her again full-time, just as I had whenever I'd taken some trip out of town that had separated us for a few days. In the meantime, she chose to keep to herself. Homer was only six months old and still malleable in his affections. He was having the time of his life roughhousing with Jorge's friends, who'd become something of a Homer fan club—admiring the spunk, daring, and dexterity that I'd come to know and love, but that the uninitiated always found surprising in a blind kitten. As for Vashti, she was in her element having a few men around after months with no one but my girlfriend and me to pay attention to her.

"It's great having them here," Jorge concluded. "Thanks for giving me time with them again."

The last thing I did before leaving was to let Vashti out onto the screened-in sun porch. It had always been her favorite room in the house when we'd lived there; she'd loved to sunbathe and chase after the geckos that are ubiquitous in South Florida. But even though she frequently caught the small lizards, she never actually hurt them. She'd walk up to me with a lizard dangling from her velvet-soft mouth, I'd grasp the scruff of her neck until she dropped it, and off the gecko would scurry—looking thoroughly disgruntled but otherwise unharmed.

I had a wisp of a thought as I turned back at the front door for one last look at Vashti, scampering happily in her beloved solarium. I wondered if maybe . . . just maybe . . . I was doing the wrong thing for my cats in bringing them to my parents' house—forcing them to live with two dogs, confined to my bedroom, bathroom, and a portion of a hallway, without access to anything remotely like a sunporch. Might they not be better off, after all, here with Jorge?

I didn't know if Jorge would be willing to keep them permanently. I didn't allow myself to think that far. But the mere, passing idea that my cats might do better without me was very nearly—on top of my recent breakup, my floundering career, and the necessity of moving back in with my parents—a crippling blow.

Vashti couldn't have known what I was thinking in that moment. Nevertheless, perhaps she'd seen something in my face during that last look we'd exchanged. Or maybe it was just that I'd come to the house and then gone again, leaving her behind. Whatever it was, something had obviously led Vashti to fear that her stay with Jorge—and only Jorge—might become a permanent one, because I got a call from Jorge before nine a.m. the following morning.

"Scarlett did it again," he announced.

My brain didn't kick fully into gear before noon on Sundays, and I had no idea what Jorge was talking about. "What did she do?"

"She peed on that same spot on the couch last night," Jorge said. "And then, this morning, she peed in my laundry basket with all the clean clothes I'd just taken out of the dryer. It's practically all the clothing I have."

There was no longer any reason to maintain the charade that Scarlett had been the perpetrator all along, so I told him, "I think it was Vashti."

"*Vashti?*" Jorge appeared to momentarily consider, and then quickly reject, this new idea. To my way of thinking, the fact that Vashti was too gentle ever to hiss, bite, or scratch was actually *more* evidence that she was our mad pisher—because what other method was left to her for expressing dissatisfaction? Jorge, however, saw her surface sweetness and looked no further. "No way. It was Scarlett."

There was even less point in arguing about it now. After profusely apologizing on behalf of whichever cat was the culprit, I got down to the two brass-tacks questions: How much did I owe Jorge for the cleaning of couch and clothing, and did he want me to come pick up the cats today, even though they'd originally been scheduled to stay with him for another week?

To Jorge's credit, and despite this recent round of malicious mischief, he seemed reluctant to part with the cats before their scheduled departure date. After pooh-poohing my offers to pay for the cleaning (probably feeling that Scarlett, whatever her own preferences, was still nearly as much his cat as mine), he said, "Hopefully she's gotten it out of her system. Let's see if she settles down."

Two days later, however, he called in the late afternoon with a fresh report. "She peed on my leather jacket this time." It was January, and not only was that jacket expensive, it was a necessity; even in Miami, it was chilly in those first weeks after the New Year. "That's my *only* jacket," Jorge reminded me. "I wear it every day." It was clear, after this latest assault, that Jorge was now ready for the cats to leave—immediately.

As it happened, I had a part-time job that night helping coordinate a local fashion designer's publicity event, which I hoped would turn into a full-time entry-level job with the marketing firm that was producing it. It would take at least three hours in rush-hour traffic to drive from my parents' house in Aventura down to Coral Gables to pick up the cats, then back up to my parents' house to drop them off, and *then* out to South Beach where the event was being held. And if I showed up late to the event, there wouldn't be any job—part-time or full-time—at all. After again apologizing, and pleading for twenty-four hours' clemency, and insisting on covering the cost of a new jacket, we agreed that I would pick up the cats after work the following evening.

"It *was* Vashti," Jorge declared immediately upon greeting me at the front door the following night, as I held my checkbook in one hand and three cat carriers in the other. "I caught her peeing on the kitchen stove."

"Wait—*what?*" This new information cast things in an entirely different light, and for the first time I questioned my previously firm belief in Vashti's guilt. I had never once seen Vashti jump onto a kitchen counter. I'd never once seen her even *attempt* to jump onto a kitchen counter. Not if there was an open can of tuna left out on it, no matter how desperately Vashti might want some of that tuna, and not if the kitchen faucet was running—even though Vashti was obsessed with running water, "asking" me to turn on the bathtub faucet for her several times a day and standing at my feet to gaze longingly at the kitchen sink whenever I turned the water on. It was news to me that Vashti was even capable of making it from floor to countertop unassisted. "Are you *sure?*" I asked.

"Positive." Jorge sounded grim, and more than a little betrayed. "She waited until I walked into the kitchen, so I could see her when she did it."

It was then that a cascading series of epiphanies began to dawn on me—realizations that seemed so incredible and improbable, yet at the same time so manifestly true, that I was staggered. Setting the carriers on the floor, I looked down at Vashti, who'd immediately raced over to stand behind my legs when I walked in.

What struck me in that moment was a single, crystalline certainty: Vashti had embarked on a strategic, long-term (for a cat) plan to get herself kicked out of Jorge's house.

She hadn't simply been "acting out"—urinating in some random place, or in some spot where it might make her feel more secure to find her own scent, or in one location that she thought might especially irritate Jorge (as when a cat pees repeatedly on a dog's bed out of spite). There was an unmistakable *escalation* to each of the successive spots she'd picked. Having first set out to systematically destroy everything she thought Jorge loved, she'd gone on to try to take the very food out of his mouth.

The couch had been Vashti's opening salvo, an arrow fired across the bow. Jorge had been angry when she'd defaced that same spot once before, and while it hadn't been the end of the world then, perhaps it would be sufficient this time around to earn Vashti her walking papers. When that hadn't proved effective, she'd moved up to soiling the basket of clean laundry.

Peeing on the clothes while they were still dirty—given that the basket would sit there half full, for days and days, in between washings—would have been a far easier crime to pull off. But it wouldn't have been nearly as annoying to Jorge as her peeing on the clothes once he'd done the work of washing and drying them, even if that meant Vashti would have to lie patiently in wait for a brief window of opportunity in which she could strike—perhaps only five minutes between when Jorge had pulled the clothes out of the dryer and when he would return to fold them.

Still, the clean clothes would barely have smelled like Jorge (how attached could he be to something that didn't even smell like him?), and he did have others hanging safely in his closet. The leather jacket, on the other hand, was a unique and prized possession. Vashti might not have understood things like "expensive" or "hard to replace." She would certainly have known, however, that Jorge wore that jacket every day, and that it was the one thing in the house that had more of his scent on it than any other—which, from a cat's perspective, would automatically mark it as intensely dear and personal.

But the stove was the real coup de grâce—a definitive attempt to cut Jorge off at the knees. On the one hand, from a human›s point of view, it was actually the least of the damage Vashti had caused. What could be easier than cleaning cat urine from a metal stove without any pores for the liquid to seep into?

A cat, however, wouldn't see it that way. The stove wouldn't have smelled especially like Jorge, but it was where he prepared all his meals. And if there's one thing every animal understands, it's the intimate connection between food and life itself. She'd let Jorge know that she wasn't messing around anymore, that it was no longer just his "stuff" she was coming for—she had now set her assassin's eye on Jorge, himself. *I'm peeing on the place where YOUR FOOD comes from!* I imagined Vashti thinking. *You cannot possibly ignore me now that I'm taking away YOUR FOOD!*

The uncharacteristic effort she'd made—the one and only time in her whole life when she'd jumped from floor to counter! And she'd waited until he'd walked in to *watch* her do it—she wasn't even trying to get away with it! I thought of a movie I'd seen once, where a mobster, in giving orders to an underling for retaliatory measures against a rival, had roared, "I *WANT* IT TO LOOK LIKE ARSON!"

The truly astonishing thing about all this was that it showed a fundamental grasp of the principle of cause and effect—the idea that by deliberately putting a chain of events in motion, Vashti thereby increased the likelihood of someday attaining a specific goal. In this case, the future goal that Vashti had in mind was getting kicked out of Jorge's house and living with me again. It was the kind of abstract thought that a cat's brain wasn't supposed to be able to comprehend, much less act upon.

But it was so much more even than *that*! Because Vashti had made a very concerted attempt to put herself in Jorge's place— *to try to think like Jorge thought*—in planning out her Peemageddon. *If I were Jorge*, she'd asked herself after each act of illicit urination had failed to earn her release, *what would be an even worse thing someone could do to me?*

Empathy was one thing. Every animal I'd ever lived with had demonstrated empathy—cozying up to me when I was upset, or frolicking jubilantly when I was especially happy. Never, though, had I seen an animal embark upon a series of steps in a deliberate plot—executed over a period of days—to bring about a precise emotional state in someone else. There are plenty of humans who put real effort into unraveling the perplexities of feline psychology (ahem). But I'd never seen a cat delve any deeper into the mysteries of human behavior than *If I meow right now, she'll feed me.*

Perhaps I was over-interpreting (which is a thing we writers tend to do). But even twenty years later, it's the vision of Vashti atop the stove—or, at least, what I imagine she must have looked like up there—that keeps coming back to me. I would go on to live with Vashti for the remaining thirteen years of her life, and in all that time, never once—never *once*—did I see her jump onto anything higher than the level of a dining-room chair. That she'd roused herself to the effort on this sole occasion could only have been because she'd been trying to make a point.

To Vashti, Jorge had always been someone who'd threatened to separate her from the one person upon whom her life depended. In her limited understanding of the world, there was the option of living with Jorge, the option of living with me, and no other option she could think of—so if Jorge kicked her out, then being returned to my custody was a foregone conclusion. In wreaking such havoc in Jorge's life, Vashti had been fighting for her own.

Perhaps, knowing how painful I would also find any permanent separation, she'd been fighting for both of us. Her little pee spree had been, in its own pungent way, an expression of love. And it would prove to be—over a lifetime of using her own bodily fluids as a creative medium for saying the things she couldn't say in words—Vashti's magnum opus.

What even Vashti couldn't have foreseen, however, was that she'd opened my eyes to something I should have known all along. There would be bountiful times, and there would be lean times, but never again would I think that my cats might be happier without me. The four of us would always be at our best together. We were a family.

My three cats returned with me to my parents' house that very night. Having reacted so badly to less than ten days with Jorge, Vashti's potential response to a newly limited space—and two dogs, to boot—at my parents' house left me more than a little nervous. Despite my apprehensions, though, Vashti and her siblings would go on to spend the better part of two years—two surprisingly happy, bone-dry years—with me in my childhood home.

Driving them over that night, with Vashti on the passenger seat ensconced in her carrier, reaching longingly toward me through its grating with her little white paws, I glanced over at this small, evil genius beside me, clothed in the angelic form of a pretty but otherwise ordinary-looking white cat, and wondered, *Who are you? Where did you come from?*

MORE THAN A DECADE LATER, AFTER I'D PUBLISHED A MEMOIR about Homer, and pictures of all three of my cats were in wide circulation both in the book and online, a reader sent me an email about Vashti. *She's a Turkish Angora*, the reader proclaimed with great confidence, providing a helpful link to the breed's Wikipedia page. Among photos of cats who looked uncannily identical to Vashti, I found this intriguing observation under the section labeled "Behavior":

Turkish Angora cats are playful, intelligent, athletic, and involved. They bond with humans, but often select a particular member of the family to be their constant companion. They are in turn very protective of their person. They seek to be "helpful" in any way they can with their humans, and their intelligence is at times remarkable, showing basic problem-solving skills.

It seemed unlikely that a descendant of one of the most ancient breeds of domestic cats—cats originating naturally in the mountains north of Ankara more than a thousand years ago, who had once been the prized companions of emperors and queens but whose numbers, in recent years, had dwindled so low that the Turkish government had established a protective breeding program—would find herself as a tiny, abandoned kitten, covered in mites and starved half to death, roaming the streets of Miami all alone.

Still, the circumstantial evidence was compelling.

IT WAS A GLORIOUS DAY WHEN, AFTER TWO YEARS, I FINALLY LEFT my parents' house and moved into a South Beach apartment of my own. Like anyone living by herself for the very first time— without parents, roommates, or boyfriend—I put a lot of time and effort into selecting the apartment itself, and also into carefully allotting my savings for the furniture and decorative flourishes that would make the place comfortable for all four of us without breaking my budget.

So it seemed an especially cruel twist of fate when, only three months after I'd moved in—just when I'd finally gotten the place to feel like "me"—my apartment was broken into.

In my memoir about Homer, I wrote at greater length about the night of the break-in—how I'd awakened in pitch darkness and turned on the lamp to find a strange man looming over my bed, and how Homer (blind, tiny Homer!) had attacked the intruder viciously, driving him out of our home while giving me the chance to call 911.

In the book, the story had ended with the welcome sound of the police knocking on our front door. Safety had been restored, Homer had earned his creds as a bona fide hero, and that was where I, as the storyteller, allowed the curtain to drop.

But, of course, in real life curtains don't drop at the end of crucial or dramatic moments—things just keep happening. And what happened next was that, once I opened the front door, six police officers burst into the apartment. Two of them searched my home for the burglar, despite my having seen him leave before the police had even arrived. ("Clear!" yelled Officer One from my bedroom, while Officer Two, scoping out my small living room/kitchen, also yelled "Clear!" That was the whole search. It wasn't a very big apartment.) Two of them radioed back to the police station to give them an update. And the other two busied themselves taking my official statement.

Vashti was beside herself with excitement and dismay during these proceedings. Excitement, because here were *six* men—more men than she'd ever seen at one time in her whole life!—standing in our apartment. And dismay, because not *one* of them was paying any attention to her. Nobody had so much as murmured her name appreciatively, or had the decency to remark on her beautiful green eyes and snow-white fur. She was normally subtler in her approaches toward men, but all the surplus testosterone in the air must have driven Vashti wild. Standing in the middle of the living-room coffee table in what I called her "Abominable Snow Kitty" pose—reared up on her hind legs, exposing the thick, white fluff of her belly while her front legs pawed frantically at the air—Vashti worked desperately to get the attention of these inexplicably insensitive gentleman callers. (*Notice me! NOOOOOTICE MEEEEEEE!*) Finally, one of the cops took pity and stroked a grateful Vashti on her back, saying, "You're a pretty little thing, aren't you?" Vashti cooed and modestly cast her eyes to one side, as if to say, *Who . . . me?*

Our home may have just been broken into, our lives endangered while we'd slept, but still—Vashti had her priorities.

If a cat could possibly be described as a flirt, then Vashti was the Scarlett O'Hara of cats (with all due respect to the actual, and forever surly, Scarlett who lived with us). But, like any true temptress, Vashti could easily turn fickle toward her prey once she'd lured them in—which was something we'd all learn the hard way when, a mere seven months after the break-in, a job opportunity had me moving with my three cats up to New York.

When you live in New York and have a circle of friends based in Miami, inevitably you end up with more than the usual number of overnight houseguests. Budget-conscious friends heading north for weddings, class reunions, or job interviews, or those simply looking for a few days of fun in the Big Apple, will unerringly claim "crash pad" rights, and—especially during that first year after you move—you'll likely miss the old gang enough to welcome the intrusions.

What initially seemed like a cost-saving option for traveling friends, however, more often than not turned out to be a much pricier scenario for me—and my checkbook got quite a workout during those first few years of Manhattan living. The move from Miami to New York City, that well-known breeding ground for artists of all stripes, seemed to have reawakened Vashti's creative impulses. If I'd been the actual parent of a gifted child, I couldn't have been called upon more frequently to exhaust my slender bank account in underwriting her artistic experiments.

Or, in more down-to-earth terms: making right with my cash whatever fresh wrongs Vashti had done with her urine.

With the passage of nearly three pee-free years, I'd come to regard Vashti's early forays into peeing-with-a-purpose as no more than the extremes of youth—a circumstantial reaction to the unique threat that Vashti had thought Jorge represented. Cats, I believed, were apt to forget such early traumas over time.

But I think that Vashti remembered Jorge for years and years, long after he'd exited our lives for good. At the very least, she appeared to have maintained a fixed idea that men—however desirable they may have been as courtiers paying homage to her beauty—were dangerous where I was concerned. She may have been all soft purrs and tempting coos of welcome when a man first came into our home, but the internal climate of her heart cooled considerably if he signaled anything that Vashti construed as an intention to hang around long-term.

Female guests had nothing worse to fear from Vashti than a certain chilliness in her attentions. She didn't alternate between hiding under the bed and lashing out at them with her claws, the way Scarlett did. She didn't follow them doggedly into the bathroom, as Homer liked to do (Homer, as dictated by cat logic, always regarded a closed bathroom door as a personal affront). Beyond a cursory sniff of inspection when they first arrived, Vashti left female guests and their belongings alone. My mother, sister, and various girlfriends came for a few days and left again without any greater reaction from Vashti than her deigning to allow them to pat her on the head when—and only when—she was in the mood to tolerate it.

With men, however, it was a different story. As far as Vashti knew, any male houseguest might become a conquest of her own, but he might also be a new Jorge in the making— someone who had the potential to come between her and me and maybe even part the two of us forever. Accordingly, men who stopped by for an afternoon visit or an evening cocktail were welcomed with all the warmth—in the form of coos, purrs, affectionate head bonks, and demonstrative swishes of her magnificent tail—that Vashti could muster. Any man who brought a suitcase or duffel bag and proceeded to spend the night, however, was made to understand in no uncertain terms that he'd exceeded Vashti's strict boundaries and overstayed his welcome.

The men whom Vashti seduced and then ultimately betrayed could never quite believe that she was the culprit behind the deliberate destruction of their cherished possessions. It wasn't just that her seductions were always so convincing. (*Nobody will ever love you like* I *love you,* the naked adoration in her wide green eyes seemed to promise.) It was because Vashti looked, for lack of a better word, so *classy.* The sort of creature who would engage in anything as unseemly as public urination could only be described as NOCD ("Not Our Class, Dear"), whereas Vashti looked like a high-society *grande dame*, rolling by in a Bentley while swathed in furs and jewels—or, at the very least, like the kind of cat such a lady might keep.

But however sweet and flowery an act she might have put on, Vashti was no fainting Southern belle or cloistered Park Avenue debutante. She was a vandal, a street punk, a graffiti artist. She hailed originally from the wild and wooly pavements of Miami—and she had no compunctions whatsoever about dirtying her lily-white paws (or other people's belongings) when dirt was called for.

Eventually, I found that it saved a great deal of time, money, and irritation on everybody's part to write down a list of basic rules that had to be observed while staying in our apartment, and to leave that list with my doorman, along with my spare keys, for any overnight male visitors who were likely to arrive before I'd gotten home from work to give them a full orientation. The list went something like this:

- *You should immediately store your suitcase and/or garment bag in the closet. NEVER leave it open on the bed or floor or anywhere outside the closet even if it's closed. Vashti will pee on it.*
- *Hang your coat in the closet as soon as you walk in. Never leave a coat, sweater, shirt, or any article of clothing— including a sock—on the floor, on the bed, or draped over a couch or chair. Vashti will pee on it.*
- *I've left you a towel on the bed. After showering, please immediately hang the towel over the shower. If you leave it lying around once it's used and smells like you, Vashti will pee on it.*

THE PICASSO OF PEE

- *If you decide to take a nap before heading out into the city, please strip the sheets and comforter, fold them up, and put them on the top shelf of the closet before you leave. If the bed smells like you, Vashti will pee on it.*
- *When you leave at the end of your visit, please place your used towel and sheets in the laundry bag, seal the laundry bag tight, and stick it in the closet. If you leave it out and full of things with your scent on them, Vashti will pee on it.*
- *If you've brought anything of value not covered in the above list (briefcase, computer bag, etc.), either keep it in the closet at all times or else leave it with the doorman downstairs to hold during your visit—because if you love it, and you leave it anyplace where Vashti can get to it, she WILL pee on it!*

I probably don't need to add that each item on this list was there in direct response to some hard-won and financially costly bit of knowledge gleaned from a previous friend's visit. Once I knew that Vashti would pee into an open suitcase, for example, it didn't immediately occur to me that she would do so even if the suitcase were closed. I learned that she would pee on a garment bag, but didn't realize that the tuxedo or suit jacket contained within it would also be fair game if left lying on the bed. And surely Vashti wouldn't soil the bed itself, where *I* slept when we didn't have guests, just because the sheets temporarily smelled like someone else. (It occurs to me as I write this that my elementary school teachers may have been wrong all those years ago, and that I was in fact neither "a fast learner" nor "especially bright.")

Like many a beautiful woman before her, every so often a man would enter Vashti's life firm in the belief that he was the one who could "tame" her. One particularly optimistic customer in this department was my dear friend Frank. Back when I was working for a Miami nonprofit, Frank was my counterpart in the organization's Boston office. We had become fast friends over biweekly status phone calls, and had met in person more than a few times over the years, as work-related or personal travel had brought us into each other's orbits. Even long after I'd left the organization, the two of us remained in touch—although by then our lives had diverged in very different directions: I had moved to New York and into private-sector marketing communications, while Frank had moved even deeper into charity work.

Nominally, Frank's home base was in Alaska, where he lived in a one-room cabin in the middle of a remote forest without electricity, heat, or running water. Mostly, however, Frank traveled the world. He was a computer genius—the kind of guy who big companies line up to throw six- and seven-figure salaries at. But Frank had turned them all down, opting instead to travel to third-world countries where he helped small villages build up their computer infrastructure in exchange for token sums that worked out to less than a twentieth of the current US minimum wage.

In addition to his work on behalf of humankind, Frank was also a tremendous lover of nature and animals—and, with a certain amount of fairness, considered himself to have an above-average rapport with the four-legged among us. He'd stumbled upon more than one black bear, for example, in the woods of Alaska, and had managed to get away from these encounters entirely unscathed. Sometimes this was with the aid of a repellent spray called Bear-B-Gone (although Frank was the first to admit that often the best deployment of Bear-B-Gone was simply to startle the bear by chucking the entire can in its general direction). More usually, however, he'd managed—with a gentle tone and calm demeanor—to persuade the wary bear that he meant it no harm.

Even Scarlett, when Frank arrived on our doorstep for a few days' visit, was charmed by him—or, at any rate, as close to charmed as Scarlett was capable of being. She wasn't affectionate, exactly, but she didn't run away from him, and even permitted Frank to stroke her forehead without bloodying his fingers in return. Homer and Frank, it goes without saying, immediately got along like a house afire.

Vashti also appeared to adore him, looking up at him with her heart in her eyes and nuzzling her head into the palm of his hand. I tried to give Frank the usual warnings about safeguarding his few belongings from Vashti's wrath, but he tut-tutted me. "Vashti and I are going to get along just fine." He said this to me, but mostly to her. Vashti appeared to echo this sentiment with an innocent little squeak—so cool, butter wouldn't have melted in her mouth. "We're not going to have any problems."

The next morning found a sadder-but-wiser Frank standing over my bathtub, wringing the cat urine from his favorite sweater. I watched from the bathroom doorway, my pen and checkbook in hand. "So . . . should I just make this out to 'Cash'?"

The one thing for which I must—grudgingly—give Vashti credit is that she made me far more selective in my romantic life than I might otherwise have been. During the first three years that I lived in New York, I had only one serious boyfriend—and then for only about six months. Homer had already forced me to set a pretty high bar in terms of whom I allowed into my home on a regular basis. Such a person had to be, at a minimum, conscientious enough never to leave the balcony door open and unattended, or to strew items in unusual places that might trip up a blind cat who wasn't expecting them to be there.

By the time I also factored in Vashti's reaction, and considered the hassle of stripping the bed every morning and remaking it every evening that my boyfriend spent there, and mentally ran through the lengthy checklist of dos and don'ts I'd have to give him, and *then* calculated the likelihood that eventually he'd forget at least one of those dos or don'ts—requiring me to bear this hypothetical boyfriend's probable anger plus the cost of replacing whatever Vashti had destroyed—it rarely seemed worth the effort. Going out for dinner with a group of friends or catching up on *The Sopranos* at home alone were infinitely easier options.

So it was with more than a little trepidation, when I first started dating Laurence, the man I was to marry, that I welcomed him into our lives and then eventually moved with my three cats into his apartment. Laurence was a man who'd never lived with even one cat, and he wasn't at all sure that suddenly living with three was a swell idea. But he loved me, and I loved my cats, and so he conceded that he was willing to give it a try . . . for my sake.

LAURENCE HAD LIVED IN THE SAME RENT-CONTROLLED, THREE-bedroom, two-bathroom apartment for seventeen years—with roommates initially, although for the past decade he'd lived alone.

Moving in with my three cats was an uneasy transition for all of us at first. Definitively not a "cat guy," Laurence seemed inclined to give the three felines a wide, wary berth—an inclination that at least two of my cats reciprocated. Homer, who bonded instantly with most people, turned unexpectedly skittish in the face of Laurence's booming, basso profundo. (Laurence's rich, ringing, almost preternaturally deep voice was one of the things I loved most about him—but it was easy to see how it might spook a blind cat at first.) As for Scarlett, she couldn't quite believe that, after nearly seven years, I was once again forcing her into the horrors of living with *two* humans instead of just one.

But where Homer and Scarlett saw a potential adversary (one that Homer dealt with largely by avoiding him, and that Scarlett handled by angrily slashing at him with her claws whenever she thought he was standing too close), Vashti shrewdly surmised an opening.

She may have been "the pretty one," but it was Homer who'd always gotten the lion's share of attention from newcomers. Once people oohed and aahed over Vashti's beauty, they fell to watching Homer, fascinated to see a blind cat going through the simple, everyday motions of retrieving a favorite toy or walking across the room unassisted.

But Laurence—with whom I'd been best friends for nearly three years before we started dating—had met Homer before, and had long since gotten used to hearing me insist that Homer was a perfectly normal cat despite his blindness. Accordingly, Laurence wasn't inclined to be unduly impressed when Homer did normal cat things.

From Vashti's perspective, this presented a golden, once-in-a-lifetime opportunity: the chance to have, for the very first time, a human who was all her own—one she wouldn't have to share with any other cats.

As with anything that grows surely but imperceptibly, it's hard to look back and know exactly what the earliest overtures were. Did Vashti creep over to stand at Laurence's feet as he sat on the sofa alone one night after I'd gone to bed, weaving affectionately—with many a dazzling tail flourish—around his ankles? Did she jump up on the couch and lean oh-so-tenderly against his shoulder while he watched a Jets game and I read a book in the bedroom? It's impossible to say. But I do remember very clearly, perhaps a month after we'd moved in, walking into the living room to find Vashti firmly ensconced in Laurence's lap—Laurence, Mr. I'm-Not-A-Cat-Guy, who'd once upon a time said, *I'm not sure that living with cats is for me.* "You're a pretty girl, aren't you?" Laurence now crooned as he scritched Vashti beneath her chin. For her part, Vashti looked as pleased and proud as the cat who'd swallowed a man-sized canary. "A pretty, *pretty* girl . . ."

So much for Vashti's long-standing mistrust of my boy-friends! I knew for sure that Vashti's conquest of Laurence (and vice versa) was a fait accompli when, one morning, I walked into the kitchen and saw Laurence at the table eating scrambled eggs while Vashti sat at his feet, daintily scooping up the little bits of egg that Laurence, in response to the gentle pressure of Vashti's paw on his shin, dropped to the ground for her enjoy-ment. "Laurence!" I scolded. "It's taken me *years* to train them not to beg for food at the table!"

Laurence at least had the decency to look shamefaced. "But she's so pretty, and she likes me."

Laurence is also a writer and has a way with words—but, in that moment, he was just another guy, aptly summing up fifty millennia of masculine wrongdoing in a single sentence.

Vashti soon had Laurence wrapped firmly around her fuzzy little paw. Laurence was a film journalist who hated nothing more than being interrupted while watching a movie—but he'd jump up from the couch half a dozen times over the course of a two-hour film to turn the bathtub faucet on or off for Vashti upon hearing her soft squeak of command. He was forever buying her new toys, or bringing home little delicacies from the local gourmet deli that he thought she might enjoy. Scarlett and Homer also got their share of the bounty, and—much sooner than I could have hoped for—the rough edges of our initial transition to living together with three cats were quickly smoothed over. Even Scarlett, appreciative of Laurence's largesse (and not caring that she was only its secondhand beneficiary) would occasionally allow Laurence to brush within a few inches of her when passing in the hallway without lashing out at him with her claws.

Vashti seemed grateful for the unexpected good thing she'd found in the slavish attentions of this devoted new man in our lives—rewarding Laurence with adoring looks and loving cuddle sessions. And yet, for all the happiness it brought us, this blossoming man-feline love affair also introduced its own, entirely new, set of problems. Laurence would also offer his guest room to the occasional friend visiting from out of town. And whereas it had once been only men who'd aroused Vashti's territorial instincts, she now turned gimlet-eyed (and bladder-ready) upon the arrival of female visitors as well.

By Vashti's calculations, one woman in his life was all Laurence ought to need. She barely acknowledged even *my* claim on him. I don't know that Vashti ultimately understood male-female sexual dynamics, but, at a minimum, she knew that her sole competitor for Laurence's attentions was me, and I was a woman. So throwing yet another woman into the mix couldn't possibly be a positive turn of events.

It shouldn't have surprised me, then—though it did—to find myself, at 6:31 Halloween night, scavenging through a thoroughly picked-over costume shop with one of Laurence's out-of-town friends, trying to find a hasty substitute for a "sexy angel" costume that was neither sexy nor angelic now that a pungent yellow circle of cat pee adorned its shimmery white folds.

Then there was the memorable Friday afternoon when Laurence and I had to rent a car and drive all the way up to Buffalo (six hours! each way!). Buffalo was the location of the one and only David's Bridal in the entire Tri-State area that could, on such short notice, offer us the exact size and style bridesmaid dress needed to replace the one that Laurence's visiting college friend was expected to arrive wearing at the Tribeca Rooftop by four o'clock the following day—and to which Vashti had made some last-minute "enhancements" in the form of a Pollock-esque, lemon-yellow spatter across its front. We sent the bridesmaid herself off to the rehearsal dinner, assuring her that all would be well and urging her not to trouble the bride the night before the wedding with this teeny-tiny little hiccup. (*Don't worry! We can totally fix this!*) My friend Anise—an MTV fashion stylist with two temperamental cats of her own—took Laurence's

friend's measurements before we left and rode along with us, hand-stitching the final alterations to the replacement dress in the car's back seat as we drove through the night.

You did have to give Vashti credit for the unerring instinct that had led her to bypass mundane garments like jeans and nightshirts, and strike her perceived foes precisely where it would hurt the most.

I'd never thought I'd see the day when Vashti would appear to be as attached to anyone else as she was to me—and I wasn't always sure how I felt about it. On the one hand, I was thrilled for her obvious happiness—Vashti, the classic middle child—in having a person of her very own who she didn't have to share. And there was no question that this bond between Laurence and Vashti, in giving Laurence a reason to enjoy living with the cats beyond making me happy, had made my life infinitely easier.

Still, I couldn't help feeling wistful as I remembered a time, not very long past, when Vashti had given me fresh and emphatic evidence every day that, as far as she was concerned, there was only one human for her—and I was it.

If I occasionally felt a little jealous of Vashti's relationship with Laurence, that feeling was absolutely a two-way street. Even when it was just the five of us—Laurence and me and the three cats, without any pesky houseguests—Vashti's eagle-eyed watch over Laurence never entirely abated. She'd squeal with outraged jealousy if she happened to walk into a room to see the two of us embracing, racing over to paw frantically at Laurence's leg and wriggle her soft, white body between ours.

Laurence thought that Vashti's possessiveness was adorable (and more than a little flattering), and he'd often go out of his way to make a big show of hugging and kissing me for Vashti's benefit. It was adorable, that is, until the time when Vashti—rather than trying to separate us—promptly and pointedly strolled from the living room to the bedroom, where Laurence's leather jacket was tossed carelessly over the bed, and peed on it with angry abandon.

"She never seems to pee on anything of *yours*," Laurence grumbled. Which was true. She never once did.

Still, I argued in her defense. "It was an act of love, don't you see?"

"What, like she was trying to punish me for paying attention to you?" Laurence, understandably, found it difficult to be sanguine under the circumstances.

"Maybe," I agreed. "Or maybe she was trying to 'mark her man.' She found the one thing in the whole house that smells the most like you, and she put her scent on it, too. To show that you belong to her." I was forced to interpret for Laurence, but I'd understood loud and clear the message Vashti had intended to convey: *He's MY boyfriend! Not yours: MINE!*

Laurence looked around what had once been the decidedly masculine living room of a bachelor living alone. Sports memorabilia had gradually given way to small vases filled with fresh flowers. One of my handbags rested on the new rosewood coffee table—which had replaced a thick, unappealing slab of dull-green faux marble—and a pair of my high heels had been kicked carelessly underneath it. Two large "kitty condos" were now as prominent in the room as the entertainment center—and although neither obscured the view of the TV, the rug before the TV was strewn with catnip toys, colorful little balls of yarn, and the old shoeboxes we left lying around because the cats so thoroughly enjoyed sleeping in them.

"I guess love makes everyone do strange things," Laurence observed.

I<small>N LOOKING AT THE STORY OF</small> V<small>ASHTI'S LIFE ALMOST EXCLUSIVELY</small> through the prism of her pee, I realize that I've done her something of a disservice. Her only true crime, in the end, was loving those she loved a little too much—of loving us so much that she would insist, however accommodating she was most of the time, that we love her and each other to the exclusion of all outsiders. Vashti's greatest and only real fear was that someone or something might break up her family. It would be heartless to blame her too much for such a thing as that.

In many ways, Vashti was the very heart of our home, the glue that held us all together. She was the only cat who was willing to play with Homer, the only cat Scarlett was willing to play with, and Laurence's link to the cats who'd so thoroughly invaded his life. The soft warmth of her white fur against my cheek, the gentle weight of her small body resting on my chest, had gotten me through many a day that was darker than I cared to remember. She would always be my own little foundling, who'd crawled into my arms and my heart on that very first afternoon in Miami— my mysterious Turkish princess, covered in rags and ashes until the moment had arrived for her to reveal her true glory.

So it broke our hearts, thoroughly and completely, when, a few months before her fourteenth birthday—two years after

Laurence and I had married, and five years after we'd moved in together—Vashti was diagnosed with chronic renal failure. We didn't know how much time we'd have left with her, but we did know that the diagnosis was fatal.

Vashti had hyperthyroidism as well, and the two conditions combined brought a slew of additional complications. Vashti lost weight at an alarming rate. She became anemic and developed high blood pressure as her heart worked harder to pump out all the toxins her kidneys no longer filtered effectively. The acids created by those toxins backed up into her tummy and sharply curbed her appetite.

For nine months, I forced pills down Vashti's throat twice a day and gave her two shots (one for her anemia and one for her high blood pressure). We also had to administer—with a needle and IV bag—subcutaneous fluids every other day, to give her kidneys extra support. Vashti hated this, as any cat would, but she hardly struggled—although she'd make me chase her around the living room for a good half hour first (Vashti was unexpectedly wily when it came to duck-and-weave evasive maneuvers). But never did she scratch or bite me, not even by accident, once I'd captured her. The same was true of the professionals at our local animal hospital, where Vashti was now a frequent visitor. All the vet techs were ready to swear that Vashti was the sweetest cat they'd ever treated, and I certainly wouldn't have argued with them.

After she'd been diagnosed with CRF, Vashti's peeing outside the litter box became less a pointed choice and more a thing that just happened. Perhaps she associated her new discomfort with the litter box itself and thought that going someplace else would feel better—or possibly, with age and illness, her mind simply wasn't as sharp as it had once been. There were a few places she appeared to favor more than others (our most expensive area rug, for example), and we bought additional litter boxes to place in those spots—and I really do think that Vashti tried to use them. She'd creep into the new litter box, but her little tush would still be hanging outside of it—which meant that her pee landed in the spot on the rug right in front of the litter box, rather than in the box itself. The scrub brush and a bottle of Nature's Miracle became my two best friends during this time.

Eventually, Vashti took to the bed in the guest room and hardly ever left it. We moved her litter box so that it was directly next to the bed, but Vashti would still pee on the bed itself as long as there was anything soft or cushiony for her to go on. Day by day and one by one, we removed first the comforter, then the sheets, then the pillows one at a time, until there was nothing left on the bed but a rubber sheet and Vashti's favorite blankie, which I dutifully laundered and returned to her every day.

Then one day, Vashti stopped eating altogether. For four days we upped the dosage of her appetite-stimulant pill and waited, hoping for some improvement. But we hoped and waited in vain. On the fifth day, Laurence and I looked into her face. In the dulled green eyes she turned our way, we saw no trace of the Vashti we'd known and loved.

That was when we knew.

We arranged an appointment at the vet's office for the following morning, and I made up the bed in the guest room so I could sleep with Vashti that night. Vashti might not have been the first cat I'd adopted, but she was the first I would lose—my first profound loss of any kind as an adult. Looking back from the perspective of almost-forty, I could see that I'd been barely more than a child when Vashti and I had come into each other's lives. I hadn't even been able to take care of myself without my parents' help for two whole years of Vashti's life. Back then, Jorge had had more money, a stable and growing career, a spacious home—things I hadn't been able to provide. And yet, Vashti had chosen me anyway. She had, in a way, been the first to believe in me and in my potential, long before I'd been able to believe in myself—and I knew that when Vashti left me, she would take a piece of me with her. One that would never come back.

My loss of Vashti was specific and new, but cradling her in my arms in the wee small hours of our final night together, my want was universal. Whether it's the loss of a cat or a parent or a beloved friend, everybody wants the same thing as you clutch their hand (or paw) in those last moments together. You want to know that the one you're saying good-bye to is there with you. That the moment is a shared moment, the feeling a shared feeling. That whatever may have come before, over the years, in the way of temporary struggles or momentary anger—and whatever might still be yet to come, once you've been left alone with your grief—in that instant, the two of you are one heart, two parts of one whole, there together in a single, perfect moment.

The tears from my eyes overflowed as I pressed Vashti tighter against my chest. "Vashti," I murmured. "Let me know that you know how much I love you—how much I've always loved you. Let me know that it's okay for me to let you go."

Vashti, of course, had no words to give me. Even if she had, it was a thing beyond words, what was happening to us here in the darkness of our last night together.

But Vashti had always been a creative spirit. She'd always found a way to express the contents of her innermost heart, words be damned.

Even now, she was creeping slowly up my torso to curl beneath my chin, harkening back to our very first days together, when Vashti's and my finding each other and her very survival had seemed improbable and wondrous and meant to be. I murmured her name and allowed the tears flowing from my face to bury themselves in the thick white of her fur. Rising again, she crept further up my body until her belly rested against my face, absorbing my tears as quickly as they fell. She was going to crawl all the way up to the pillow above me, I thought, to mold herself around the top of my head like a crown as she'd done in her younger days, and make the circle of our beginning and our ending complete.

Oh, my Vashti, I continued to murmur, *My beautiful girl, my beautiful, beautiful girl . . .*

Vashti braced herself against me with one hind leg resting on each of my shoulders. I could feel, in the way her legs trembled, how much this effort cost her. Still, it was with exquisite tenderness and delicacy that she squatted down, lowering the bottom half of her body until my chin rested on her warm belly.

And then, in a scalding-hot stream, Vashti peed directly onto my neck.

The pee struck me with surprising force, running sideways from beneath my chin into my hair, and down the front of my nightshirt to the blanket pulled across my chest. And even as I sputtered and squealed my surprise, and plunged—after carefully dislodging Vashti—out of bed into the darkened hallway toward the bathroom for my first-ever three a.m. shower ("What happened?" Laurence called in alarm from our bedroom, and I shouted back, "*VASHTI JUST PEED ON ME!!!*"), even then I had to admit that Vashti had saved her very best for last.

As I stood in the shower that night, crying and laughing until I could no longer tell which was which, I realized that Vashti had, in her own inimitable way, given me a gift: the certain knowledge that some of us, if we're extraordinarily lucky, might someday be vouchsafed the blessing of getting to die as we lived. That some essential, immutable core of who we *really* are—and always were—will, in the darkness of our last hours, beam out strong and sure and bright as a lighthouse. That whatever else time and age may take from us, they can never rob us entirely of our true selves.

Her final creative effort would be her most dramatic—the one she would always be remembered for. In choosing to go out with a bang and not with a whimper, Vashti had crafted a legend that would live forever. She'd ensured that I would tell her story over and over and over again, long after she was gone. In the face of death, Vashti—a little white cat from the streets of Miami—had attained immortality.

What more could any artist ask for?

"Cat Lovers Don't Read Books"

Famous cats weren't a *thing* back in 2007 like they are today.

In November of that year, when I first began writing the proposal for a memoir about Homer, the blind black cat I'd loved and lived with for more than a decade, there was no such thing as cat cafés (at least, not outside of Japan). Cat videos hadn't yet taken over the web. The "Friskies 50" list of the internet's fifty most-influential cats was years away not only from execution, but also from any relevance. If you had proposed an idea for something like CatCon—a huge, Comic-Con-type convention where ailurophiles from all over the world take over an L.A. convention center and pose for selfies with their favorite social media "celebri-cats"—concerned friends might have made serious inquiries about your mental health.

Of course, everybody knew about famous *cartoon* cats, like Garfield, Tom, Sylvester, and the perennial Hello Kitty. And there were instantly recognizable commercial pusses like 9Lives' Morris and the elegant Fancy Feast Persian—although they were "played" by a succession of different cats, more brand icons than actual felines. But there didn't seem to be any real-life famous cats, cats who were also members of real-life human families.

Except, that is, for one cat I'd read about in a recent newspaper article—a cat who'd lived in a library in small-town Iowa, and whose human caregiver had just sold a proposal for a book about his life for more than a million dollars.

My own first book, a novel about South Beach (my hometown), had been published a few months earlier. Now I was trying to figure out a second book. I didn't think I could earn anything close to a million dollars for any book idea I might have, but I remember putting down the newspaper and looking across the living room at Homer—who was, at the moment, visible only from the waist down, the upper half of his body buried under the sofa as he struggled to retrieve an intriguing new belled toy that had rolled away from him—and thinking, *I bet I could write a book about Homer. Homer's a pretty cool cat . . .*

I've lived in New York for more than fifteen years now, but I adopted Homer in Miami in 1997, when he was only three weeks old—a tiny, abandoned stray fresh from the surgery that had removed his untreatably infected eyes, forever taking his vision for the sake of giving him his life.

I was the very last person that my vet (who had performed the surgery on the kitten pro bono, hoping she'd later be able to find him a home) had on her list of potential adopters, knowing how precarious my own life was at the moment. I was in my mid-twenties at the time, still recovering from my recent breakup with Jorge, the man I'd lived with for three years and had thought I would marry. I was staying in a friend's spare bedroom with the two rescue cats my ex and I had adopted together—a fluffy white beauty named Vashti and a moody gray tabby named Scarlett. But when everybody else refused to take a chance on an eyeless kitten, she called me as a last resort.

I wasn't sure that I was the right person for this kitten, either. But from the very first moment when I went to meet him at my vet's office—when I picked up the wee ball of black kitten fuzz, and he crawled from my arms up the front of my sweater to the bend of my neck, nestling there and purring like a race car—I knew that the two of us were meant to belong to each other.

The doctor warned that Homer would likely always be a timid cat, never quite as brave or self-sufficient as his sighted counterparts. In fact, over the years, the opposite had proven true. Even when fully grown, Homer was never very big—no more than five pounds at his peak—but he had all the courage and brio of a cat ten times his size. He scaled seven-foot bookcases with ease, caught buzzing flies in mid-air—a blind cat!—with nothing but his ramped-up sense of hearing to guide him. An outgoing "people cat," he eagerly made close and affectionate friends-for-life with every new person who came into our home.

And then there was the unforgettable night in the summer of 2000, when Homer saved my life by chasing off a four a.m. burglar.

It was the sound of agitated growls coming from Homer, who had been sleeping next to me on the bed, that first awakened me. Alarmed at hearing my normally sociable, happy-go-lucky little guy in obvious distress, I reached over to flip on the bedside lamp.

A man—a man I'd never seen before in my life—was standing at the foot of my bed.

My own first reaction was frozen panic. Homer, however—tiny, five-pound Homer—was already stalking slowly across the bed toward the intruder, teeth bared, hackles raised, his ebony tail puffed up to about three times its normal size. (I'd always thought that Homer, who'd never been able to see how small he was compared to others, believed himself to be bigger than anyone. He made others believe it, too.) When I grabbed the bedside phone to call 911, the man said, "Don't do that," helpfully giving Homer the audio cue he'd needed to pinpoint the man's precise location. With a furious snarl and a flash of claws, Homer launched himself directly at the intruder's face—at which point the man turned and fled. He ran right out of my apartment, I called the police, and what might have been a story with a much different (and far grimmer) ending became instead the tale of how, once upon a time, I'd saved a blind kitten's life—and of how, years later, he'd returned the favor.

Thinking about that night after the fact, it made sense to me that my normally friendly cat—usually the first to extend a warm welcome to new people—had, on that one occasion, reacted with such uncharacteristic aggression. Perhaps inevitably, Homer and I had grown so attuned to each other's moods and thoughts that it had become difficult over the years to tell where his ended and my own began. After all, when Homer had first come to live with me, he'd needed to stick as closely to me as my own shadow, to listen anxiously for every clue I could give him about our surroundings with the varying pitch and inflections of my voice, to follow my footsteps so intently, as he learned his way around, that if I was walking and happened to stop short, his little nose would run right into my ankle. And it goes without saying that I'd paid almost painfully close attention to Homer at first. A tiny, three-week-old blind kitten couldn't be left unattended to fend for himself.

But even when we were years past the point where Homer needed to rely on me as his "seeing-eye human"—after we'd moved six times, and from Florida to New York, and Homer had long since proven his expertise at learning his way around new spaces all on his own—and even when I'd come to understand that I didn't need to worry about Homer any more than any other "normal" cat (although not worrying about Homer was easier said than done), our hyperawareness of each other had become a permanent, and defining, feature of our relationship. When I was happy, Homer rejoiced. If I was in a bad mood, Homer also took to moping around the house. And, apparently, when I felt threatened . . . that was when Homer became enraged.

So it seemed to me, in November 2007, that if publishers were looking for stories about cats, here was one begging to be told. It would be a book filled with warmth and humor, with thrills and daring and gripping adventure. It would come complete with a Hollywood-ready, inspirational underdog (under-*cat?*) who'd found triumph in adversity and overcome seemingly insurmountable obstacles to not only survive but thrive, and live the happiest life a cat could possibly live. Best of all, it would be the single greatest love story about a girl and her cat ever published (an especially easy hurdle to clear because . . . y'know . . . there hadn't really *been* any other memoirs published at that point centering on a girl-meets-feline love story).

That was how I saw it, anyway. Alas, I was of the minority opinion. Of the twenty publishers to whom my literary agent submitted my proposal for a book called *Homer's Odyssey*, eighteen rejected it roundly. Broadly speaking, these rejections fell into two categories. The first were those who said that, while they were intrigued by the idea, ultimately Homer wasn't an "interesting" cat.

Homer would usually be doing something that *I* thought was very interesting—or, at a minimum, entertaining—whenever one of these letters would come in. I remember that when I got the first one, Homer had just liberated a bagful of catnip toys I'd recently stocked up on. I'd double-wrapped the toys in two plastic bags, hidden those bags inside a duffel bag, and secreted the whole thing underneath a mound of clothes in the bottom of the closet, so that I could distribute them one at a time as the old ones wore out without the cats' pestering me to death. But Homer's unerring nose—a nose that was capable of identifying tuna while it was still sealed in the can (Homer may have missed his true calling as a bomb-sniffing cat for the TSA)—had found them anyway. He'd burrowed assiduously into that mound of clothes intended for the laundry—kicking dirty socks and underwear heedlessly behind him—unzipped the duffel bag with his teeth and claws, and torn through the first plastic bag. Looking for all the world like Santa Claus, Homer now pranced down the hall and into the living room with the remaining sack, still full of toys, between his teeth, the other two cats following eagerly as they waited for him to distribute the booty.

The other objection my agent and I tended to hear pertained to the alleged reading habits of my target audience. Editors informed us with great confidence that animal lovers only wanted to read books about dogs and horses; or that animal lovers didn't want to read animal books at all "in our current tech-centric environment"; or that animal lovers were only receptive to picture books. One editor informed us matter-of-factly that "cat lovers don't read books." *Why do you think there aren't more cat books?* he asked with perfect catch-22 logic. Another said that, sure, maybe cat lovers read books, but they don't read memoirs. A third was confident that while cat lovers might read books—and while some of those books might even be memoirs—they definitely wouldn't read *cat* memoirs. (I wish I could say I was making this stuff up.)

Prior to writing my first book, I'd spent eight years as a marketing executive for various magazines and online publishers. The crux of my job had been the analysis of market research on our readers' consumer-spending habits, and the "Marketing Analysis" section I'd written for the *Homer's Odyssey* proposal had been exhaustive. I'd provided data on the percentage of cat-owning Americans (roughly one-third of all U.S. households); the dollars spent per year by those households on cat-related products and services (well into the billions); and, specifically, the higher-than-average propensity of a wide swath of the U.S. cat-owning population to spend their disposable income on entertainment-related purchases—including dinners out, movie tickets, *and books.*

"If there's any hard data out there supporting the hypothesis that 'cat lovers don't read books,'" I'd say to Laurence, the man I'd married only a month earlier, "I'd be pretty darn interested in seeing it." (Except I generally used a saltier word than *darn.*)

There were, however, two publishers who actually liked the idea. After a few days of back-and-forth with my agent over numbers, one of them made us an offer—not the million-plus

dollars the book about Dewey the Iowa library cat had sold for, but enough, if I was thrifty, to cover basic living expenses for a year. I was ecstatic.

The paperwork for *Homer's Odyssey* was finalized in late October 2008, and the book was scheduled for publication in August 2009. It seemed a long way off. But to make that publication date, I would have to write the entire book by the end of January. I buckled down, and by working fifteen-hour days, I managed to have my complete first draft written and submitted by Monday, February 2.

Homer would have his first professional photo shoot later that same day.

BY THEN, THE BOOK ABOUT DEWEY HAD FINALLY BEEN PUBLISHED, and it was a big hit. Suddenly, the conventional wisdom on whether or not there was a market for cat memoirs had shifted. Between that and the success of *Marley & Me*, pet memoirs were the hot new thing. And *Homer's Odyssey*, which had begun as the small passion project of one cat-loving editor, was now worthy of the full weight of my publisher's serious attention.

I had taken numerous photos of Homer when I'd first started working on the book proposal, in order to submit them along with the writing. They had been deemed "just darling" by my editor, yet none were of the professional caliber required to grace the cover of a book my publisher now hoped might be one of its bigger Fall 2009 titles. A professional photographer was therefore dispatched to our apartment with all due haste—and an entirely new phase in our lives began.

I had understood, in a sort of general way, that in publishing a book, I was also accepting all the risks—and rewards—of potentially becoming a public figure. It was obvious to me that any author who wrote a book did so with at least the partial hope that it might gain a wide readership someday. What I hadn't fully considered, however, was that by writing a book about my cat, I had effectively agreed to make him a public figure as well. It was a thought that had literally never occurred to me. After all, who had even heard of such a thing as a "cat celebrity"?

People who came to see us had always been interested in Homer. He was (the opinion of certain editors notwithstanding) an interesting little guy. But now began an influx of visitors to our home who were interested *only* in Homer—the photographers who came to create Homer's glamor shots and publicity stills, along with the print, television, and online journalists who arrived on our doorstep in a steady stream via my publisher's publicity department. They came from *People*, from *USA Today*, from *Ladies' Home Journal*, from *Time* and *Time for Kids*, *Cat Fancy*, *Best Friends*, the Associated Press, *National Geographic*, Animal Planet, People Pets online, and more blogs, vlogs, and e-zines than I could count. I may have been the one who'd written the book, but from the moment that first photographer knocked on our door, my role diminished to little more than glorified gatekeeper.

Actually, it was worse than that. I had become that most-dreaded of all show business figures: I was Homer's stage mom.

You've probably heard that stars aren't born, they're made. Well, I'm here to tell you that it's true. Behind every star is an entire team of people invisible to the public. Not just the photographers, the editors, the lighting assistants, the stylists (or, in the case of a cat, professional groomers—although they quickly learned that *our* star strongly preferred *not* to have anyone but mom trim his claws or touch his paws, thank you very much). There are also agents, managers, publicists, personal assistants, and—yes—stage moms and lackeys whose job it is to keep the star happy and engaged, to get him out of his trailer in time for the shoot and in a suitable emotional state to work, and to run and fetch whatever the star may want to eat or amuse himself with.

When it came to making Homer a star, all of those latter roles were filled by me, with an occasional assist from Laurence—who was, fortunately, also a writer working from home. "Managing" Homer quickly became my full-time job. It was my responsibility to set his appointments; to thoroughly brush and groom him ahead of time, so that his coat would shine with a high gloss and without any pesky stray bits of fur that might dangle from his haunches and ruin a shot; to make sure he got plenty of rest before a shoot began; to keep us stocked up on the tuna, turkey, and toys required to keep him happy and playful; to wrangle him from spot to spot as the daylight, or the whims of whoever was shooting him, changed.

I had to pop open cans of tuna when they wanted Homer to raise his head and perk up his ears, and then dip toys and bits of sisal rope in the tuna oil whenever Homer's interest in them began to flag and he'd trot over to me. *Why aren't you playing with any of this cool stuff, Mom?*

I had to gauge when it was finally time for Homer to retire to the sanctity of his cat tree for a quick, replenishing catnap. I'd gently suggest to whoever was in charge that Homer really *could*

use a bit of time to himself—at which point he or she would cry, "That's lunch, everybody!" and the cameramen, the sound crew (if it was a video shoot), the lighting techs, the groomer and stylist, the field producer, and the field producer's assistant would ask me to recommend a nearby restaurant. And would I mind terribly calling ahead for a reservation, since they'd need a large table?

It was my job to do all these things and more and then . . . to get out of the shot.

I used to joke that I might as well change my name to Gwen "Thank You Now Please Get Out Of The Shot" Cooper. "We'd like to shoot Homer in front of the bookcase," they'd say. "He's adorable with all those books behind him! Thank you so much, but"—after I'd lured Homer to the desired spot with a cheerful, *Come on, Homer-Bear!*—"could you move juuuuuuust a little to the left? A little more? We can still see part of your arm."

Or, "I'd like to get Homer in front of the window. He'll look so *majestic* with the Manhattan skyline behind him. Could you get him to . . . yes . . . perfect, that's it! But your hair is so curly and it's blocking Homer's light—could you pull it back?"

Far be it from me to block Homer's light!

If Homer had been a different kind of a cat—a cat like my surly-girl Scarlett, for example—all the "managing" in the world couldn't have made these shoots possible. But Homer had always dearly loved attention. He was intriguing to people not just because of his blindness, but because he had real charisma.

That might sound like an odd word to apply to a cat. Charisma, though, is little more than the ability of some people (or cats) to make you feel—even if only for the span of a few minutes—as if *you* are the most fascinating thing going, the very person they'd been hoping to get to spend time with.

Homer had that ability in spades.

Every strange person who came to our home and crawled on their belly holding a camera before them—so as to shoot Homer at his own level—was one more friend for Homer to make, one more cheerful greeting for him to bestow and receive a playful scritch behind his ears for in return. Scarlett and Vashti ran for the hills whenever our apartment was thus inundated, but Homer could never get over how much cool *stuff* these people brought with them! Cartons and crates, lighting reflectors, boom mics, snaking cables and power cords, fat rolls of backdrop paper to hang from tall stands so that Homer could pose before them, duffels for Homer to crawl in, around, and over. His nose and whiskers would twitch nonstop as he tried to process all the exotic new smells of equipment bags that had been on airplanes, in studios, and out on location shoots, perhaps even (as in the case of the crew from Animal Planet) in the homes of other cats.

The camera crews came to our home as a team of seen-it-all professionals, out on just another job—and an annoying one at that, because what could be more irritating (or less interesting) than working with a *cat?*—but they left as new members of an adoring cult. Each photographer and videographer was convinced that he or she had formed a unique and special bond with Homer over the course of the shoot, that some magical *thing* had happened between the two of them during those few hours they shared.

Homer could make you feel that way. It was his gift. It was as if he knew precisely when they wanted him to sit as still as a statue and look regal, to chase around toys in goofy, kittenish fashion, to run or jump or flip around on his back with un-self-conscious abandon, to turn his head shyly a little to the side, as if to say, *I'm strong, but also vulnerable.* Maybe he even *did* know. Homer was a sensitive cat, one who'd always paid close attention to the people around him.

Do you see this? they'd demand. *Do you see how he's responding to me?* Click-click, the camera would go. *He's a great cat, Gwen. A really exceptional cat.* And then they'd remind me for the umpteenth time to—please!—get out of the shot.

I knew that I hovered. Part of it was my old overprotectiveness, which reared up again and was hard to suppress as I watched strangers cluster around Homer, amidst walls of gear five times his size. As our living room furniture was pushed this way and that in order to clear space for lighting trees and camera stands, creating strange configurations far different from the ones Homer had long ago memorized, I worried that it might be too disorienting for a blind cat who relied on order and consistency, above all things, to get through his days.

Homer, however, was almost never nervous with all the activity going on around him. All he needed in order to find these unprecedented new experiences completely enjoyable was the knowledge that I was near. But with so much going on— with so many people and so much equipment crammed into a relatively small space—it was difficult for him to catch my scent if I wasn't standing close by. And trying to calm him by speaking to him in a reassuring voice wasn't a great option, as it tended to cause him to leave off whatever he'd been doing and head in my direction.

And as soon as Homer wasn't sure I was there anymore—as soon as the horrifying thought that I might have left him *alone* with all these strangers appeared to cross his mind—he was capable of being as uncooperative as any temperamental star. The fur on his back would start to rise, and he'd twist his head wildly in unphotogenic postures, nose in the air as he tried to figure out my location. I'd rush over to pet him and smooth down his fur. *I'm not going anywhere, Homer-Bear. I'm right here with you.* Thus calmed and restored to cheerful good humor, Homer would once again return to the work at hand as if he'd been born to do it.

If I'm being honest, I have to admit that sometimes . . . *sometimes* . . . back when I was writing the book—grubbing around, like many a writer on deadline, in my PJs or sweatpants with bird's-nest hair and a handful of Doritos, trying to remember if it had been *this* morning or *yesterday* morning when I'd last showered—I'd slip into rags-to-riches, Cinderella fantasies. Fantasies in which my book was already published and a huge smash, and I was the one in front of the cameras—impeccably coiffed and impossibly glamorous—posing for pictures, giving thoughtful (but also down-to-earth) answers to interviewers' questions, and ever-so-graciously thanking whatever minions had been dispatched to bring me a salad or some mineral water with which to refresh myself between takes.

Such delightful daydreams! They popped like so many soap bubbles as, in the here and now, I pulled my hair back from my sweat-streaked face into an untidy ponytail—and hastened, once again, to get out of Homer's shot.

ALL THIS NUTTINESS TOOK PLACE OVER THE SPAN OF JUST UNDER seven months in the run-up to the book's publication. Once

Homer's Odyssey finally hit stores in August 2009, it seemed—for a brief time, at least—as if our lives would return to normal. I did a few in-studio television and radio interviews on my own while Homer snoozed safely at home. There were still a few new bloggers and online journalists scheduled to come over to meet him, but this second wave of press was much mellower than the first had been, requiring far less of Homer and me. Usually it was just one person with a handheld recording device, or perhaps one additional person to hold a video camera. Homer was able to interact with these people with nothing more than his usual level of friendly interest—although I do remember one blogger in particular for whom Homer went absolutely wild.

I've never been nearly as aware of people's differing scents as Homer was (Homer being able to instantly identify the people he knew and liked with nothing but his sense of smell to guide him). But this specific blogger had an especially . . . pungent . . . aroma that even I could catch from across the room. She smelled strongly of patchouli mixed with insufficiently masked body odor—which is really only worth mentioning because Homer was as fascinated by this woman as I'd ever seen him with anyone before. It was impossible to keep him off her, to prevent him from crawling up and around her as he tried to take in her scent from all conceivable angles, burying his head in her hair and burrowing his nose insistently into more private areas.

"He's certainly a *friendly* cat, isn't he?" the blogger observed, trying unsuccessfully to angle Homer's snout away from her crotch.

"That he is." I was mortified. "Homer! *Homer! Come. Here!*" I spoke in the through-clenched-teeth guttural voice that my own mother had used to rein me in when I was small, and some bit of inappropriate behavior had seemed in danger of causing public embarrassment.

Homer, however, was not to be deterred. "I'm *so* sorry," I apologized. "I don't know what's come over him." Homer's head was still neck-deep in our guest's nether regions, and finally I went over and lifted him from her, one hand under his breastbone for support while the other took the scruff of his neck in a manner meant to indicate, *I am NOT kidding around!*

Homer wriggled out of my arms and boomeranged right back to his intrusive examination of every square inch of the blogger's body. "I can put him in the other room, if you'd like," I offered. *Please don't blog about this,* I thought. *Please don't blog about this!*

"No, don't worry about it!" I may have been appalled at Homer's bad behavior, but the blogger herself seemed unruffled. "Maybe we should open a window, though?" she added. "Your face looks a little red."

This, however, was one hour of consternation in what otherwise felt like a blessedly ordinary three-week period. There was great rejoicing in our home—and a healthy helping of extra goodies and treats for the cats—when my editor called to inform me that, after only one week on sale, *Homer's Odyssey* had made the *New York Times* bestseller list. Beyond that, though, those few weeks right after the book was published didn't feel all that different. It was an unusually interesting time with my work, perhaps, but nothing that ultimately changed the day-to-day rhythms of my real life.

It wasn't until gifts for Homer—sent to us by readers— began to arrive, about three weeks after publication, when I fully grasped that something fundamental had shifted, permanently, in the landscape of our lives.

At my publisher's suggestion, I went out and rented a P.O. box dedicated to the intake of Homer's presents and fan mail. The letters, cards, and parcels arrived at a rapid clip and in mountains more towering than I would have thought possible. Hand-crocheted balls stuffed with catnip, little satin-enclosed catnip pillows with each of the cats' names embroidered on them, hand-knitted and hand-sewn kitty blankets, colorful new bowls for food and water, bags of treats, and belled, noisy playthings—ideal for a visually impaired cat—came by the sack full.

Scarlett and Vashti got their fair share of the bounty and may, I think, have enjoyed the bonanza even more than Homer did. All the soft blankets—that were just her size!—were a profound joy to Scarlett, who'd always been something of a prima donna and adored all things plush and luxurious. To have something soft and warm to claim for her very own, small enough for her to guard from encroachment by the annoying other cats she was (for some inexplicable reason) forced to live with, was a gift from above. And Vashti was even wilder about catnip than the other two (although they were pretty 'nip crazy themselves). For his part, Homer seemed most enamored with the shipping boxes these gifts came in. He enjoyed them all so much that I couldn't bear to take any away from him—until our living room began to look as if we were in the process of moving. It was at this point that Laurence tactfully suggested that it might be time to throw a few away.

In addition to the gifts, we received hundreds of letters and emails from newly minted Homer fans. Many of them brought me to tears with their obvious love of Homer and his story and the ways in which they'd found both inspirational. Some letters, however, contained fervent special requests that ranged from the entirely understandable to the decidedly odd. There were people who wanted "pawtographed" photos of Homer, to be made personal by our pressing his paw onto an inkpad and then applying it to the picture (not something that Homer, who was morbidly sensitive about his paws, was likely to tolerate . . . but, sure, I could see why someone might want that); people who wanted tufts of Homer's fur that they could then have pressed into keepsake jewelry (while there was apparently an entire sub-culture of small businesses that would do this for you, it struck me as kind of a weird thing to want from a cat you'd never met); and people who were planning upcoming trips to New York and were hoping they'd be able to swing by our home and spend some one-on-one time with Homer himself (definitely off-putting—as if, I'd observe to Laurence, Homer was some sort of NYC tourist attraction, like the Statue of Liberty).

As few famous cats as there were at the time, there had never, to my knowledge, been a famous special-needs cat before Homer. And so Homer became something of a "poster kitty" for the cause of adopting animals once thought unadoptable. I began to understand something that I'd never thought about before: the deep chord that *Homer's Odyssey* would strike in the animal rescue community. Homer represented any number of cats who rescuers would cry themselves to sleep at night think-ing about—cats who were sweet and friendly and loving, cats who these rescuers worked with every day and who they knew would make a wonderful companion to anyone lucky enough to adopt them, but who, nevertheless, were consistently passed over for adoption—as Homer himself had been—because they were blind, or deaf, or needed extra care for ongoing medical issues, or simply because they had aged out of kittenhood and were now "too old."

Gratitude poured our way in the form of cards, crinkle balls, and home-grown catnip, and of course such largesse deserved acknowledgment. This presented a bit of a puzzle, however, since—as far as I knew—Emily Post had never covered the etiquette of writing thank-you notes for gifts to one's cat.

"Should I write as just me, thanking them on Homer's behalf?" I'd ask Laurence. "Or should I write as if I were Homer thanking them himself?"

This was a legitimate question, because within only a few months of the book's publication, "Homer the Blind Wonder Cat" had (again, at my publisher's suggestion) his own highly active social media presence. There was Homer's Facebook page and Homer's Twitter account and Homer's Pinterest collection, and naturally there was also Homer's dedicated online fan site, which featured Homer's very own online superhero comic. (Title: *The Handicats!* Tagline: *They're not just handi-capable . . . they're handi-kickass!*) Eventually, Homer's social media footprint would grow to something like a combined million-plus fans and followers. But even in their nascent days, when they were still relatively small, Homer's various accounts kept me busy.

These were Homer's pages, not mine, and so I wrote on them in Homer's voice—not his actual voice, obviously, but the way Homer had always sounded in my head. I'll admit that I'd never been much for personal photographs, but now we were snapping photos of Homer, Scarlett, and Vashti constantly. I never tried to arrange the cats in staged poses, or force them into some nonspontaneous "adorable" activity, or dress them up in hopes of capturing a photo that would go viral online. I took the same kind of amateurish, vaguely sloppy but ultimately affectionate candid shots that people took at family picnics or kids' birthday parties for private use. I tried to mine our everyday lives for the kinds of things that I thought might help people who'd read the book, and now wanted to keep up with the ongoing adventures of our feline family, feel connected to Homer and the gang on a day-to-day basis. *Oh boy! Turkey for dinner!*, I'd write above a snapshot of Homer doing his best to steal a bit of food from Laurence's plate. Or, **My* little bag of catnip! MINE!* along with a photo of Homer crouched protectively over one of the small bags of homegrown 'nip a reader had sent from her own cat-filled hobby farm.

I had a hard time explaining to my mother, when she asked what my work now consisted of, that I spent a significant portion of my days pretending to be Homer online.

My poor mother was always looking for new fodder about her "successful" daughter to bring to her weekly card and mahjongg games—and I wasn't doing a great job of supplying her with impressive-sounding ammunition. I had grown up in an extraordinarily competitive neighborhood. Although I'd attended a public high school rather than one of Miami's fancy private academies, my school had still managed to turn out an astonishingly large number of high-profile graduates. Heck, I was only one of three or four *New York Times* best-selling authors in my graduating class. Among my fellow alumni were lawyers arguing cases before the Supreme Court, high-ranking entertainment-industry executives, engineers, research scientists, C-level execs at *Fortune* 500 corporations, and a smattering of wealthy tech entrepreneurs.

Then there was the Very Famous Person I'd gone to school with—a person so famous that you would surely recognize their name in an instant (which is precisely why I can't share it here). Suffice it to say that this person's two-years-younger sibling, the one who'd graduated my year, was now chief of pediatric neurosurgery at one of the nation's most prestigious hospitals—and was generally acknowledged to be the *less* successful of the two. My mother would run into their mother ("Still very gracious and down-to-earth," she'd concede) every so often on the neighborhood canasta circuit, and they'd reminisce about the old days when we kids would all carpool to after-school activities together.

You can see what I was up against.

"So, what you're doing now for work," my mother would ask, trying to wrap her head around the idea, "is you pretend to be a cat on the internet?"

"Well . . . I mean . . . not *just* that," I'd hedge. What the entirety of Team Homer (meaning my publisher and me) had agreed upon as a sound business strategy dwindled into absurdity when put that way, and I'd find myself scrambling for a plausible defense. "I also travel a lot, visiting shelters and speaking at their fund-raisers and, you know, bringing attention to the issue of special-needs pet adoption."

"And these people you talk to on the internet when you're pretending to be Homer," she'd continue, blowing right past my stammering (albeit truthful) attempts to puff up the importance of my own work, "they do know that it's really you they're talking to, right?"

"It's what you'd call an open secret," I'd deadpan.

"But the book is still selling thousands of copies, and it's being published in all those different countries?" Foreign rights to *Homer's Odyssey* had, by this time, sold in seventeen languages and counting.

"That's all still true," I'd assure her.

She would ponder this for a moment. "All right," she'd finally say, with a determined-to-make-the-best-of-it sigh—a general marshaling her resources for a particularly hairy battle. "We can work with that."

I WOULD LOOK AT HOMER SOMETIMES—AS HE ENTHUSIASTICALLY chased one of his big sisters down the hallway, or jumped onto my desk and did his best to keep me from typing, or simply curled up peacefully in my lap for a snooze—and I would marvel. It was an impossible—an incomprehensible—thing to try to fathom, that so many thousands of strangers all across the globe cared for Homer, followed him online, knew all about him. Knew him and loved him. He was, after all—first, foremost, and forever—*our* cat. Our happy, high-spirited little boy. He had been with me for so long! And while I would never say that I took Homer for granted, he had become as essential, yet also as mundane, as the beating of my own heart.

And yet, sometimes, I would think back and remember one moment—one specific instant a few weeks before *Homer's Odyssey* was even published—when I'd had a sudden flash of bone-deep knowledge that, in the end, this was how it would be. It was the day when we'd recorded the book trailer—a promotional video commissioned by my publisher for placement on YouTube and other websites—and it was, by far, our craziest shoot.

It was one of only two off-site (meaning, outside our own home) publicity sessions that Homer would have to endure. My publisher had taken over a two-bedroom suite at the Hotel Pennsylvania, across the street from Madison Square Garden, where many a visiting rocker had stayed and partied back in the hotel's glory days. Homer was reluctant to get into his carrier that morning, and it was raining as I dashed as quickly as I could from our apartment building to the waiting Town Car my publisher had sent for us. (Homer caught a few drops on the way, which didn't improve his mood.) The driver helped me load in all the gear I'd thought necessary to bring along if we were going to be out of the house for an entire day—a litter box and litter, food and bottled water and bowls for both, a sack of catnip, a bag of Pounce treats, and a large trove of rolling-and-belled toys. We had an early-morning call time— before seven—and I'd requested that as few people as possible be there when we first arrived, so that Homer could acclimate to this new place before it was time for the hair-and-makeup person to go to work on me, and the groomer to go to work on him.

A single cameraman was there to greet us when we knocked on the door of the suite. He'd beaten us to the hotel by only an hour, having landed at five a.m. on a red-eye from L.A., which he'd taken just so he could be there to record Homer's first hour of exploration. I set up food and water bowls for Homer in the kitchen, and placed the litter box there as well, setting Homer in the box first—as was our custom whenever I brought him someplace unfamiliar—so that he wouldn't have to wonder where it was.

"I've never seen such big aural canals in a cat," the cameraman noted. "You can see all the way down into his ears. They're huge!"

"Homer's hearing is off the charts," I agreed. Homer's head perked up at the sound of my saying his name, and he turned the ears we'd just been discussing in my direction.

"Are you sure he's never been here before?" The cameraman was watching as Homer—nose to the ground—began to figure out the suite and its various rooms. He didn't bump into a single thing, not a wall, not a sofa, not the cabinets in the kitchen or a lamp in the suite's living room. Homer's sensitive nose and remarkable whiskers gave him all the information he needed to navigate seamlessly—just as he'd done time after time in the homes we'd moved in and out of over the years. After about a half hour of thorough investigation, Homer happily took up play with a catnip ball, fascinated with the way it ricocheted off the bottom of the kitchen cabinets and into the living room. He chased it in and out of the bedroom, under tables, and around the sofa and floor lamps without losing track of it for even a moment.

"I can't believe he's *blind*," the cameraman marveled. "Don't take this the wrong way, but if it weren't for the fact that his eyes are gone, I'd say you were lying."

I laughed. "My husband says the same thing," I told him. "To this day, he swears that Homer's faking blindness."

It was the start of a long day. As the morning wore on, the suite began to fill up. The next to arrive were Homer's and my respective groomers, followed by another cameraman, a lighting tech with trees and enormous reflective panels ("It's hard to get the lighting just right on a black cat," he explained—which I already knew), a sound person with boom mics, a producer, the editor who'd first acquired the rights to *Homer's Odyssey* and had remained an integral influence on every word I'd written, and my publisher's vice president of marketing, who had arrived to supervise the shoot personally. But with all the primping and preparation, with all the setting up of equipment and moving of furniture, with all the phone calls and consultations and last-minute disagreements about the shot list (which detailed the specific things they wanted to capture Homer doing), it was hours before the shoot proper—wherein I would answer questions about Homer and the book, while Homer did various adorable and active things in the background—even started.

By then, as was his preferred habit on rainy days when thunder rolled with a pleasant faraway rumble beneath the sound of drops splashing against the windows, Homer wasn't interested in doing anything but napping. He wasn't upset. He was as friendly as ever when new people came over to greet him and introduce themselves. He was simply *bored.* All the hoopla over the last few months, all the duffel bags and equipment and strangers and cat treats, all the new toys and the cameras following him to catch his every movement as he sat or ran or stretched or jumped or rolled over, had become old hat. All Homer wanted to do now was curl up quietly on the couch, the way we did on rainy days when we were home alone, and snooze peacefully beside me while I read a book.

Everybody's eyes were on me. But, as every cat person knows, there's only so much you can do with an uncooperative cat. I tried opening a baggie of catnip and wafting it under his nose. Nothing. I tried jangling a belled toy next to his ear. No response.

I got up and walked across the room. "Homer," I cooed gently. "Homer, come over to Mommy."

Homer flicked one ear lazily in the direction of the sound of my voice, but didn't stir. *Nah*, he seemed to say. *Don't wanna.*

"Homer-Bear," I sing-songed. I tried rattling a bag of Pounces. "Do you want a treat, Homer? Do you want to come and get a kitty treat, baby boy?"

Homer yawned mightily and extended his front and hind legs in a long, languorous stretch. He flipped onto his back momentarily, then curled back into a ball and continued to nap.

And so, there we were. A room full of people, a crew of professionals who'd flown through the night all the way from the West Coast, my publisher's VP of marketing (upon whom, I couldn't help but feel, I was making a very bad impression), all the treats and toys any cat would want—all of us here for Homer, and *only* for Homer, and Homer himself couldn't be bothered. He'd already been there. He'd already done that.

"Let me make a call," I told the room, and went to dig my cell out of my purse so I could phone Laurence at home.

"I need you," I told him as soon as he answered. "We need half a pound of that sliced deli turkey Homer likes, and a whole bunch of those little cans of tuna. Do you think you could go to the grocery store and then bring it all here?"

"Yeah, sure." I heard him rifling his desk for a pen and paper to jot my instructions down. "What do you want, Chicken of the Sea?"

"No, no." I was beginning to sound frantic. "Not Chicken of the Sea! He likes Bumble Bee, Laurence! *Homer likes Bumble Bee!*"

There was a pause, and then we both began to laugh. We laughed until we were almost crying. Tears ran down my face and my stomach began to ache, making it hard to breathe as I tried to suppress the laughter, aware that all the people in the other room could probably hear me.

Our lives *had* gotten a little nutty. But Homer wasn't some diva, and we weren't his flunkies. Homer was still just *Homer*— the good-natured, occasionally frustrating, but always lovable little cat we fondled and cooed over at home, in private, as soon as the cameras were packed up and gone.

I'd been making myself crazy in part because—yes—I desperately wanted my book to be a success. What author doesn't want that? Petty as it may have been, I had something to prove to all those editors who'd told me that *Homer isn't interesting* and *Cat lovers don't read books*. And I knew how rare it was for a publisher to put this kind of effort and attention into a book, that this particular moment in my life was fleeting and one I needed to enjoy as it was happening, because Homer and I wouldn't be the flavor of the month forever.

But it was more than that. I was also *proud* of Homer—and not just of the ease and dignity with which he'd acquitted himself as all these unusual and unprecedented things were happening to us. I was proud of who he was. And I wanted others to see that. I wanted the whole world to see—naysayers I'd never even met and probably never would, who nevertheless would think, *Why would anybody want a blind cat?* I wanted everybody to view for themselves what a blind cat—*my* blind cat— could do. The veterinarian from whom I'd adopted Homer was writing the foreword to *Homer's Odyssey*, and I had an idea that some of the people who'd had the chance to adopt him but turned him down, all those years ago, might read this book. They might put two and two together and realize what they had discarded as if it were something of no value at all. Their loss had been my infinite gain, but still I wanted them to view Homer with amazement, to read his story with envy and think, *That could have been me.*

Before any of that could happen, however, there was still our immediate problems to contend with: a cat already bored with a fame he technically hadn't attained yet, and the necessity of recapturing his interest long enough to make it through this last shoot.

"I'll be there as soon as I can with turkey and tuna," Laurence said, when we had finished laughing.

"Thank you," I told him. "Oh—and make sure it's the fancy albacore. That's his favorite."

Laurence ran out to the grocery store in the rain, waited forever to find a cab—which was always tougher on soggy days—and sat in the heavy crosstown traffic for over half an hour as he crossed from Second Avenue to where we were waiting at the Hotel Pennsylvania on Seventh. Once he arrived, we had to open a slew of those little cans of tuna before the sound of cans opening and the aroma of fish filling the room intrigued Homer enough to rouse him from his slumber. Laurence went into the suite's kitchen and rattled the deli paper Homer's favorite turkey was wrapped in, actually going through the motions of making a sandwich until Homer rose languidly from the sofa and trotted into the kitchen to paw at Laurence's leg. *Hey—is that turkey?*

The shoot ran longer than scheduled, but in the end we got the footage of Homer we needed. I took a look at the demolished suite as I was packing up Homer and his gear to head back home. Furniture had been pushed around haphazardly. Lampshades were cocked at odd angles, positioned this way and that to better reflect the light off Homer's black fur. Cameras and lighting reflectors were lying on the floor or leaned against end tables. Every window's blinds or shade had been pulled up and askew, each at its own varying height, as if a frenzied paranoiac had raced through, unable to decide which precise eye level would best keep *them* from seeing in. Nearly two dozen half-opened cans of tuna were scattered across every available surface, and uneaten bits of turkey were strewn across the floor, placed strategically to tempt Homer into various spots. The whole space was torn apart; it looked as if a bomb had gone off in a bodega.

I shook my head in amazement as I took it all in, thinking, *I guess we've finally arrived.* And it was in that moment, although I couldn't have expressed it in words at the time, when I foresaw Homer's destiny—saw it whole and round and glistening before me.

Homer had trashed his first hotel room. He was a star.

THEM!
A Story in Five Parts

1. THE BOWL BOY

Laurence and I uncovered an infestation of moths in our closets and drawers a few weeks ago. It was the kind of thing I thought only happened to people in sitcoms and movies—having never personally known anyone with a moth-ridden house in real life. Turns out, it *does* happen in real life. When I first started finding holes in the cashmere sweaters I was prepping for summer storage, I blamed the cats—Fanny, in particular, who dearly loves sleeping on articles of my clothing, especially when that clothing is made of cashmere or angora (Fanny having very posh tastes). I've occasionally observed her remorselessly "making biscuits" on said clothing—her claws at full extension—preparatory to lying down. It seemed like a plausible theory.

But when I then found identical holes in T-shirts, sweatshirts, silk blouses, pajamas, socks, workout togs, and all manner of other clothing that neither Fanny nor Clayton had access to, I began to doubt the cats' guilt. And when I finally noticed two teeny-tiny moths, perched upside down on the bedroom ceiling above my head, I knew I'd found my culprits.

Tearfully, I consigned a large pile of expensive cashmere sweaters—accumulated over some fifteen years—to the trash, the holes in them so numerous that no amount of clever crocheting could have salvaged them. I walked from the bedroom closet to Laurence's home office, right next door to our bedroom, cradling in my arms the moth-eaten corpse of a much-beloved cranberry cowl-neck as tenderly as if it were the bullet-riddled body of a comrade fallen in battle. Throwing it across the desk where Laurence was working, I informed him of the moth-y new development in our lives. "We must kill them," I announced. My voice quavered with the intensity of my desire for vengeance, and I struck my fist on Laurence's desk for dramatic emphasis. *"We must kill them with fire!"*

The only ones who seemed pleased at this turn of events were the cats. My manic tear through our closets and drawers, after I'd discovered the first moth holes, had sent airborne perhaps another half-dozen moths who'd been disturbed from the cool, dark comfort of their hiding places. Small as they were, their frantic, looping cartwheels in the air around us made the catching of them a delightfully tantalizing prospect for Fanny and Clayton.

Poor, stocky Clayton, who has only one hind leg, is a mediocre jumper at best, and most of the moths evaded him easily enough. But his littermate, Fanny—slender and leanly muscled—is our resident jock. Able to leap from a starting point on the ground to the height of my hairline, with as much dazzling speed as if she were a black-furred bolt of lightning, Fanny was in her element as she made short work of one moth after another.

It's possible that Fanny is the actual sweetest cat in the world—a devoted lover who coos and cuddles and looks at me with her whole heart in her round, golden eyes—but she is, conversely, also the most murderous cat I've ever lived with. If Fanny has a bucket list, that list consists of only one item: to kill something worth killing before she shuffles off this mortal coil. Every spring, when the sparrows who nest in the eaves of our Jersey City brownstone push their fledglings down into the little patch of grass in front of our bay window, I have to lock Fanny in the upstairs bedroom for a couple of days, legitimately afraid that she might crack her skull from striking it repeatedly against the bay window's panes, so desperate is she to dispatch those temptingly plump and flightless baby birds as they hop around helplessly on the other side of the glass.

As a strictly indoor cat, Fanny never gets a chance at the birds or squirrels who seem to take a certain delight in taunting her from safe perches just outside our windows. And since I've never seen a rat or a mouse in any home I've shared with my cats—not even when we lived in Manhattan, dubbed "Worst Rat City in the World" in 2014 by Animal Planet (presumably the rodents catch our home's cat smell and clear a wide berth)— Fanny is forced to expend her bloodlust on toy mice and whatever live insects manage to make their way indoors. The moths, therefore, were a bonanza for her.

They were, however, anything but a bonanza for me. I hadn't been kidding when I'd proclaimed, "*We must kill them with fire!*" A cursory check of Google revealed stories of people who'd been fighting moth infestations *for years*. I quickly outlined for Laurence what seemed to me an entirely rational plan of attack, involving roughly a metric ton of kerosene and a single lit match.

Cooler heads eventually prevailed, however. We ultimately embarked on a far more sensible course of action, purchasing dozens of boxes of mothballs, plastic zip-up storage bags, cedar hangers, two cans of repellant cedar spray, and another two cans of a pet-safe insecticide. We backed these up by emptying every single item out of every single closet and drawer and either putting them through three entire laundry cycles or, in the case of delicate fabrics, sending them out to the dry cleaner. Once everything had been cleaned, I then completed a thorough visual exam, sitting beneath a strong lamp with a magnifying glass in my hand as I pored over sweaters and wool dresses like a Talmudic scholar, searching for any telltale signs of moth larvae.

Having undertaken such an early and unexpectedly aggressive round of spring cleaning, Laurence and I decided we might as well give the entire house a thorough scrubbing from top to bottom and, in the process, dispose of all the superfluous *stuff* we'd accumulated over the years. Since we were, thanks to the lepidopteran pestilence visited upon us, getting rid of so many things we actually cared about, what was the point in hanging onto things we were indifferent to?

And here's where an old and familiar series of arguments began: Is it technically fair to call something "unused" if *we* never use it ourselves, but the *cats* use it all the time in some way other than its original intended purpose?

"You made me go out and buy that special cast-iron frying pan so you could make us omelets," I said to Laurence, "and we've still never had a single omelet in this house. The pan's been gathering dust on top of the kitchen cabinet for three years now."

"You really think we should get rid of it?" Laurence gestured across the room to indicate Fanny who, as if on cue, made a nimble leap from kitchen counter to cabinet top, then stepped neatly into the middle of the frying pan in question, "Someone might object."

It's true. Fanny has a fondness for high places—probably because the higher up she is, the less likely that Clayton will be able to pester her—and that frying pan had become her favorite kitchen napping spot. And I'll confess that, once I noticed how much she loved curling up there, I'd lined the pan with an old T-shirt, hating the thought of Fanny trying to make herself comfortable in a "bed" of cold, hard metal.

"What about that huge 'decorative bowl' you made us buy for the middle of the kitchen table?" Laurence suggested. "It doesn't *do* anything. It just sits there until we push it out of the way at dinnertime."

"No way!" I protested. "That's Clayton's favorite place to sleep when he's in the kitchen."

"He only ever comes down to the kitchen when we're not eating so he can bother Fanny," Laurence pointed out.

"Exactly," I replied. "And when he can't get to her, because she's on top of the cabinet in her frying pan, he goes to sleep in his bowl, and everybody's happy. I thought *you* thought it was so adorable of him," I added wistfully. "You always call him the 'bowl boy.'"

Moving through the house with an eye toward ridding ourselves of the unnecessary, it was astonishing to realize how many things had long since ceased to be of any practical value except insofar as the cats got some enjoyment out of them. For example, the gel pads I'd bought to support my wrists while I was typing, when I'd felt the earliest twinges of incipient carpal-tunnel

syndrome (an occupational hazard for writers). Clayton, who likes to sleep next to me on my desk while I work, had immediately claimed them for his own, clawing at them until the gel oozed out to form sticky patches. This had rendered them unfit for my own use, obviously, but—once the sticky patches had attracted enough of Clayton's shed fur to make them more fuzzy than gummy—they made for ideal catnap pillows. I didn't really want to take those away from him, did I?

Then there was the recumbent exercise bike I'd installed in a corner of our bedroom, intending to ride it during the breaks I managed to snatch for reading a book while on writing deadlines. I'd ended up discovering, however, that I much preferred a couple of hours of dedicated gym time to twenty-minute increments here and there over the course of the day. Still, I'd been loath to try to resell it, because it was Clayton's favorite bedroom perch once we'd all turned in for the night. In any event, he'd "marked" the bike's faux-leather seat with his claws until it was so torn up that we probably couldn't have resold it even if we'd wanted to. There was plenty of room for it in the bedroom, so it was hard to see what harm we were doing by just letting it stay there.

We had empty shelves mounted on walls throughout the house, having planned once upon a time to display our knick-knacks on them. But Fanny, with her love of high places, was apt to sleep on those shelves, and Clayton—when it came to the shelves he could actually climb up to—had a habit of pushing any knickknacks he encountered onto the floor. So the shelves remained empty, devoid of any justifiable use to our home's human inhabitants and making it look as if we were in a perpetual state of either moving in or moving out. Fanny was happy, though, which was the thing that really mattered.

THEM!

There were two plush blankets that Laurence's sister had given us as holiday gifts last year— intending, I think, for Laurence and me to snuggle beneath them together while watching movies from the couch. But the cats adored all soft things, and the second we'd placed the blankets on the couch, Clayton and Fanny had sprawled out on them, rolling around ecstatically on their backs as they luxuriated in the plush texture. Now the blankets were thoroughly be-furred and wadded up on the ground, one in our third-floor bedroom and one in the book room on our middle floor.

"If anything's going to attract moths, those blankets will," Laurence said.

"Moths don't eat polyester," I replied.

Like all cats, Fanny and Clayton loved cardboard boxes more than just about anything. Accordingly, a few old shoeboxes had taken up a permanent residence on our living-room floor. "We can finally get rid of *those*—can't we?" Laurence suggested, pointing to two boxes that the cats happened to be sleeping in at that exact moment. As if they understood what we were saying, Clayton and Fanny looked up at us, anxious pleas for clemency written in four identical golden eyes. *You're not going to take away our shoeboxes that we love soooooo much . . . are you?*

"You're a monster," I told Laurence.

Similar stays of execution were also granted to a few stray plastic bottle caps ("Fanny loves 'hunting' them, and she never gets to hunt anything real," I implored); a nest of inkless pens that Clayton, unbeknownst to us, had been hoarding beneath the couch (I tried to get rid of them, really I did—but Clayton had hippity-hopped after me, as I clutched his treasure trove of useless pens, with such a persistent and plaintive chorus of *Meeeeeeee!* that I'd been forced to relent); some old rolls of wrapping paper that didn't have enough paper left on them to wrap another gift, but that nonetheless delighted the cats with the crinkling sound they made when they were knocked onto their sides and batted across a tile floor; and a couple of ancient bed pillows that were well past any ability to provide comfort to human heads, but that the cats thought were absolutely *purr*-fect spots for a long siesta, once Laurence and I were up and out of bed for the day.

In the end, we got rid of two huge trash bags' worth of moth-chewed clothing and a far more modestly sized bag of broken hangers, old papers, and the like, culled from our cleaning efforts throughout the rest of the house. "It's not as much as I thought it would be," I admitted to Laurence, who sighed and agreed, "Yeah . . . it never is."

Our first battle against the moths was over. The war, however, had only begun.

2. FANNY FRENZY

It's hard to imagine two creatures whose lives more closely resemble an airtight cocoon of security and love than my cats. They came to us as a "bonded pair" of littermates and best friends, and—except for the two weeks Clayton spent recovering from the surgery to remove his bad half-leg—the two of them have never been separated since the day they were born. They live with a pair of humans who dote on them to a fairly ludicrous degree and who work from home, ensuring that Clayton and Fanny have a near-constant stream of attention and affection pretty much on tap. Our leafy street in Jersey City is generally quiet and serene, and the rhythms of Clayton's and Fanny's days—varied mostly by whether and how many squirrels and birds perch on our windowsills to tempt our little would-be predators—have the sort of comforting and predictable sameness that would be the envy of most other cats. And life, for the most part, has always been good to Clayton and Fanny. Unlike so many rescue cats, they never spent a single day of their existence confined to a cage in a shelter. They were found at two weeks of age in the backyard of a kindly cat rescuer who turned them over immediately to a foster network he volunteered with, called Furrever Friends, which placed the two kittens in the home of an experienced kitten foster mom. From what I could tell in our conversations prior to my adopting them, she lavished on Clayton and Fanny (then named Peeta and Katniss—possibly the only genuine hardship they've ever had to endure) nearly as much slavish adoration as Laurence and I do now.

It's true that I can't account for anything that may have happened to them during the first two weeks of their lives. But, then, I doubt that Clayton and Fanny would have much information to offer about those two weeks, either.

So it irks me, probably more than it should, when the two of them get more skittish than a given situation seems to call for. I expect—and accept—a certain amount of hissing from Clayton when I run the vacuum cleaner. But I'll admit that I get a wee bit impatient when I hear that same wild flurry of hissing upon snapping open a plastic garbage bag ("When," I'll ask Clayton, "have I ever allowed *a single bad thing* to happen in this house?"). Or when Fanny, the quintessential "daddy's girl," bolts in terror at the sound of Laurence's footsteps—his tread undeniably heavier than my own—coming up the stairs. Usually, once she's gotten a few feet away, she'll boomerang back around to greet Laurence properly, as if having realized mid-flight, *Oh, wait— that's not the Apocalypse. It's just Laurence walking upstairs!* But after six years of hearing that exact same footfall, you'd think she'd have learned to recognize it instantly by now.

Then there was the time when Fanny got a tiny price sticker—picked up heaven knows where—stuck to one of her front paws. I found her in the hallway trying furiously, and unsuccessfully, to shake it loose. Intending only to help—and not thinking much of it—I picked her up with one hand, pulled off the sticker (it came off very easily, I should note, and didn't take a single strand of fur with it), and placed her back on the floor. The whole thing took about two seconds. Nevertheless—I kid you not—Fanny hid under the bed or ran to hide in a closet whenever she saw me coming for the next five hours. *Five hours!* The same cat who spends half her day napping sweetly in my lap while I write—a cat whom I've never once touched with anything other than gentleness and love—was now fleeing from me in abject panic because I'd pulled a tiny sticker off her front paw. The nerve of it! The drama! "Fanny!" I pleaded, watching her scuttle out of my path, eyes wide with fear, as if I were Carrie at the prom. *"What is your problem? Nothing bad has EVER happened to you!"*

So I knew we were really in for it the Saturday afternoon that Fanny got her exceptionally long, snaky tail caught in one of our moth traps.

If Phase One in our war on the moths had been a general carpet-bombing of drawers and closets with moth spray, then Phase Two was all about hand-to-hand combat. Once our arsenal of mothballs and cedar hangers and a generous application of cedar spray had made life in closets and drawers thoroughly untenable for the invaders, they began showing themselves out in the open, in plain sight. One of them, in a frenzied flight away from a plume of cedar spray, flew right up Laurence's nose. "I think it came out my ear!" Laurence sputtered, pressing his finger against his nose to hold one nostril closed as he exhaled furiously through the other—until, finally, he saw the welcome sight of the moth exiting (considerably worse for wear) the same way it had entered.

For a good few days, it seemed as if the air in our house was thick with minute gray wings. We went on something of a rampage, whacking them with rolled-up newspapers and T-shirts—whatever was close by, basically, that could be used to crush an errant moth against a wall or the floor without damaging either. The cats were alarmed at first by the constant hiss of spray and *thwack!* of newspapers that filled our home—although they, too, were eager to get in on the action. Fanny and Clayton sometimes made their kills individually and sometimes worked as a team, with Fanny leaping high to force a moth into a downward trajectory while Clayton waited on the ground beneath her to scoop up the befuddled insect in his jaws.

In addition to the mothballs and insecticides we'd already acquired, we purchased—on the advice of several online posters who'd also dealt with moths—a slew of moth traps, which were triangular cardboard tents with sticky interiors that operated on the same premise as Roach Motels: They enticed the moths inside with a moth-attracting scent (undetectable to the human nose) and then held them fast.

We placed the moth traps atop our tallest bookcases and highest shelves—higher, we thought, than even Fanny was able to go. Clearly, however, we had underestimated the zealousness of Fanny, our little huntress, in her pursuit of airborne quarry.

Laurence and I were downstairs on the living room couch watching a movie when we first realized something was wrong. Ever the film buff, Laurence had curated a collection of giant-bug movies from the '50s for us to watch during this, our time of insect affliction. With a new appreciation, we rediscovered (or, in my case, discovered for the first time) such noteworthy entries in the subgenre as *The Deadly Mantis, Earth vs. the Spider, Tarantula!, The Wasp Woman*, and, of course, the classic *Them!*, which was about a swarm of giant, irradiated ants that sprang up in the New Mexico desert, near the nuclear test sites.

Clayton was sound asleep on my lap, so when we first heard the rapid-fire thudding of feline paws on the floor above our heads, we assumed it was, as we call it in our house, a "Fanny Frenzy"—which is when Fanny goes to town on Rosie the Rat (her favorite plaything), swatting and tossing the toy from one bedroom to the other in a burst of hyperactivity. But then we heard the clatter and thump of unknown objects flying from their perches, and the crash of a bedside lamp hitting the floor. Those noises weren't at all typical of a Fanny Frenzy. Swiftly dislodging a thoroughly unhappy Clayton, I leapt from the couch and ran upstairs to see what was going on.

The sight that greeted me as I entered our bedroom looked like a crime scene. The pillows on the bed and the pictures on the walls were all askew. Everything that had once been on top of a piece of furniture now lay in a heap below it—books had been swept from the bookcase and were lying open and bent upside down with their pages wadded up; pens and earrings had been tossed from the top of the dresser onto the floor; the lamp, clock radio, and tissue box that customarily resided on the night table were lying at odd angles on the ground. In the midst of all this chaos, Fanny was crouched on the floor. Her pupils were so dilated with fright that her golden eyes appeared black.

Glued firmly to the end of her long, long tail was one of our tented moth traps. Unable to detach it, she'd obviously tried to outrun it instead—alas, to no avail.

"It's okay, Fanny." I deliberately made my voice low-pitched and calm as I walked slowly toward her, not wanting to alarm her further. "It's okay, baby girl. Let Mommy help you."

Laurence came up the stairs behind me just in time to see Fanny turn her all-pupil eyes briefly in my direction (*Don't come any closer! I REMEMBER THE STICKER!*) before darting under the bed, the triangular moth trap still stuck to her tail skipping merrily across the floor behind her. In vain, Laurence and I knelt on opposite sides of the king size bed and then lay down on our sides, trying to get to Fanny so we could pull her out. But neither of us had arms long enough to reach the spot in the middle where she'd curled herself into the tightest ball she could manage. The only way reaching her might have been possible would have been if Laurence lifted the bed, and it seemed unwise to risk adding the complications of a back injury to the problem we already had.

So, for the moment at least, Fanny had us at a stalemate. "She'll have to come out eventually," I finally said with a sigh. Bending down, I picked up the lamp and clock radio and restored them to their appointed spots on the night table. "And she'll probably be calmer when she does."

Fanny had bolted under the bed at around one o'clock in the afternoon, and it was nearly midnight before she finally reemerged. She'd missed both her lunch and dinner—although

I'd done my best to tempt her out of hiding, carrying the cans up two flights from the kitchen to the bedroom, just so I could open them next to the bed. In my experience, the sound of a can opening and the rattling of a treats bag are the two sounds likeliest to summon even the scaredy-est cat. Accordingly, I'd also gone up periodically to shake the bag of Greenies in the hallway just outside the bedroom. But Fanny had remained unmoved by either of these lures.

Some calls of nature, however, are harder to resist than others, and I think Fanny was heading for the litter box, some eleven hours later, when she finally crept down the stairs. But the sound of the moth trap dragging behind her, thumping against each step as she descended, sent her into another, quite literal, tailspin.

Fortunately for us, though, this time Fanny didn't head up and back toward the bed. Instead, she flew down the remaining stairs and began running in desperate circles around the living room. Up and over the couch, across the coffee table, onto the mantelpiece, then back down to the floor—the triangular trap on her tale a whirling mace that sent throw pillows, coasters, coffee-table books, and framed photographs into brief, dizzying flights before they crashed to the ground. Laurence and I threw up our hands to protect our faces from any flying shards of glass from the picture frames, only lowering them once Fanny was safely earthbound again among the wreckage as her spinning continued.

Clayton, clearly laboring under the misapprehension that Fanny had invented some fascinating new game (*We're running in pointless circles! Wheeeeeeeee!*) hippity-hopped after her, working

desperately hard to keep up and make sure he didn't miss out on any of the "fun." I don't know if Fanny thought that Clayton was chasing her, or if his presence simply egged her on, but the harder he pursued, the faster she ran. The moth trap still attached to Fanny's tail bounced gaily between them, like a child's pull-toy.

I knew that Fanny's inevitable next move—once the futility of running in circles had fully revealed itself to her—would be to try to get back upstairs and under the bed. Accordingly, I stationed myself in front of the staircase and hunkered down like the catcher in a baseball game. Soon enough, Fanny came winging toward me. Upon seeing me waiting for her, she tried to make a last-minute swerve beyond the reach of my arms. But this time I was quicker than she was and—at last!—I scooped her up in my arms.

Shooing Clayton away with one foot, I cradled Fanny against my chest for a moment, both hands supporting her from beneath as I pressed my cheek against the top of her head and tried to slow the anxious pounding of her heart with the calmer rhythm of my own. "I've got you, Fanny," I murmured. "I've got you, little girl. It's all going to be okay."

Gesturing Laurence toward the middle of the living-room rug, I carried Fanny over and sank slowly into a cross-legged position. Holding Fanny out at both arms' length for a moment— the moth trap now dangling limply from her tail like a flag that's lost its wind—I turned Fanny around and pressed her against my side, so that my hands were still supporting her beneath her chest and hindquarters, her head was wedged firmly beneath my elbow, and her backside with the sagging moth trap was facing toward Laurence, who was now seated across from me.

"I'm going to kind of squish her against my side, so that she feels a little safer and doesn't see what's coming," I told Laurence. "And *you* are going to rip that wretched moth trap right off her tail."

Laurence, his eyes passing over Fanny as she continued to squirm, looked dubious. "I don't want to hurt her."

"It'll be fine," I assured him. "Ready?" I pressed Fanny a bit more tightly against my side.

Laurence grasped the end of Fanny's tail and, with agonizing slowness, began to peel it from the inside of the moth trap, one strand of fur at a time. Fanny struggled in earnest now, one of her hind claws raking through my shirt and into my skin. Although we kept her claws fairly well trimmed, she dug in hard, and I knew it would leave a nasty scratch.

Gritting my teeth against both the pain and Fanny's tussling, I said to Laurence, "You have to rip it off in one clean shot, like tearing off a Band-Aid."

"But I don't want to hurt her," he repeated.

"*She's* hurting *me*," I told him. "Just get it off already."

Laurence's hold on Fanny's tail tightened, as did his grip on the moth trap in his other hand. He hesitated for a second and then, with one decisive tear, tail and moth trap were finally separated. I loosened my own grip on Fanny just a little, but that was all she needed to wriggle free. Racing back upstairs, I could hear the sound of her claws skidding across the floor above us as she once again retreated under the bed. I knew we wouldn't see her again for the rest of the night.

When I examined the moth trap, I found a fuzzy black strip that Fanny's tail had left behind but, fortunately, no skin and no blood. I, however, hadn't fared as well. A few dots of blood from the scratch Fanny had given me seeped through my nightshirt. Laurence noted it, too.

"I'll go get the alcohol," he said, standing up and helping me to my feet.

"Rubbing or drinking?" I asked, hoping for the latter. And Laurence laughed, replying, "Why not both?"

By breakfast-time the following morning, Fanny and I were friends again. A good night's sleep and the welcome aroma of food after her unplanned fast the day before (Clayton, it would appear, had eaten Fanny's food as well as his own when she'd failed to show up for her meals) had done most of the work of restoring the balance between us. After her post-breakfast siesta, Fanny returned to stalking moths through the house. Laurence and I were pleased to note that their numbers were in a definite decline. And the retreat continued even after we disposed of the rest of the moth traps—which, we were forced to admit, hadn't been nearly as effective a moth deterrent as Fanny was, anyway.

People with black cats are apt to refer to them as "house panthers." It's an epithet I'd certainly never apply to my roly-poly Clayton, crazy as I am about him. But in Fanny's case, the comparison between her and her "big cat" cousins seemed apt: the precise symmetry of her lean muscles beneath her glossy black fur; the flawless grace and balance when she leapt from floor to bookcase; the hypersensitivity of the ears, eyes, and whiskers that didn't miss a single thing that moved, crept, or flew in the terrain around her.

I realized, watching Fanny prowl through the house with as much unthinking confidence in her own prowess as any panther ever had, that the constant stream of sensory input and physical awareness—which made her such a ruthlessly efficient hunter—were also the root cause of the overload that occasionally made her spook a little too easily.

You couldn't have separated the one from the other, couldn't have changed the balance without throwing the entire mechanism off its axis. Without question, Fanny could be a pain in the neck sometimes. But she was *our* pain in the neck, which was precisely why we loved her as much as we did.

And she was still—as we recognized that laundry and pesticides would take us only so far—one of the best weapons we had in our ongoing assault against the moths.

3. SCENE FROM A LOST HAROLD PINTER PLAY

ACT ONE – SCENE ONE

INT. GWEN AND LAURENCE'S THREE-STORY BROWNSTONE IN JERSEY CITY – A SUNNY WEDNESDAY AFTERNOON

LIGHTS UP ON DOWNSTAGE LEFT: GWEN sitting at a sleek black desk in front of her laptop computer. With one hand on the keyboard, another tapping on the desk, and her eyebrows scrunched as she gazes at the laptop's screen, she's obviously deep in thought. CLAYTON, a three-legged black cat, is splayed out on her lap.

LIGHTS UP ON ELEVATED PLATFORM, DOWNSTAGE RIGHT: LAURENCE has just sat down at an old wooden desk in front of a large desktop computer. As he arranges himself on the

THEM!

chair, FANNY, another black cat, eagerly
leaps onto his lap and daintily makes herself
comfortable. LAURENCE shifts to accommodate
her as he turns his head toward the offstage
door and shouts to GWEN, who is one floor
beneath him.

LAURENCE: Hey! One of the cats threw up in the
kitchen!

GWEN: Okay.

LAURENCE: Okay.

GWEN: And . . . ?

LAURENCE: You should clean it before it sinks
into the tile and makes a permanent
stain.

GWEN: Can't you clean it? With all the
moth *mishegas*, I'm behind on my
deadline.

LAURENCE: I thought you'd want to look at it
first.

GWEN: Why would I want to look at it first?

LAURENCE: I don't know . . . I thought you
might want to check viscosity and
breakdown.

GWEN: What does "viscosity and breakdown"
even mean?

LAURENCE: It's from that old motor oil
commercial—remember those
commercials?

GWEN [muttering]: You and your old
commercials.

LAURENCE: What'd you say?

GWEN: I have to turn in this story to my
editor tomorrow. Are you going to
clean it or not?

157

LAURENCE: I really think you should examine it first.

GWEN: They probably just ate too many moths or threw up a hairball or something.

LAURENCE: It doesn't look like moths or a hairball.

GWEN: How would you know what a hairball looks like? You never clean up their hairballs.

LAURENCE: Because I always think you'll want to look at it first.

GWEN: *Why* do you keep saying that? *What* do you think is so compelling about a puddle of cat vomit that I have to drop everything and race over like it was a flash sale at Barneys?

LAURENCE: What if one of them is sick?

GWEN: Cats throw up sometimes. It's what they *do*. I'm sure it's fine.

LAURENCE: But you don't know that it's fine—you don't even know who threw up.

GWEN: What am I, a cat CSI unit? How am I supposed to know which cat threw up? Was one of them standing near it?

LAURENCE: They were both gone by the time I found it.

GWEN: Found it and left it for me, you mean.

LAURENCE: I can never clean it as well as you can.

GWEN: Oh, come *on*!

LAURENCE: It's true! I'm not as good as getting it all up as you are.

THEM!

GWEN: Well, as my mother used to say, *practice makes perfect*.

LAURENCE: Did she?

GWEN: She *also* used to say, *God gave you two arms and two legs*. Didn't your mother ever say anything like that?

LAURENCE: Don't bring my mother into this.

GWEN: I'm sure she'd agree that you're a full-grown man who's perfectly capable of cleaning up cat vomit all by himself.

LAURENCE: But I'm on the third floor. You're so much closer.

GWEN: Wait . . . you're *upstairs*? I thought you were still downstairs. How'd you get all the way *upstairs*?

LAURENCE: I walked on the two legs God gave me.

GWEN: Sarcasm's definitely your best play right now.

LAURENCE: Why are you asking a question you already know the answer to?

GWEN: So . . . you saw the throw-up on the first floor, decided to leave it for me, walked all the way past me on the second floor without saying a word, and now you're on the third floor?

LAURENCE: I can make you a sketch of my route, if you'd like.

GWEN: Very cute.

LAURENCE: Well, I'm obviously too far away to do anything about it now.

GWEN: Only because you walked up two whole floors before you said anything!

MY LIFE IN A CAT HOUSE

LAURENCE: What's done is done. Besides, I thought you'd want to look at it first.

GWEN: Stop saying that!

LAURENCE: It's true!

GWEN: Like I don't know that this whole *you should look at it first* routine is just so you can stick *me* with a gross job.

LAURENCE: My intentions were pure.

GWEN: *Pure?!*

LAURENCE: Not to mention that Fanny's already so comfortable on my lap. It would be cruel to disturb her.

GWEN: Don't use Fanny against me! And anyway, Clayton's on *my* lap. So we're even.

LAURENCE: But I'm up on the third floor. What am I supposed to do about cat throw-up that's all the way downstairs?

GWEN: It's too bad we had those one-way-only stairs installed. How will you *possibly* get "all the way downstairs" ever again?

LAURENCE: Now who's being sarcastic?

GWEN [mimicking him]: *Now who's being sarcastic?*

LAURENCE: I heard that!

GWEN: Isn't it enough that I just did, like, fifteen loads of laundry to get rid of the moths? Can't you do this *one* thing when you know I'm on a tight deadline?

LAURENCE: Fine! I'll go down and clean the cat vomit. Go back to your writing.

> **GWEN:** FORGET IT! I'VE ALREADY LOST MY
> TRAIN OF THOUGHT!
>
> **LAURENCE:** This is going to end up in your new
> book, isn't it?
>
> **GWEN:** Don't be ridiculous . . .
>
> *Scene.*

4. PING!

Ahoy! Bless your eyes, here's old Bill Barley. Here's old Bill Barley, bless your eyes. Here's old Bill Barley on the flat of his back, by the Lord. Lying on the flat of his back like a drifting old dead flounder, here's your old Bill Barley, bless your eyes. Ahoy! Bless you.

—Charles Dickens, *Great Expectations*

I always say that when I turned forty, it was like a warranty expired. There wasn't any single catastrophic failure, but all kinds of little things started going wrong in unpredictable ways. The gradual breaking down of my previously resilient body began, in point of fact, on the night of my fortieth birthday itself. Laurence and I were celebrating in Paris and had gone out for an extravagant dinner at an over-the-top restaurant (Napoleon had courted Josephine there, our guidebooks breathlessly informed us), and the six-course meal left me—despite having always prided myself on my billy-goat stomach—wide awake and tossing for the better part of the night with the kind of intense heartburn I'd never even suspected was possible.

As the months went by, new and unmistakable signs of aging cropped up. I'd find dark hairs sprouting on my chin, whereas the hair in other, more private, regions began to fall out.

Suddenly I had knees that could forecast the weather: I'd feel a certain twinge in the right one and be able to inform Laurence, with near-perfect accuracy, "It's going to rain tomorrow." Getting around New York and environs was definitely more of a challenge than it had been in younger, sprightlier days. Upon reaching the top of the endless flights of stairs at the Christopher Street PATH station in the West Village, for example, I'd find myself too winded to speak for a good minute or two.

This catalog of minor grievances could go on, but you get the point. Still, nothing truly *awful* had gone wrong until one afternoon, about a month into our moth infestation, when I was in hot pursuit of a particularly large and resilient moth that Fanny had flushed out in the living room. I had a rolled-up newspaper in one hand, and had just bent over to swat the bugger as it made a sudden dive toward the floor, when I felt a *ping!* in my lower back. And then, everything stopped.

More specifically, my legs stopped. Working, that is. The last thing I remember thinking, as I fell to my knees and cried out for Laurence, was that aging is the absolute worst thing in the world.

Well . . . except for the alternative.

A visit to our neighborhood chiropractor revealed no injuries of a serious nature—no herniated or slipped disk, or anything requiring drastic intervention. "Just a good old-fashioned pulled muscle," was the chiropractor's diagnosis. After cracking my spine a few times, he advised, "Spend as much time as possible lying flat on a firm surface. A firm mattress would be ideal. Everything should settle back into place within a day or two."

THEM!

At the risk of making my cats sound heartless, it must be said that Clayton and Fanny are always positively elated when I'm sick enough to require a full day in bed. It's usually a cold or flu that takes me down, and the cats take great pleasure in requisitioning my heating pad (to lie on) and my box of tissues (to tear to shreds). The aspirin bottle I'll keep on the bedside night table for easy access makes a charming rattle when peremptorily swatted *off* the table to roll around on the floor—and, no doubt, my cats must ask themselves whether it wouldn't be more sensible on their humans' part to simply keep this enthralling cat toy easily accessible on the night table all the time.

But the very best part of my being sick, from the cats' point of view, is that they get to join me in bed for a full day, or—if I'm *really* sick and the cats are *really* lucky—maybe even two full days. Clayton and Fanny are longtime practitioners of snooze-all-day-ism, and they seem to regard my sick days as a possible—and promising—first step toward a permanent embrace of their lifestyle. They'll pile into bed with me, and frequently *on* me, like senior members of a cult keeping close tabs on a new initiate, making sure she doesn't begin to have second thoughts or stray from the path. If they sense that I'm about to get out of bed, one or the other of them will climb onto my chest and bring a whiskered black face as close as possible to my own. *You can't quit now,* they always seem to be saying. *You're doing so great!* And if I'm sick enough to run a fever, so much the better. Burrowing under the blankets with me, they add the not-insignificant warmth of their own furry bodies to my heightened body heat, until the space beneath the covers

feels like a sauna—one that vibrates with the strength of my cats' purring contentment.

The day that my back went out, however, wasn't quite like my usual sick days. For one thing, I had no interest in lying under the covers and had Laurence shove them entirely to one side of the bed—along with the piles of clothing we were still cycling in and out of the laundry in an effort to rid ourselves of moths once and for all. Even worse, I never once turned onto my side for a delightful session of cuddling one or the other of my cats in a spoon position. I just lay there sprawled out, flat on my back, in a kind of *Vitruvian Man* pose. I lay so flat that I couldn't even see the TV screen across the room, or much of anything other than the ceiling. The number of moths we'd spot fluttering around the house had abated almost entirely but, from time to time over the course of that day, I'd spy one or two hovering above me. Fanny spotted them, too, and leapt onto my belly in order to use my motionless body as a springboard heavenward in her pursuit, each time prompting a loud "Oof!" from me.

Convenient a launching pad as my inert body made, it wasn't exactly Clayton's or Fanny's notion of the ideal day spent in bed with Mom. Nevertheless, there was plenty to be happy about on any day that saw me spending so much time with them. And the heating pad had been duly taken down from its closet shelf and was turned over to Clayton or Fanny every twenty minutes or so, whenever I felt I'd used it long enough for the time being. That, at least, was something.

The only real moment of consternation on that first day came in the evening, when Laurence helped me into a hot bath that I hoped would help soothe my knotted back muscles into something resembling their previous shape. Proper baths—as opposed to showers—are a rare event in our house, and Clayton and Fanny peeked anxiously over the side of the tub, occasionally daring to rise up on hind legs (or hind leg, in Clayton's case) and dip a tentative front paw into the water before quickly withdrawing it. Their little brows furrowed in anxiety and confusion. *Whatcha doin' in all that water, Mom? IT'S WATER!!!*

Eventually, however—having clearly concluded with a mental shrug that humans were just *weird* sometimes, and there was no explaining them—they sprawled out in front of the tub like two ebony-carved centurions. Perhaps they'd decided that, with my having taken this foolishness into my head, *someone* had to make sure I didn't drown. In any case, their refusal to leave the tub area so long as I was still in there made Laurence's job getting me *out* of the tub, a half hour later, needlessly complicated. ("Just step around them," Laurence kept saying patiently. While I—trying vainly to move sideways a leg that refused to go in any direction other than backward or forward—replied through gritted teeth, "I can't step *around* anything!") The cats seemed relieved as, with Laurence's help, I finally hobbled back to the bedroom and the three of us settled into bed.

They weren't nearly so sanguine, however, by the following morning. Like all cats, Fanny and Clayton are wedded to the routines that make up their typical day. One of the most important items on our daily agenda is when I get out of bed at five a.m. precisely and head down from the third-floor bedroom to the first-floor kitchen to give them their breakfast—tossing Clayton's toy mouse for a few preliminary rounds of fetch along the way.

Even when I'm down with a cold or flu, I still manage to sneeze and cough my way downstairs to feed the cats on time.

So nothing in their previous experience had prepared them for this first morning after my back injury. The pain in my lower back did feel distinctly lessened when I initially woke up— although possibly that was the lingering effect of the Vicodin (left over from some dental surgery Laurence had had a few months earlier), which I'd taken before going to sleep.

Nevertheless, I couldn't sit up. I had to sort of rock from side to side until, eventually, I rolled out of bed and onto the floor in a semi-crouching position, at which point I stood up as straight as I was able and limped to the bathroom at the end of the hall. After that, staggering back to bed was all that I could manage. Walking down two flights of stairs to feed the cats— and then two flights back up again—was as unattainable a goal as climbing Everest.

The cats appeared flabbergasted as I got back into bed without having fed them. Laurence was sleeping in the guest bed in his office next door—to allow me the full and undisturbed span of our bed—and I'd advised him the night before to keep his door closed, anticipating that, when the cats found me unresponsive, they would be disinclined to wait for him to wake up on his own. There was a solid five minutes of caterwauling in the hallway as the cats did their best to rouse at least one of us—but Laurence, a sound sleeper, kept dozing undisturbed. Thanks to his closed door, they were unable to deploy any of their more aggressive tactics, like stomping onto his chest and meowing loudly into his ear.

They could, however, still use both maneuvers on me. "Laurence will be up soon, you guys," I assured them over the loud and increasingly desperate cries that were beginning to make my eardrums hurt (although I knew that "soon," given that

THEM!

Laurence kept a much more normal schedule than I did, wouldn't be for at least two more hours). "You'll get your breakfast—I *promise* you will."

Vexed and baffled by this unprecedented state of affairs, they were obviously working hard to figure out a way of getting me onto my feet, down the stairs, and pointed in the direction of the pantry where their food was kept. Clayton seemed to be of the opinion that if *he* kept doing the things that he normally does in the morning, then inevitably *I* would also fall back into my normal routine. Accordingly, he kept bringing over the rattling toy mouse he likes to play fetch with, hauling himself up onto the bed so he could rattle it a few times in his mouth and then drop it into my hand. I would toss it half-heartedly as far across the room as I could without moving any more of my body than my arm. Clayton was patient with me at first as he dutifully retrieved the mouse, climbed back onto the bed, and dropped it into my hand once again. *No, see, you're doing it wrong. You're supposed to* get up *and throw it for me—and then you're supposed to keep walking.* After four or five repetitions, however, he was stumped. He looked over to Fanny for guidance. *Got any ideas?*

Fanny is unquestionably the smarter of the two. She had evidently reasoned out that I couldn't solve *their* problems until my own mysterious problem—whatever it was—had also been solved. She leapt nimbly from the bed, and I heard her descending the stairs. She returned a few moments later and, with the "hunting" cry that generally meant she was about to leave Laurence or me a "gift" (usually Rosie the Rat, which she thoughtfully places on our pillows every night before bedtime), returned to my side and gently deposited a white plastic spoon on my stomach. She watched me expectantly for a few seconds, seemingly disappointed that her gift had produced no immediate effect beyond my saying, "Thank you, Fanny," and handing the spoon back to her. Undeterred, however, she departed again and returned with another white plastic spoon—and then, about three minutes later, with yet another.

I'm still not sure what these plastic spoons symbolized to Fanny (or even where this stash of hers was being kept, given the thorough moth-related housecleaning we were still in the process of undertaking). Perhaps, I reasoned, trying to follow the logic, she knew that humans use spoons for eating and thought that if I ate something, I might be able to get up? Whatever effect she'd hoped the spoons might produce, when it failed to occur she must have decided that a more drastic intervention was called for.

It was perhaps a half hour later, and I'd just drifted back into sleep, when I was roused once again by the sound of Fanny ascending the stairs with her hunting cry. I felt her land beside me on the bed, and she once again placed something on my belly. I blearily half-opened my eyes and raised my head as far as I could without engaging any more of my beleaguered spine than the very top portion of my neck. It was hard to make out what it was at first, although . . . was I imagining it? Was whatever it was *moving?* The room was still dark in the pre-dawn hours, so I switched on the bedside lamp.

It took me a second to realize what it was—primarily because my brain, for a moment, flat-out refused to confirm the report my eyes were sending. What Fanny had so lovingly deposited on my stomach was an enormous palmetto bug— otherwise known in the Northeast as a "water bug," or simply a "huge ugly cockroach"—on its back *AND STILL ALIVE* as all six of its legs waved feebly in the air.

THEM!

Now, I was born and raised in South Florida. I've seen plenty of giant cockroaches in my day. I've seen—and dispatched without flinching—cockroaches so big you could've saddled and ridden them in the Kentucky Derby. I had even, once or twice, awakened with a kind of prickly sensation on my arm and realized it was just such a cockroach crawling across me.

And, as would normally be the case in finding an enormous cockroach on my person, my instinctive first response—which, without thinking, I immediately undertook—was to attempt to bolt upright into a sitting position so as to dislodge the thing and *get it off me.*

Except that I *couldn't* bolt upright. I couldn't sit upright at all. The instant and painful wrench I felt in my lower back as I tried to rise quickly—an effort that would end up costing me another two days in bed—was a forceful reminder of just how futile this attempt was. "*Son of a—!*" I swore loudly, as I fell back into a supine position.

So there I was, flailing about helplessly on my back, while the giant cockroach on my belly was *also* flailing about helplessly on *its* back, the two of us acting out a scene from some cat-and-cockroach remake of *Misery,* in which Fanny was playing the Kathy Bates role and either the cockroach or I—or both of us—were James Caan.

Ultimately, the palmetto bug was more successful than I was. It soon righted itself and began a rapid scurry up my body in the general direction of my neck. I tried to brush it off with the back of my hand but, with a brief flutter of wings, it scuttled right over the top of my hand, down my palm, and—clearly as startled and disoriented as I was—continued its trajectory up my torso with an increased dash of frenzied speed.

I had a friend in Miami who'd once awakened in the middle of the night to find that a palmetto bug had crawled into his ear, and both his own and the cockroach's combined efforts had been unable to get it back out. He'd wound up in the emergency room where the doctors irrigated his ear canal—effectively drowning the palmetto bug while my friend was forced to listen to its excruciating death throes *inside his own head*—before they were finally able to extract its corpse from his ear, chunk by chunk, with a small pair of forceps.

This palmetto bug—the one that *I* was dealing with in the here and now—was closing the distance between itself and my chin at an alarmingly swift pace.

"*Laurence!*" I shrieked. "*LAAAAUUUUUUREEEEEENNNCE!!!*"

Fanny and Clayton—who'd been sitting next to me with an eager air this whole time—darted off and under the bed so quickly, they practically left spinning dust clouds behind them. From the guest room, I heard the sound of feet hitting the hardwood floor and then a rapid thud of footsteps. In a flash Laurence was standing in the bedroom doorway, clad only in his boxer briefs and brandishing the baseball bat he always kept next to him while he slept (a holdover from having first moved to New York in the '80s, at the height of the crack epidemic).

So poised and ready did Laurence look to club somebody bloody with that baseball bat that I had a wild, momentary fear he might use it on the cockroach while it was still on top of me.

"Get it off me," I whimpered, gesturing to the bug on my chest. "*Get it off me!*"

Dropping the bat with a clatter and grabbing a handful of tissues from the box on our night table, Laurence snatched up the hapless cockroach. He clenched his fist with a satisfying crunch and swept it from the room, the sound of the toilet flushing a moment later confirming that it had been given a burial at sea.

"How did it get all the way up here, anyway?" he asked, as he returned to the bedroom. During the warmer months, we were usually good for one or two palmetto bugs a week squeezing into the basement-level kitchen through the French doors that led out to our tiny backyard. But the only time we ever saw one up on the third floor was in pieces, after Fanny had thoroughly mauled it and left its remains for us as an offering.

"Fanny brought it up," I confirmed. "I think she thought she was 'helping.' She didn't even eat any of it before she gave it to me." The thudding of my heart had finally slowed to its normal rhythms, and I smiled at Laurence. "That was damn manly, by the way—how you raced in here ready to beat an intruder to death to protect me."

Laurence smiled back. "I probably would've tried to talk my way out of it first."

Clayton and Fanny, having determined that the coast was clear, peeked out from beneath the bed's dust ruffle, then tentatively crept over to sit in front of Laurence. They craned their necks to gaze up into his face, their yellow eyes wide and hopeful. "You know," I suggested, "as long as you're awake . . ."

Laurence looked down at the cats. "Come on, guys," he said, his tone resigned. "Let's go get breakfast."

Fanny gave Clayton a look that could only be described as triumphant. *See? I knew I could get at least one of them out of bed!*

As the three of them headed downstairs, one lone moth fluttered out of a dresser drawer to perch on the ceiling above my head—a solitary soldier in the enemy army taunting me, a fallen warrior, as I lay helplessly on my back remembering the day, one pleasant but otherwise ordinary day, just over a year ago when the whole thing had started.

5. IN THE BEGINNING . . .

It was a dreamily perfect spring afternoon. The sky outside the window of my writing nook was as pure and crystalline a blue as God had ever intended. The tiny pink roses on the climbing bush, wending its way up the wooden fence enclosing our small backyard, were in full, festive bloom. After a particularly cold and difficult winter, the entire backyard had exploded into a riot of glorious green leaf and multihued flower. I'll admit that there are still days when I think to myself that nothing will ever be better than living in Manhattan. But, on days like that one, I can't imagine any place on Earth I'd rather be than in my lovely little brownstone, here in Jersey City, with Fanny napping on the sunlit windowsill of my writing nook and Clayton dozing peacefully on the desk beside me.

A sudden commotion of sparrows split the silence outside, and I swiveled in my desk chair to see what had them so agitated. A wispy, fast-moving cloud of some kind was rising from the other side of the fence that adjoined our neighbor's yard. I couldn't tell what it was at first, but I soon detected the fluttering of small, almost imperceptible wings. It looked as if an egg sac of infant moths had burst open into the stillness of the springtime air—and the sparrows, grateful for the bounty, had stationed themselves in a cluster around the newly hatched insects, gobbling up as many as they could in their small beaks as the moths tried to beat their way skyward.

THEM!

The sound of sparrows tittering in the backyard had wakened Fanny and Clayton from their slumber, and they took up side-by-side positions on the windowsill for a better look. My wall-unit air conditioner faces out onto the backyard, and soon I noticed three or four of the minuscule moths—small enough to pass through the filter—fluttering their way through the air conditioner, into the house, and around the cats' heads.

It was the birds my cats wanted, not the bugs. But the cats were already up, their appetite for hunting whetted, and the baby moths were better than nothing. Rising up on her hind legs, Fanny tried to grab at them with her front paws, while Clayton made a few half-hearted hops, attempting to catch one or two in his mouth before they got away.

But the moths were so small—so very, very tiny—that it was nearly impossible to keep track of them among the dust motes also dancing in the sunlight that fell through the window. Almost before Clayton and Fanny had even started to try to catch the insects, before I could think of finding something to swat at them with myself, the wee creatures had flitted out of sight. And even though they hadn't tried *very* hard to nab the moths, Fanny and Clayton still looked disappointed.

"Aw, don't worry about *them*, you guys," I said, giving each cat a sympathetic scritch on the head. Fanny and Clayton looked up at me drowsily from heavy-lidded golden eyes, purring lightly at the touch of my hand. "Those silly moths weren't worth trying to eat, anyway. There'll be plenty of bigger and better things for you two to catch someday. You'll see . . ."

Cat Carrier
Tango

I was reading a book recently (*The Friend*, by Sigrid Nunez) in which a doctor acquaintance of the narrator explains to her that during the psychiatric rotation of his residency, he'd been taught that having multiple cats could be a sign of mental illness. Observing that one does occasionally hear about cat hoarders, and expressing a general approval that this was something health-care professionals were being trained to look out for, the narrator asked her doctor friend what number of cats would be considered the "tipping point" as a possible indicator of insanity. And the doctor replied, "Three."

I was glad that I first encountered this in the privacy of my home and not, say, sitting in a bookstore audience somewhere, hearing the author read it aloud. I'm positive that I would have laughed long and hard (as I did when reading it to myself), and maybe it would have been one of those uncomfortable moments where you're the only one laughing in a roomful of silent, serious people. Because maybe "three" wasn't supposed to be the punch line of a joke. Maybe it wasn't a joke at all. Or maybe it was, but the joke was on *us*—the "crazy cat people" of the world (*Look at those wacky people with as many as* three *cats!*).

I mean, c'mon . . . *three?!* Three is nothing! In my world—being in daily contact with any number of people who work in animal rescue—it almost isn't even worth noting how many cats a person has until the number gets into double digits. And even then, so long as that number doesn't climb much above a baker's dozen, and you live in a home sufficiently large to give everyone their space, you're probably okay. Two of my closest friends live on a hobby farm in Tennessee with *eleven* cats—along with eight cows, four horses, a constantly fluctuating number of chickens, an apiary full of honeybees, and one three-legged dog. As a longtime urban apartment dweller, I've always loved hearing their "crazy" stories about life on the farm. But I've never thought of them as being *actually* crazy.

Still, I'd be lying if I said that there were never days, back when I had my "first generation" of three cats—Scarlett, Vashti, and Homer—when I felt like I might be cracking up, or wondered if maybe I needed to have my own head examined. It was possible that I'd gone 'round the bend a long time ago, and that my friends secretly wished I'd get myself to a therapist's office posthaste without their having to intervene.

This impulse to consult a trained psychiatric professional was never stronger than on days, like the one back in 2005, when I had to take all three cats to the vet's office at the same time.

A three-cat vet visit was a physically unwieldy and decidedly unpleasant eventuality that I tried to avoid whenever possible. Although I'd adopted my cats over a three-year period, each a year apart from the other, their birthdays fell close together on the calendar—May for Scarlett and Vashti, and July for Homer (peak "kitten season" months, as anyone in rescue will tell you). This meant that the timing of their annual physicals also fell close together. Nevertheless, it was worth the effort of making two or three separate trips rather than bringing them in simultaneously.

Just getting the three of them into their carriers all at once was an ordeal. I had to take the carriers out of the closet the night before I planned to use them, because Scarlett and Vashti would go into deep hiding for hours once the carriers made an appearance. (I think Homer knew they were there, but maybe they didn't freak him out because he was blind and thus couldn't see them.) Right before I planned to load them in, I had to lure the cats into the living room/kitchen area with a rattling cat-treat bag and then close the doors of bedrooms and bathrooms, once they'd assembled and gotten their first round of treats, to bar any potential escape routes. Homer would happily munch away on his, blissfully unaware of what was about to happen. But as each door in the apartment closed one by one, with the three carriers looming in a row before them, the expressions on the faces of the other two cats would flicker from surprised gratitude (*hey! treats!*) to betrayed wariness (*oh . . . that's why we're getting treats*).

I always started with Vashti, because she was, surprisingly, the most difficult to catch. I'd spend a good five minutes chasing her up and down the hallway; over, around, and behind the furniture; and underneath the dining-room table—requiring me to shove it out of the way and thus allowing her to escape (a ruse I invariably fell for). I always heard the *Benny Hill* "Yakety Sax" music playing in my head as my fleet-footed feline nimbly evaded my grasp time after time, her fluffy white tail flying out behind her like a comet, until—with a desperate lunge—I'd snatch her up at last. Once caught, while I tried to hold the soft carrier open with one hand and shove her into it with the other, Vashti would splay out her hind legs like a jackrabbit, thwarting my efforts by making herself too wide to fit through the carrier's opening. By the time I finally managed to prop the bag open with enough stability that it stayed that way on its own, one of my hands holding Vashti's rear legs together and the other firmly clutching the scruff of her neck as I wrangled her into it, I was already panting and exhausted—and I still had two cats to go.

Scarlett was on the chubby side and, although she'd put up a token effort at running away, far easier to catch. Still, her wild hisses and snarls as I corralled her into her carrier informed me in no uncertain terms that I was the Cruella De Vil of cat moms. Homer, who never shied away from confrontation, didn't run away at all. Once I had him in my hands, he simply transformed himself—Tasmanian Devil–like—into a whirling mass of fur and claws. I didn't so much place Homer in his carrier as blindly aim him in its general direction, holding him out at full arm's length, until the physics of it aligned by pure chance and he was somehow safely inside, slashing frantically and popping his head out through the opening to the last as I held him down and zipped the flap shut above him. (A few years later, I would make the mistake of scheduling a routine vet appointment for Homer ten days before my wedding—and then spend those ten days with my hands covered in honey, because I'd read someplace that honey helped wounds heal faster, and the uncomfortable stickiness of it, even amid all the last-minute stress of wedding planning, still seemed preferable to standing up in front of everyone I knew, in my exquisitely pristine gown, while Laurence tenderly placed a wedding ring onto a hand as scraped and scabby as a tomboy's kneecaps.)

Even under normal circumstances, I was never at my coiffed and perfumed best by the time I finally sank into a chair in the vet's waiting room. But this particular day had been far from normal. My hair was frizzed up to outrageous heights, my mascara had puddled in black pools under my eyes, and I don't know if you could really call what was happening on my sweat-soaked shirt "pit stains," given that the wet patches radiated out from my actual armpits to meet in the middle of my chest.

And their exams hadn't even started yet! Vashti was a good-enough patient (she'd struggle a bit, but ultimately let the doctors and techs do whatever they needed to do without a fight). Scarlett and Homer, however, were not. Homer was a thoroughly bad patient, truth be told. The only shot I had at keeping him calm enough for the exam even to take place without some hapless vet tech getting hurt was to hold his carrier in my lap while we sat in the waiting room. Accordingly, I now had one wounded hand inserted through the flap of its zip-up top to gently stroke his head. I'd arranged Scarlett and Vashti on the chairs on each side of me, turned so they could see me smile at them reassuringly through the front mesh of their carriers.

But they all knew where they were—even Homer, who may have been blind, but still knew exactly what a vet's office smelled like. The three of them wailed their misery to the waiting room, their cacophony of moans, growls, and yowls—each one of my cats, upon hearing their siblings' anguished cries, louder than if they'd been there individually—drowning out the tweets, purrs, yips, and yelps of the semi-full room's other patients. Their owners gazed at me—sitting there alone, taking up three chairs, cat carriers surrounding me like a pillow fort—and then down toward my bare ring finger with an air of bemusement and pity. *How is it even possible,* I imagined them thinking, *that some lucky person hasn't already snatched up this gem?* I felt a childish, almost irresistible impulse to cry out, *I do so too* have someone! *He just isn't with me right now, is all.*

I hadn't planned to be in that waiting room alone with my cats that day. But it was a day when nothing had gone as planned . . .

IN MY ORIGINAL BLUEPRINT FOR THAT AFTERNOON, LAURENCE WAS supposed to be there with me. The only reason I'd booked all three cats for their annuals on the same day was because we'd agreed that, under the circumstances, it was a necessity—one that Laurence would help me execute.

I had moved, a month earlier, into the apartment where Laurence had lived for seventeen years. He was in possession of the Manhattan equivalent of the Holy Grail, the kind of thing you heard urban legends about, but never expected to see in your own real life: a rent-controlled, three-bedroom, two-bathroom apartment *with a terrace,* in a Midtown doorman highrise, for a three-figure monthly rent. (Eight years later, our unit would phase out of rent control and the rent would skyrocket to six thousand a month—at which point Laurence and I made a beeline for Jersey City.)

Technically it was a "no pets" building, but the rent was too insanely good not to at least try to make it work. On my move-in day, we'd tipped the super for use of the freight elevator (located in the rear of the building), and I'd managed to sneak in the three cat carriers among my boxes and suitcases without having to worry about the scrutiny of the lobby staff.

Nevertheless, the possibility of discovery was an ongoing concern. I had some savings, and Laurence—having lived so inexpensively for so long—had a lot more. We had more than enough between us, in other words, to finance a hasty move if we were suddenly evicted for illicit cat possession. And Laurence, who'd been there far longer than all but a handful of the other tenants, knew and was liked by everyone who worked in the building. Various maintenance men had come and gone over the past few weeks, and—while we'd locked the cats in a bedroom, not wanting to be *too* obvious—the clearly audible sound of three outraged felines, who were unused to being restrained, had passed unremarked. The maintenance guys had simply made whatever repairs they'd come to make, accepted our cash tip when they were finished, and left without comment.

Still, it seemed wise not to flaunt the cats where flaunting was avoidable. So when the time for their annual exams rolled around, I booked a single three-cat appointment with a new vet (our old vet now being a forty-minute, twenty-dollar crosstown cab ride away), figuring it made more sense for Laurence and me to hustle the three cats quickly through the lobby and past the doorman in one straight shot, rather than trying to do so on three separate occasions. Plus, we reasoned, our new doctor might as well meet them all at once.

But, as the saying goes, man plans and God laughs. At the last minute, Laurence, who was a film journalist with *Variety* at the time, got assigned to cover the press junket for the new *Zorro* movie. He'd have to attend a private screening of the film uptown, following which he'd head for a suite at the Waldorf Astoria to sit for a roundtable discussion with one of the principals—just Laurence, three other reporters, and Catherine Zeta-Jones, hanging out to talk about whatever movie stars and movie reporters talk about when they get together.

"So what you're telling me," I said to Laurence, "is that you want me to lug all three cats to the vet's office *by myself*, so you can spend the afternoon with Catherine Zeta-Jones."

"It sounds bad when you put it that way," Laurence admitted.

We briefly considered changing the appointment, but it wasn't as if I'd never managed on my own to get all three of them to the vet at once. Granted, the last time had been four years ago, when I'd brought the cats to our Miami vet to get their airline travel certificates so they could ride with me in the plane's cabin during our move to New York. And things had been different back then in certain crucial ways, although I didn't stop to think about that before agreeing to send Laurence off to Catherine Zeta-Jones and go it alone. I'd been living in a pet-friendly apartment building, for one thing. And for another, I'd had my own car.

Neither of those was the case now.

The first hurdle was clearing the lobby of our building without arousing the doorman's suspicions. It was early fall—not yet true coat weather, but not the kind of broiling-hot day that would make coat-wearing overly suspicious. The original plan had been for Laurence to hide Vashti and Scarlett's carriers under his coat, and for me to carry Homer under my own, until we got outside.

CAT CARRIER TANGO

Now I had to find outerwear that could effectively hide three cat carriers on its own. I had a vintage swing-coat of my grandmother's, made in the '60s, that I thought might do the trick. Its great swath of cherry-red fabric fell from a high leopard-print collar into a wide, beltless balloon, which Laurence claimed made me look like Emma Peel from *The Avengers* whenever I wore it.

Checking myself out in the hall mirror before I left—with Scarlett's carrier slung over one shoulder under the coat, Vashti's over the other, and Homer's clutched in my hands in front of me beneath the coat's girth—I didn't look a bit like Emma Peel. I looked armless and startlingly obese, my legs descending beneath the coat's knee-length hem like two toothpicks supporting a bowling ball.

Actually, I assured myself, the bowling-ball comparison wasn't entirely fair. Bowling balls don't meow, after all, whereas a raucous and colorful string of feline oaths was already emerging from beneath my coat's copious folds. Homer, in particular, was swearing up a storm as he loudly—and repeatedly—let me know exactly what he thought of this nonsense.

Well, I thought, *at least I'm not conspicuous.*

"Be cool, you guys," I pleaded with the cats, speaking down to them through the coat's high collar as I emerged from the elevator into the lobby. The sound of cars whizzing by on Second Avenue from beyond the building's front doors momentarily silenced them, for which I was infinitely grateful. I could walk neither well nor quickly, laden down as I was beneath my heavy coat and nearly thirty pounds of catflesh, so I did a sort of quick-time waddle past the doorman's desk.

The doorman regarded me quizzically for a moment before his face broke out into a broad smile. "Look at you!" he exclaimed heartily. "Congratulations!" I had no idea what he was talking about, as he continued to beam at me, until he added, "When are you due?"

Nothing makes a woman feel better than being mistaken for pregnant when she's not. But I didn't know how much longer my cats would remain silent, and I certainly wasn't looking to prolong the conversation. So I said, rather lamely, "No sooner than I have to be" (even I wasn't sure what that meant), and waddled even faster toward the lobby's front door.

"Oh, no—allow me," the doorman insisted, racing from behind his desk to open the door for me, then plunging himself into the gray, overcast afternoon and the whirl of Second Avenue traffic to flag down a cab. I waited until I could see he was safely back inside and out of eyeshot—pausing to give me a friendly goodbye wave as he disappeared back through the front door—before I opened my coat and began arranging the carriers on the cab's back seat.

"It's like a clown car in there," the cabbie observed cheerfully, as one cat after another emerged from the inner recesses of my outerwear.

I hadn't anticipated finding myself in the back of a cab with such speed and ease, and my relief was great enough that I let the comment go by. "We're going straight down Second Avenue," I told the cabbie. Pulling Homer's carrier onto my lap and checking that Scarlett's and Vashti's were still securely closed, I leaned back and closed my eyes. The hardest part was over.

CAT CARRIER TANGO

IN THE FLUSTERED HASTE TO GET OUT OF THE APARTMENT, I HADN'T noted the exact address of our new veterinary clinic. But a newly launched web mapping service called Google Maps had revealed St. Mark's Veterinary Hospital to be on the northwest corner of St. Mark's Place (another name for Eighth Street) and First Avenue.

The East Village, as the area was known, was an older, pre-skyscraper section of Manhattan, and St. Mark's Place had once been the flashpoint of New York's counterculture. Although slowly gentrifying, it still retained something of its bohemian charm and was colorful and crowded as a Moroccan bazaar, albeit one that had been taken over by hippies, artists, and hawkers of tourist tchotchkes. There were also plenty of increasingly expensive apartments in the East Village's aging brownstones and tenements, at least some of which, presumably, housed conscientious pet custodians. And, of all the veterinary practices within a reasonable distance of the cats' and my new home, St. Mark's Vet seemed the most beloved by its clientele, judging by online reviews.

Laurence and I lived at Twenty-Eighth and Second. We could make it down to St. Mark's Place in about half an hour on foot, and even in the stop-and-go traffic on Second, I didn't think it would be more than a fifteen-minute ride. Still, I'd left home at 1:45 p.m. for our 2:30 p.m. appointment, assuming it would take me longer to find a cab than it ultimately had, and also because a certain compulsiveness when it came to punctuality had been baked into my DNA. Even when going to her nail salon, a three-minute drive from her house, my mother down in Florida would first check rain forecasts, traffic reports, construction updates, the air level in the tires of her car, the very wind velocity for all I knew—and then still leave a half hour early because "you never know *what's* going to happen with all the idiots driving around Miami."

We crept along for about ten blocks, the cabbie hitting the brakes hard every minute or so as the cars in front of us ground to a halt. Every time the cab stopped, a cat would start to wail, but only one at a time, as if they'd agreed upon a particular sequence beforehand. (I found this fascinating and tried to figure it out—were they going oldest to youngest? largest to smallest?—but couldn't detect a pattern.) I'd gotten so used to the rhythm of go/stop/cat cry, go/stop/cat cry that—when I heard a dull crunch of metal and was suddenly flung forward against the plastic divider separating the front seat of the cab from the back, then backward against the back-seat headrest—I didn't register at first that anything odder than a particularly hard slam of the brakes had occurred. Then I realized that I had a painful lump blossoming on my forehead, and that Scarlett's and Vashti's carriers had lurched forward and were now wedged between the divider and the edge of the back seat. Homer's, fortunately, was still safely in my lap.

A quick check revealed all three cats to be unharmed. Nevertheless, the immediate roar of their caterwauling nearly drowned out the cabbie's loud curses as he threw the car into park, turned on his hazard lights, and flung open the driver's-side door, leaping out to confront the driver who'd rear-ended us. It was difficult for the cats to make themselves heard over the angry blare of horns that rose from the cars behind us. But my cats were pros. They managed.

Shhhhhhh . . . it's okay . . . everything's going to be oooooookay . . . I murmured in the most soothing voice I could muster. But my cats argued stridently and persuasively that it most definitely was *not* going to be okay, with Homer, who always did have the most expressive cat voice I'd ever heard, making a particularly compelling case. My only hope was that the damage would prove minor enough for us to continue on our way. That hope was dashed, however, as the cabbie returned to dig out his cell phone from the front seat. "I'm calling the cops," he told me. "You should probably go find another cab."

I was momentarily nonplussed, possessed by the swift, wholly irrational feeling that I would rather do anything— literally, *anything*—than get out of that cab, shoulder my three cats, and go looking for another ride. "Don't you need me to stay and be a witness for the police report or something?"

The cabbie gave me a look that eloquently expressed his rapidly diminishing opinion of my intelligence. "Did you *see* anything?"

"Well . . . no."

"Just go. And don't worry about the fare," he added (rather graciously, all things considered) as I opened my purse to dig around for my wallet.

Heaving a sigh, I hoisted Scarlett's and Vashti's carriers over the shoulders of my unbuttoned coat and cradled Homer's in my arms in front of me, stepping out into the gray day and walking along the sidewalk backward as I scanned Second Avenue for another available cab. Even Vashti—patient, squeaky-voiced

Vashti—had been pushed beyond endurance, lowing her misery to an indifferent universe in deep, wrenching tones. Their complaints only rose in volume as I felt first one raindrop, then a second splash onto the top of my head before the clouds that had been piling up all day in an ever-angrier blue-black bruise finally opened, and it started to rain in earnest.

Of *course* it started to rain.

Ducking under an awning, I divested myself of cats and coat so that I could reassemble everything with all three carriers once again secured beneath the coat's folds, this time to protect them from the deluge. In the process, I attracted lively interest from the patrons of the bakery behind me, whose awning I was temporarily sheltering beneath. As they comfortably sipped their coffee and ate their scones and pointed me out to companions in backward-facing chairs who swiveled around for a better view, I had an urge to wave my arms around and holler, *LOOK AT ME, EVERYBODY! LOOK AT THE CRAAAAAAAZY CAT LADY! TWO BITS A GANDER!* But I restrained myself and merely sighed again, dashing back out into the rain once the cats were settled. Carrying Homer beneath my coat with both hands meant I didn't have one free to make use of the fold-up umbrella in my purse, but by then I was already so thoroughly soaked that it hardly seemed to matter.

I tottered along awkwardly for about three blocks without seeing a single available taxi. I watched as one occupied cab after another crawled by, muttering darkly under my breath about the callous insensitivity of a city where not *one* person was willing to stop and split their fare with a fake-pregnant lady stuck in the rain. My damp hair plastered itself against my face, and I thought ruefully of the high and wild "Jew-fro" I was sure to have once it was dry again. The cats, who were now putting up an active revolt from within their carriers, felt decidedly heavier than they had when I'd first started out—and, despite the rain and early-autumn coolness, I perspired heavily beneath my coat. The ache in my shoulders intensified as the cats twisted and turned in their confines, shifting their weight unevenly from front to back and side to side as they sought in vain for an escape. By all rights, on a rainy day like this one, they should have been warm and dry at home, snoozing blissfully in front of the heater. I can only assume they thought I'd woken up that morning possessed of a perverse and irresistible desire to ruin their lives and that, after much consideration, I'd finally hit upon the perfect plan for doing so.

Water was filling up inside my fashionable ankle boots ("fashionable" here should be read as shorthand for "impractical for walking in the rain"), and I was just about to dash under another awning and wait out the downpour, our scheduled appointment be damned, when a battered Lincoln Town Car that had seen better days—very obviously a gypsy cab— pulled up alongside me. The driver rolled down his window and shouted, "You headed downtown?"

In the days before Uber, gypsy cabs were basically random guys with Town Cars who cruised around the city looking for (illegal) fares among the sidewalk downtrodden—people who either weren't savvy enough to avoid gypsy cabs or who lacked better options. I avoided gypsy cabs on general principle. In the first place, their fares were almost always outrageous (see above re: naïve and desperate clientele). And, in the second place,

I had a long-standing wariness—impressed upon me since childhood—of getting into cars with strange men.

But there I was, standing in the middle of a downpour with three livid cats—mad as hell and hot as radiators—stashed beneath the sopping and sweaty coat I now fully intended to burn when I finally got back home. I looked first at the mustachioed driver, and then at the bobble-headed cat statue that bounced merrily on his dashboard. I think it may have mesmerized me. *Go ahead,* it seemed to whisper. *What else are you going to do?*

I took a step closer to the car. "How much to go to Eighth Street and First?"

"Twenty dollars," the driver said immediately.

"*Twenty dollars?*" I screeched. "To go *ten* blocks? That's crazy!" The driver didn't even bother responding. I was in a fix, and we both knew it. I reluctantly conceded, "All right," opened the door to the back seat, and once again started unpacking my cats from beneath my coat.

"Wait, you've got *animals* in there?" the driver protested. "I don't want them messing up my car."

The Town Car's gray interior had a reek of cheap air freshener unsuccessfully masking onions, and had been inexpertly patched in numerous places with fraying electrical tape. Was he kidding? Biting back a sharp retort, however, I observed wearily, "They're in carriers. They won't mess anything up. I promise."

"It'll be an extra ten dollars," the driver informed me.

"Fine, *whatever.*" I loaded the cats into the car and flung myself in behind them, imagining the coronary Laurence would have if he knew I was preparing to hand over thirty dollars to a gypsy-cab driver to travel a distance of only ten blocks. "Just get us to Eighth and First."

I expected the oniony stench—never a favorite with my felines—to provoke a fresh round of complaints. But the cats had apparently entered into a state of trauma-induced catatonia and were silent. The only sound to be heard, aside from the pounding Middle Eastern electronica coming from the car radio—which seemed to pulsate in tempo with the lump on my forehead—was the ringing of my cell phone from within my purse. Laurence had just gotten out of his movie and was awaiting the arrival of Catherine Zeta-Jones.

"How's it going? Are you at the vet's office yet?"

"Not yet. We hit a few snags," I told him. "How's it going there?"

"It's great," Laurence said cheerfully. "I just heard someone say they're bringing in sandwiches from Carnegie Deli."

"Lucky you," I replied wistfully, and heard a faint corroborating rumble from the vicinity of my stomach.

"I can bring a sandwich home for you," Laurence offered.

Traffic had eased considerably once we'd gotten past Fourteenth Street, and the Town Car was now closing in on Ninth. "That sounds good," I told him. "I'll see you at home."

"See you at home," he said.

The downpour had stopped by the time we reached the corner of Eighth and First. Gathering the folds of my wet coat around me, I felt reinvigorated at the prospect of my long, painful journey to the vet's office having finally reached its conclusion. Even handing over the staggering thirty-dollar fare (*Don't you dare tip him,* I could hear Laurence admonish) wasn't as onerous as I'd thought it would be. "Here we go, guys," I told the cats happily as I lifted their carriers for our short walk to the clinic. "Time to meet your new vet!"

TWENTY MINUTES LATER, WE WERE NOW OFFICIALLY FIVE MINUTES late for our appointment—and apparently no closer to St. Mark's Veterinary Hospital than we'd been when we'd first left home nearly an hour ago.

I'd gotten out of the car with my cats at the corner of Eighth and First, and hadn't seen anything remotely resembling an animal hospital among the rainbow of storefronts and restaurants that dotted this stretch of St. Mark's Place. Reassuring myself, with the remembered vision of what Google Maps had shown me, that it was probably only a little farther down, I'd hobbled along the street as best I could in my water-stiffened boots, which were now raising blisters on my ankles, and my sopping-wet coat—and with what felt like a permanent hunch forming in my upper back as I bore the weight of three wretched cats who seemed, through sheer spite, to have somehow willed themselves into being heavier than they actually were.

Having resumed their insistent wailing, they had shifted their tone from plaintive and cajoling (*Please, pleeeeeeeease, let us out, Mommy . . .*) to distinctly hostile (*Up yours, lady!*). Scarlett, my "surly girl" who could sound downright mean-spirited when she had a mind to, kept up a continuous, cantankerous, and guttural stream of personal insults that would undoubtedly be unprintable if translated from feline to human. "Stop *yelling* at me, Scarlett!" I kept shouting. "I can't *think!*" That was when I wasn't hollering at my fellow pedestrians, who persistently bumped into me—a limping hunchback smothered in cats—as a not-so-gentle reminder that my shuffling pace was slowing down the flow of traffic. "Hey!" I heard myself snarl at their retreating backs. "I'm walking here! *I'm walking here!*" I felt a sudden stab of sympathy for those people you saw from time to time, wandering the streets of New York alone, hands balled into fists as they raged and raved at nobody in particular. Maybe they all had grousing cats stuffed beneath their coats, too.

I peered up at every sign and into every doorway that I passed as I waddled up Eighth Street. By the time I made it all the way to Second Avenue—with Gem Spa (an ancient newsstand and home of the world's best egg cream) and Love Saves the Day (my all-time favorite vintage store) swimming before my bleary eyes—I knew I'd overshot the mark.

The lump on my forehead throbbed dully. It occurred to me that if I hadn't possibly concussed myself earlier when the cab was rear-ended, I would've already come up with the bright idea of digging out my cell phone and calling Information for the exact address. Setting Homer's carrier on the ground to free up my hands and clutching it firmly between my ankles (raised in Miami during the snatch-and-grab '80s, I maintained an irrational and unshakeable belief that any improperly secured bag would be stolen instantly), I swung my handbag around from its perch on my shoulder just above Scarlett's carrier and began pawing through it. I'd deliberately chosen a small bag when I'd left the house, to minimize the weight I'd be carrying around that afternoon. It didn't take more than a few seconds, therefore, to discover that my phone was nowhere to be found.

I frantically dug through all my pockets and then, moving off to the edge of the sidewalk farthest from the street, I squatted on the ground, settled all three carriers beside me, and actually emptied the contents of my purse and pockets onto the pavement. The brief glimpse I caught, in my compact mirror, of my bird's-nest hair and sweaty, makeup-streaked face was both horrifying and revelatory. Along with my scratched-up hands (from my earlier efforts to get Homer into his carrier), swollen ankles, lumpy forehead, bedraggled coat, and warped shoes, plus the effluvia from the inside of my purse spread out before me as I snatched at lipsticks and bits of paper that attempted to roll away, and my array of cranky cats—whose dour expressions made it clear that they'd rather be anywhere in the world than stuck with *this* crazy lady—my *What Ever Happened to Baby Jane?* hair and face probably explained why one well-dressed woman, barely breaking stride, went so far as to chuck a dollar bill in my direction as she strode past.

I had officially been downgraded from pedestrian to panhandler.

Still squatting on the sidewalk, I buried my face in my hands and took a deep breath—which only prompted a fresh volley of bills and loose change from passersby. A busker a few feet away glared at me, and I responded with a gesture that I hoped conveyed (among other things) that if he wanted the cash so badly, he should come and get it. *Get up*, I commanded myself. It was very clear by now that I'd left my phone in the back seat of the gypsy cab after Laurence's phone call. With no phone and dwindling cash, it still made more sense for me to try to find the vet's office—which, surely, I must be closing in on!—than to return home. I'd have to walk back to First Avenue, anyway, to catch a cab or bus that was going in the right direction to get us to our apartment. My best plan, therefore, was to ask someone for directions. One of the shopkeepers or employees along this stretch of St. Mark's Place would undoubtedly be able to tell me where St. Mark's Vet was located. Accordingly, I scooped my belongings back into my purse and hoisted my cats once again.

It seemed, however, that nobody could help me. As I limped my way back down Eighth Street, I got blank stares from the dazed proprietors of the numerous head shops I ducked into; the sidewalk vendors selling postcards and knickknacks; the girl with shocking pink hair, a pierced lip, and tattooed arms at punk-rock mecca Trash and Vaudeville; the sad day-drinkers at Holiday Cocktail Lounge. I was admonished, *You can't bring animals in here!* in a diverse array of languages at a taqueria, a stand-up pizza counter, a falafel joint, and a take-out dumpling place. Each time the aroma of cooking food hit Homer's nostrils, he began pinging wildly at the sides of his carrier, until it felt like I was trying to hold onto a super-sized container of Jiffy Pop.

It wasn't until I'd retraced my steps all the way back to the corner of Eighth and First, and poked my head into Theatre 80, that I found salvation. Laurence and I had attended many performances at the Off-Broadway theater and had struck up conversations along the way with Lorcan Otway, the old-school Quaker (I'd thought he might be Amish when I first met him, because of the way he dressed) whose family had owned the place for decades. Silently offering me a glass of water from the lobby bar when I entered, and generously refraining from any remarks on my appearance, Lorcan removed his wide-brimmed, black-felt hat to rub his head in contemplation as I put my question to him. "Oh, yeah—St. Mark's Vet," he finally said. "They moved over to Ninth Street about a year ago." At seeing my shoulders slump (while I inwardly cursed Google Maps and its outdated information), Lorcan added kindly, "They're right at the corner of Ninth and First. You're practically there already."

I was so ecstatic upon seeing the brightly painted sign that read ST. MARK'S VETERINARY HOSPITAL almost immediately upon rounding the corner of Ninth and First that I barely minded when, as I tried to navigate the narrow metal staircase leading down to the basement-level entry, the warped and rain-soaked soles of my boots slid out from beneath me. I landed flat on my backside on a hard metal step, adding a bruise on my coccyx to the one on my forehead. Fortunately, I noted as I unsteadily rose back to my feet, I hadn't dropped or fallen on any of the cats.

The landing at the bottom of the stairs was a tight space, and I had to turn and twist for a good ten seconds before finally finding an angle that would allow me to both open the front door and squeeze through with my three carriers. When the sunny receptionist chirpily informed me that I'd missed my appointment and might have to wait awhile, I didn't bat an eyelash. I was so happy to be there—*at last! at last!*—and safely beyond the reach of sudden cloudbursts or hostile pedestrians that I was tempted to leap over the counter and kiss her on the mouth.

Instead of doing that, however, I asked permission to use the office phone to call my cell. It was answered by the gypsy-cab driver, who agreed to drive over and return it to me—for another twenty dollars.

PERHAPS THE GREATEST IRONY OF THAT DAY WAS THAT THE EXAMS themselves—the insertion of needles and rectal thermometers, the prying back of reluctant lips to check teeth and gums—

turned out to be the high point. Or Vashti's and Scarlett's exams were, at any rate. After the hour spent in the waiting room with my three furious felines, the doctor's kind patience was a balm on my frayed nerves, if not my cats'. Things went swimmingly until it was Homer's turn on the exam table. A vet tech chose the moment that Homer was finally released from his carrier to enter our exam room and, upon detecting the change in the air currents when the door opened, Homer—quick as a light beam—leapt down from the high metal table and streaked through the partially opened door in a mad dash for freedom.

You'd think it would be easy enough to catch a five-pound blind cat in an enclosed space that was entirely unfamiliar to him. And you would be wrong. Homer raced down the long hallway of exam rooms and out into the waiting area, sure-footed as if he had a blueprint of the building sketched in his head. My own bruised and battered body wasn't nearly so nimble as I lurched after him. Darting perilously close to the snout of a startled black Lab before wheeling around and changing course, Homer propelled himself into a storage closet whose door had been left ajar. "Please, Homer," I begged, as Homer sat on his haunches on a shelf just above my head, wholly intractable and entirely confident in the advantage over me that height gave him. "Please come down and get your exam like a good boy, so we can all go home."

Normally, Homer would do anything I asked (other than getting into his carrier, that is) if I used the right tone of voice. But I hadn't built up much in the way of credibility over the course of that long day, and Homer wasn't buying it. *No!* he seemed to say. *And you can't make me!* I felt absurdly triumphant when I finally located a small stepladder in a corner of the storage closet. I might not have been able to outwit any of the other obstacles the day had thrown at me, but I could still outsmart my cat. Cocking one black ear in my direction and tilting his head to the side as he tried to figure out what I was up to, Homer put up only token resistance as I ascended the stepladder and pulled him from his perch. The firmness of my grip on the scruff of his neck didn't leave room for argument.

I cradled him in my arms for a moment before exiting the storage closet—an unexpected oasis of calm in our chaotic day. There had never been a day so long and so bad that holding one of my cats close couldn't make it at least a little better. Pressing my cheek to the top of Homer's head and breathing in the familiar cinnamon-and-milk smell of his neck (I don't know how Homer always managed to smell like cookies, but he did, and it was awesome), I could feel the knots in my shoulders start to unloosen. "We're still friends," I whispered in Homer's ear, "aren't we?" He appeared to consider this for a moment before mashing his entire face into the palm of my hand, our usual gesture of reconciliation. I dropped a kiss onto the top of his head, and the two of us returned to the exam room.

By the time we emerged from the vet's office, it was rush hour, which would have made finding a cab nearly impossible even if—having already spent fifty dollars on the gypsy cab and the return of my cell phone—I'd had the cash to pay for one. The bus was our only alternative. The late-afternoon sun had made a belated appearance after all the rain, and it was considerably warmer out than it had been when I'd left the apartment hours ago. Still, I didn't have the energy to take off my coat as

I slowly toted the cats up to the bus stop on Eleventh and First. *Like it matters how much sweatier I get at this point,* I thought.

The bus was jam-packed with rush-hour commuters when we finally boarded, and an elderly woman, upon seeing how laden down with cats I was, immediately rose to offer me her seat. "*Please* don't," I insisted, raising the arm carrying Scarlett to grasp one of the straps hanging above my head. Vashti continued to dangle from my other shoulder, and I settled Homer on the floor of the bus between my feet. Gesturing to the carriers and the sardine-can crowd around us, I added, "I wouldn't have any room to put all three of them down, anyway."

The woman beamed first at me, as the bus lurched forward, and then at the cats through the mesh of their carriers. She reached up to rub gently at the front of Scarlett's, and I could feel Scarlett retreating as far back into her carrier as she could, reluctant as always to engage in any unnecessary human contact. "I have three of my own," the woman confided. "Where are the four of you coming from?"

"The vet's office," I replied.

"Ah! I try to never bring my three in all together. It's hard getting around New York with three cats. Unless," she smiled up at me again, "I bring my husband to help out. You should find someone to come with you next time."

"I think you're probably right about that," I agreed ruefully.

The bus let us off at the corner of Twenty-Eighth and First, and I was so grateful to finally—finally!—be so close to home that I nearly wept. Halfway between First and Second, I paused under the awning of a medical building to once again assemble the cats under my coat, in anticipation of the return trip through my apartment building's lobby. The doormen had changed shifts by then, and the evening doorman barely glanced up at me—much less congratulated me on my "pregnancy"—as I waddled my way past the front desk.

The sound of the radio drifting toward the elevator through our apartment door, once I reached our floor, let me know that Laurence had beaten me home. Undoubtedly, he would be fresh as a daisy after a day spent being feted at the Waldorf Astoria uptown. After my own afternoon trudging around downtown, I knew I was anything but. Nevertheless, the prospect of sympathy—and a Carnegie Deli sandwich—waiting for me inside went at least part of the way toward erasing the day's awfulness.

The first thing I did upon entering the apartment and closing the door behind me was to strip off my coat and hurl it into a corner, then kneel to release the cats from the confines of their carriers. Our entry hallway opened into both the living room and the kitchen, and I headed directly for the kitchen cabinet where I kept the cat treats. I distributed them with a free hand, feeling that my cats also deserved some recompense for the miserable afternoon we'd all had. A few cursory brushes of backsides and tails against my shins let me know that I would be forgiven—eventually.

Upon hearing the kitchen cabinet open and close, Laurence called out, "You home?"

"I just walked in," I called back. "How'd it go?"

I heard the sound of Laurence rising from the couch. "It was great! Cathcrine Zeta-Jones was unbelievable. She..." Having closed the short distance between living room and kitchen and drawn near enough to take in my appearance for the first time, Laurence's voice trailed off and he whistled softly. "Yikes," he said. "Bad day?"

"Don't ask."

Laurence moved closer. "What happened here?" he asked, gently brushing a finger against the purple lump on my forehead.

I attempted a smile. "Nothing a good sandwich can't fix," I replied lightly.

Laurence opened the refrigerator and withdrew a paper bag. "Chopped liver for you," he said, "and pastrami for me."

I retreated to the bathroom and, bending over the sink, tried to wash as much of the day's grime as possible from my face and hands. I heard Laurence gathering plates and napkins as I dried off with a hand towel, and we reconvened on the living room couch.

The cats and I hadn't been living with Laurence for very long at that point, but Vashti had already learned that he (unlike mom) could be counted on to slip a few tidbits her way at mealtimes, and had accordingly positioned herself on the floor close to his feet. Homer, who adored deli meats and could put away an astonishing amount of food for such a small cat, sat on the couch between Laurence and me, his face turned toward Laurence in hopeful anticipation. After only a few weeks, he'd learned from Vashti that the long-standing rule in our home against feeding table scraps to cats was in the process of being rewritten.

Only Scarlett sat aloof, perched across from us on the coffee table with disdain plainly written on her face. She had never been a fan of human food, and thus her affections couldn't be bought as easily as Vashti's and Homer's were. To Scarlett's way of thinking, anyone living in our home who wasn't me was just another cat—and Laurence was nothing more than the largest and most annoying of all the new cats I'd foisted upon her over the years. As the self-appointed leader and maintainer of discipline within our feline ranks, Scarlett had attempted to teach Laurence his proper place in the hierarchy with a peremptory swipe of her claws whenever he brushed too closely against her while passing in the halls. Puzzlingly, however, Laurence hadn't learned to defer to her as quickly as the other two cats had. Her deep disapproval now as Vashti and Homer lowered themselves and actually *begged* this interloper for a few crumbs from his plate was nearly palpable.

"So, you didn't finish telling me how it went," I said to Laurence. "What was Catherine Zeta-Jones like?"

"She was amazing!" He tore open a packet of mustard and applied it to his rye bread, Vashti and Homer at rapt attention as he did so. "I had such a great time talking with her! She really has that movie-star *thing*."

Laurence met and interviewed celebrities on a fairly regular basis—it was a part of his job description—and it was unusual for him to sound so animated about any one of them in particular. And yet, he still wasn't finished waxing lyrical on the subject of Ms. Zeta-Jones's many charms. "When she walks into a room, you *have* to look at her," he enthused. "She just *glows*, you know?"

A quick glimpse in the bathroom mirror as I'd washed earlier up had revealed how disheveled I'd become over the course of the day: With the puddled makeup still caked around my eyes—I'd done my best to wipe it away but I knew that only

a long shower would do the job fully—I looked like an aging raccoon. My hair was a fright wig straight out of one of the witches' scenes in *Macbeth*. The wreckage of my appearance could have been described in any number of ways, but "glowing" with "that movie-star *thing*" was certainly not among them.

I'll bet Catherine Zeta-Jones has somebody to take her *cats to the vet for her,* I thought sourly as I bit into my sandwich—not knowing or caring whether Catherine Zeta-Jones even had cats. *I'll bet she has cat butlers or cat valets, or some other dumb thing only rich movie stars have. I'll bet if Catherine Zeta-Jones* does *go the vet's office, she probably comes back looking like a million freaking dollars. AND WHAT KIND OF STUPID NAME IS "ZETA-JONES" ANYWAY?*

I knew I was being at least a little childish. Obviously, Laurence hadn't intended to draw comparisons. But I couldn't help the tenor of my thoughts, which I struggled to keep from revealing themselves on my face.

Laurence was sitting sideways on the couch, partially turned to face me. He held his still-untasted sandwich loosely in one hand—the hand closest to the coffee table—and, in his enthusiasm, gestured with it as he spoke. "She's really funny, too." The sandwich in Laurence's hand moved nearer to Scarlett's nose, which was wrinkling with distaste. "So many of them have nothing interesting to say for themselves." The pastrami and rye waved even closer to Scarlett's increasingly agitated face. "But she—" With one slight, but fatal, additional motion, the sandwich drew close enough to Scarlett to brush her whiskers.

It was the last straw in a day that had, I was forced to acknowledge, been as unpleasant for Scarlett as it was for me.

I'll never know if she had drawn any connection between Laurence's last-minute absence that day and how badly our afternoon had gone—or if she was able to tell from my expression what my own feelings toward Laurence were as I listened to him rhapsodize about Catherine Zeta-Jones. Regardless, this final insult was clearly too much for her to bear. With a loud hiss, Scarlett raised a front paw into the air—and, before I could stop her, brought it down in an angry swipe at Laurence's sandwich, which tumbled from his incautious hand and landed with a *splat!* on the floor.

In a flash, Homer leapt nimbly from the couch and was on top of the remnants of Laurence's meal, nosing assiduously through its wreckage for bits of pastrami that hadn't been contaminated by mustard.

"Hey!" Laurence's eyes turned to Scarlett in astonishment, then down toward the ruined pile of meat and bread on the ground. By now, Vashti had joined Homer and was gleefully helping herself, either not knowing that Laurence hadn't intended to give it to her, or else, in her excitement, not caring. It was difficult to tell which was stronger in Laurence's voice, anger or betrayal, as he said, "What was *that* for?"

I couldn't help myself—I burst out laughing. I laughed until tears ran from my eyes to blend with the black rings of eyeliner and mascara I knew were still there. "You can have half of my chopped liver, if you want," I finally offered, when I was able to catch my breath.

Scarlett let out a harrumph-y sniff, the gray-and-black tabby-striped fur of her back twitching rapidly, as she jumped down from the coffee table. With baleful eyes she looked back at Laurence, who was still gazing with dismay at what was left of his sandwich, before coldly stalking off toward the bedroom.

"What's her problem?" Laurence asked—and it's possible that, in that moment, Scarlett and I had the same thought:

Why don't you go ask Catherine Zeta-Jones.

Fanny Trouble

Everybody serves someone, and in my house there's no question who our master is: We're all in thrall to Fanny.

Never is my serfdom more obvious than at times like this. It's five thirty on a Saturday morning, and I've had the temerity to sleep a full half hour past my usual rising time—as if, I will later remark to Laurence in my best (although admittedly still bad) Cockney accent, "I wuz the queen o' England." The cats' breakfast is therefore officially late. Although maybe I should put "late" in ironic quote marks, since it hardly seems accurate to describe anything that takes place at five thirty on a Saturday morning—other than coming home from Friday night revelries—that way. Maybe "tardy" or "off schedule."

In any case, Fanny is about to let me know definitively that it's long past time I got up.

Laurence is sound asleep beside me, flat on his back and snoring lightly. Generally he prefers to sleep curled up on his side. But that's an inconvenient position for Fanny when she's of a mind to perch on Laurence's belly and demand an ultra-intensive round of deep petting, something she insists on receiving no fewer than three or four times each night between the hours of one and four a.m. Her solution is to butt her head repeatedly into Laurence's shoulder—bracing herself and digging in hard with all the force her seven-pound body can muster—until he obligingly rolls over. As she climbs onto his now-accessible stomach, his hands will rise semi-automatically to sink into the fur of Fanny's neck and flanks for a thorough scratching session, while Fanny utters a kind of prolonged, guttural gurgle of triumph that sounds like an alien's cry from some old-time creature feature. (Perhaps this is why Laurence, from among all the various nicknames he's bestowed on Fanny over the years—including "Fanny Kittanee," "Fan Girl," and "Fandemonium"—is most apt to refer to her simply as "the Creature.")

Laurence is a better sleeper than I am and can usually accommodate Fanny without either waking up fully or having trouble falling back asleep once she's sated. But sometimes— if it's the fifth or sixth time in the same night that Fanny has required tribute—I'll hear him stir and protest weakly, "Fanny! I'm only a man!"

It's lucky for me that Laurence is capable of satisfying Fanny in this way, because if I'm up anytime past three thirty a.m., like it or not, I'm up for the day. Life would be very difficult (and exhausting), in other words, if the responsibility for Fanny's late-night rubdowns were to fall to me.

As it is, I get off relatively easy. While it's true that I have to provide Fanny with my own round of thorough, aggressive scratching once I've gotten into bed for the night, after a mere fifteen to twenty minutes of these ministrations, I'm permitted to fall asleep and remain undisturbed until her breakfast time, which is five a.m. *al punto.*

FANNY TROUBLE

It wasn't always this way. There was a time, in the not very distant past, when I was allowed to sleep as late as seven o'clock. And before the Reign of Fanny began, the one who came to wake me for the cats' morning meal (along with an early round of fetch) was Clayton. A three-legged, mushy black marshmallow of a cat, Clayton has always been, perhaps, a bit too fond of his food. Were I to try sleeping so much as a minute or two past the customary time, it was Clayton who was certain to let me know that I was trespassing too far on the cats' benevolent good graces.

(The first two weeks after daylight saving time ends every year—when the clocks go back an hour, but the cats stubbornly insist that *their* internal clock doesn't change for anything as irrelevant as a mere human's varying conception of time—is always a particularly trying period.)

But while Clayton may have been our designated chowhound, for years it seemed that the sleek and slender Fanny could take her mealtimes or leave them. Half the time, to get Fanny to even bother waking from an afternoon nap and come downstairs for lunch, I had to walk through the house chanting, "Faaaaaa-*neeeeee*! Pssss-psss-psss! Faaaaaa-*neeeeee*! Pssss-psss-psss!" until either Fanny materialized or Laurence finally cried in exasperation, "Leave her alone already! She'll come down when she's hungry!" Even at the risk of missing a meal entirely— Clayton always being happy to eat whatever Fanny left behind— she could rarely be roused from the languor of a really excellent nap to bother with something as inessential as food.

Those were the good old days—but, alas, those days are gone. Meals are now the nexus around which Fanny's day revolves. And ever since her food obsession started, the cats' feeding schedule has slipped inexorably backward. Their seven o'clock breakfast was moved up to six o'clock, and then six o'clock became five thirty, and now we seem to have landed on five. (I would try harder to negotiate a later time, but given how dismal my success has been thus far at holding the line, I'm afraid we'll end up "compromising" with four thirty—and then my life will truly be miserable.) Lunch used to be at two, but Fanny takes up such an anxious (not to mention loud) vigil in the kitchen every day beginning at noon that I feel positively heartless—like I'm running a Dickensian orphanage full of half-starved children—if I don't break down and pop open a can at one o'clock. "Her will is too strong!" is always my defense to Laurence, when I catch him shaking his head at seeing me knuckle under this way.

And while Fanny knows (she *knows!*) perfectly well that dinner isn't until ten—the entire logic of this late-night "bonus" feeding having once been that it would keep the cats from waking me for food at the crack of dawn—she comes down to the living room to commence walking all over the book I'm reading, or climbing all over the TV screen I'm watching, or loudly interrupting Laurence's and my conversations with a series of piercing, plaintive cries, at precisely eight thirty.

I'm not sure, on this particular morning, how I've managed to get away with sleeping a full half hour late. Fanny's sense of time is accurate to within five minutes, and she's strict as a schoolmarm when it comes to keeping on schedule. Deviations from our daily timetable are rarely—if ever—tolerated. But as my eyes open to a bedroom that's slightly brighter than it usually is when I awaken, a quick glance at my bedside clock confirms that I have, indeed, been allotted a luxurious extra half hour under the covers. Perhaps Fanny has decided that even the most abject of servants requires the occasional indulgence, if one is to maintain that servant's loyalty.

As I awaken more fully, I see Clayton waiting on the ground beside the bed, the toy mouse he likes to play fetch with clutched in his mouth as he readies himself to climb up the side of the box spring and mattress. But when he moves forward, Fanny pats his face a few times with a gently restraining paw. *Wait,* she seems to be saying. *Don't bother her yet.* Fanny's authority is the only one that Clayton consistently recognizes and, while clearly impatient, he sinks back onto his one haunch without protest.

Once she notes that my eyes are fully open, however, the jig is up. Fanny becomes relentless, leaping nimbly onto my chest from the floor and, using that same disciplinary paw—a bit more firmly, I note, than she did on Clayton—to bat my left ear and the left side of my face several times in rapid succession, as if I were a fainting victim who might black out again without someone to smack me into alertness. I consider closing my eyes and feigning sleep, just to prove . . . what, exactly? That *I'm* the one who's in charge? That I haven't taken orders from anyone since the day I became self-employed over a decade ago, and that I don't intend to start taking orders now from a seven-pound cat?

You're adorable, I imagine Fanny saying in response to these feeble protests. *Now get your lazy butt downstairs and fix my breakfast.*

As these thoughts run through my head, Clayton uses his powerful upper body to haul himself up the side of the bed behind Fanny—dragging my blankets halfway off in the process—still clutching the toy mouse he'll insist I toss for him as I make my way downstairs to feed them.

Throwing off the blankets entirely, I get out of bed and walk down two darkened flights of stairs to the kitchen. Fanny runs before me, tail proudly aloft, her hot-pink wazoo—always a vaguely startling sight against the coal black of her fur—guiding me through the pre-dawn gloom like Rudolph's red nose.

FANNY MAY BE THE ONLY IRONICALLY NAMED CAT I'VE EVER HAD—although the irony was purely unintentional and has its roots in initial, and absolute, sincerity.

Laurence and I named Clayton, our "tripod," for a famous one-legged tap dancer called Clayton "Peg Leg" Bates. And Clayton—Clayton the cat, that is—was a garrulous, rambunctious little ball of energy right from the start. To describe Clayton as "outgoing" would be like saying that fire sometimes has a tendency to be warm.

His littermate, Fanny, on the other hand, was a painfully shy and timid soul when we first adopted her. I realize that "shy," as applied to cats, is often a euphemism for "unfriendly" or "aloof." With Fanny, however, it was clear that she *wanted* to be friendly. Not even three months old, she would stare at Laurence and me—these strange new giants she'd been abruptly thrown together with—her golden eyes rounded into perfect O's in which hope and fear vied for the upper hand. But she was so skittish at even the slightest noise that it made my heart ache for her. She would just start to nuzzle her tiny kitten head into the palm of my hand—having been coaxed, over the course of several minutes, with a gentle, encouraging "Come here, little girl . . . nothing's going to hurt you"—when a breeze would blow through the wind chimes hanging on our balcony and off poor Fanny would scurry to hide under the nearest piece of furniture, crouching out of sight for at least half an hour.

Laurence and I both had great-great-aunt Fannys way back in our respective family trees—the younger daughters of large immigrant families, and known for the kind of shy, "feminine" circumspection that was prized in girls a hundred years ago. So when we adopted this bonded pair of kittens, we named the girl-kitten Fanny because, as I wrote in a blog post at the time, "It seems like a sweet old-fashioned name for a sweet old-fashioned girl who likes to let her big brother do most of the talking."

Which was true—at the time, at any rate. Fanny, as a very young kitten, never put herself forward unless Clayton did first, and then only if she could do so while still hiding behind him.

We adopted the two of them six and a half years ago. Not wanting to overwhelm such small kittens at first with the size of our unusually spacious New York apartment—and also wanting to give Homer, who was still with us then, a chance to familiarize himself with their scent on my hands and clothing before introductions were made—they spent the first three or four days confined to our guest bedroom. When we finally opened the door and allowed them to explore their new home in full, Clayton was out of the guest room like a shot—his half leg spinning like a tiny propeller without ever quite reaching the ground as he hippity-hopped at top speed down the hallway. He couldn't wait to see everything, to explore all the novel nooks and crannies that were now his own—and, most of all, he was desperate to claim Homer as an immediate best friend, thrilled at the prospect of having a new big brother to idolize and emulate.

But where Clayton was heedless in his enthusiasm—barreling into Homer so eagerly that he nearly knocked him over (a breach of feline protocol for which Clayton was reprimanded with a mild hiss and a paw-slap of warning)—Fanny was overwhelmed. She refused to put so much as one paw beyond the bedroom threshold, hovering in the doorway as she looked anxiously after Clayton, crying and crying in wrenching tones for the brother—with whom she always curled up when they slept, as if the two of them were still in the womb together—to come back to her.

This is my earliest concrete memory of Fanny, and for a long time, it was the dominant image I had of her: a small and frightened kitten, crying in a doorway, bewailing her beloved brother's abandonment of her as if her heart would break.

I worried so for Fanny during the two weeks Clayton spent in the vet hospital to have his bad leg removed. (Because he was such an energetic little guy, his doctor wanted to keep him confined until the stitches were out.) They'd been with us for only six weeks then, and initially we'd hoped to postpone the inevitable surgery until Clayton was fully grown. But a little scratch on his bad leg, acquired before he'd come to us, stubbornly refused to heal and eventually became infected, even after a round of antibiotics. When a culture came back positive for antibiotic-resistant staph, we knew we had no choice.

Clayton had the time of his life in the hospital—thriving on the constant stream of attention and small toys that the staff, charmed by such a cheerful and hyper-friendly kitten, couldn't resist showering him with. And though I was concerned about Clayton during his recovery, visiting him daily to check on his progress and let him know we hadn't abandoned him, it was my anxiety for Fanny that kept me up nights. To first find herself in a strange house, and then to be separated from the brother she'd always relied on for courage and security! There was no way she could possibly understand why he was gone, or know when—or even if—he was coming back. It was enough to move me to tears on her behalf as I tossed and turned in bed, disturbing the sleep of Homer, who was cuddled up next to me, visibly more relaxed now that he had only Fanny's hesitant and respectful attentions to contend with and not Clayton's playful intrusiveness.

It's probably telling that, far from turning into a shrinking violet upon being separated from her living teddy bear of a brother, Fanny finally seemed to come out of her shell during Clayton's absence. For the first time, she engaged tentatively with Homer, and explored her new home in its entirety, without hiding in Clayton's shadow. She still preferred, however, to spend most of her time in the guest room, seeming to regard it as a home base of sorts. I passed long hours in there with her, writing on my laptop or stretching out to read on the bed while Fanny— her craving for affection at last overcoming her fear—burrowed deep into my hair spread on the pillow, or into the space between Laurence's shoulder and his neck when he came in to join us.

Given how painfully shy she'd been at first, I think Laurence and I imagined that we were saving her in some unspecified way that we—and we alone—were uniquely suited to do. How many people were lucky enough to work from home, to be in a position to give Fanny the constant attention and reassurance she needed? My first three cats had had to contend with a "working mom" who was gone up to ten hours a day, sometimes even more. It seemed clear—at least, it did then—that Fanny wouldn't have thrived under the same conditions.

Looking back now, it strikes me that Fanny's fragility—or, rather, our perception of her fragility (which isn't the same thing at all)—might have been the earliest roots of her power over us, growing into its own kind of strength.

This image of a fragile Fanny, in need of extra coddling and protection because she's *just that delicate*, stuck with us long after it was applicable—years after Fanny had grown in both size and confidence, developing into the intimidatingly aerodynamic hunter who's now the scourge of any non-cat or non-human unfortunate enough to creep, crawl, or fly its way into our home. To this day, Fanny still has a tendency to spend large chunks of her time alone and hidden under a bed or buried deep in a closet upstairs. When she finally does come down to the living room to nose her way shyly into our laps (her old habit of shyness never having left her entirely), we give her the same kind of over-the-top, rah-rah greeting that Norm used to get at Cheers. "It's FANNY!" we exclaim, dropping whatever we're doing to lavish her with pettings and ear rubs—still stuck in our years-old mold of treating Fanny's every uncoaxed appearance as if it were a major milestone achieved. Even Clayton, who's loath to share attention with anyone and—for that express reason—is never more than two feet away from me, will hop down from my lap or wake up from a deep sleep near my feet to race over and greet her.

So it's not hard to see where Fanny might have developed a sense of her own importance that's just the *teensiest* bit inflated.

What initially began as genuine shyness has likely, over the years, grown into a shrewd assessment on Fanny's part as to the value of scarcity. It may be the single-greatest long con any animal has ever pulled on me. And it's a testament to Fanny's skill that, even knowing that I'm basically her sucker, I still fall for it.

Laurence is no better than I am. Much as Vashti did before her, Fanny has managed to wrap him firmly around her little black paw. Many is the time I've come upstairs to find Laurence at his desk with Fanny sprawled luxuriously in his lap as he, not realizing that I can hear him, croons, "Pretty, pretty girl. Who's my pretty, pretty girl?"

For sheer aesthetic perfection, Fanny may not quite be the equal of Vashti in her heyday (although, in fairness, who could be?). But Fanny is still an exceptionally beautiful cat in her own right, with a heart-shaped face that looks as if it were drawn by Disney Princess animators, round, lustrous golden eyes, and a little "locket" of white fur on her chest that sets off her delicate black prettiness as perfectly as a well-chosen necklace. Vashti's was the beauty of profusion—an extravagance of pink and white and a flowing abundance of silky fur. Fanny, on the other hand, is all about bone structure, looking as if she were chiseled in black marble from some idealized model of feline structural precision. Every line of bone and muscle is plainly visible, yet also coalesced effortlessly into a graceful whole—crowned by an impenetrable shell of pin-straight ebony fur, which is shined at all times to a supremely high gloss. "Snake Hips," Laurence admiringly calls her sometimes, and he's not wrong; super-models would kill to have Fanny's hip bones.

If Vashti was cast along the lines of Venus, voluptuous goddess of love, then Fanny is more of a Diana—the dazzling and terrifying goddess of the hunt. And a huntress she is, a finely tuned killing machine who manages to make even the

act of offing a palmetto bug such a study in fluid artistry that I occasionally find myself regretting (in a messed-up, Stockholm Syndrome kind of way) that she'll never have a shot at the birds we both love to watch—albeit for vastly different reasons—from inside our house. Fanny spends half her waking hours "chittering" in frustration at the birds and squirrels who hover tantalizingly just outside the windows. Sometimes, in her pointless yet still unflagging pursuit of them, she'll get a running start from across the room and spring all the way up a window that rises a good two feet over my head, hovering near the top and clinging with all four paws to the wooden slats that separate the panes, like one of those suction-cupped Garfield dolls people used to affix to their cars' rear windows. She tenders Laurence and me daily "gifts" of any bugs that get into the house and are large enough to be worth gifting—or, if she can't find anything better, makes a present of her own beloved Rosie the Rat toy—leaving these offerings on our pillows at night before bedtime or on the precise spot on the bath mat where we'll have to step when getting in and out of the shower first thing in the morning.

I used to be touched by the generosity of these unending gifts, taking them as visual proof of a deep and consuming love, or perhaps a desire on Fanny's part to go far out of her way to thank us for all the attention and care we lavish on her. Admittedly, there was more than a little condescension in my *Awwwwwww . . . Fanny thinks she's "helping" us. How cute!* perspective. Then I read somewhere that cats leave their humans "gifts" because they believe us to be hopelessly incompetent hunters who would, without their assistance, be wholly unable to take care of ourselves. This put a bit of a different spin on things. I realized that, all this time, it was in fact *Fanny* who had been condescending to *me. Awwwwwwww . . . Mom brings us back cans of food just like a "real hunter." Isn't that sweet?*

In fairness to Fanny, if we were ever to find ourselves in some post–zombie apocalypse scenario, she's likely the only one of the four of us who would flourish. There's a neighbor cat who occasionally comes to poop in our backyard, and Clayton always squeals in outrage if he happens to witness, through the French doors leading outside, his territory being defiled in this way, but that's about the extent of his interest in our local wildlife population. Clayton loves throttling his toys, but, bless his fuzzy little heart, he has no more interest in hunting an actual bird or rodent than your grandmother does. As for Laurence and me— as the old joke goes, we have no hunting skills whatsoever except, that is, when we're hunting for bargains. (Although I'd pit my bargain-hunting skills against anyone's. *Anyone's*, I tell you!)

And here, I think, we've arrived at the crux of Fanny's outsized sway over the rest of us. She's a gifted—not to mention lethal—natural athlete in a family of . . . well . . . two middle-aged bookwormish writers and a roly-poly, three-legged feline brother. Fanny is the Nietzschean *überfrau* to our uncoordinated *untermenschen*. She intimidates us with her physical superiority, while at the same time maintaining—granted, with charming and frequent displays of affection—just enough inscrutable distance to impress upon us a sense of her ultimate unavailability. She's like that really cool girl in your high school class who maybe you were technically friends with, but the friendship was never truly equal, and you were always trying harder to impress her than vice versa.

So the question isn't *How is it that Fanny manages to rule us all?* The real question is *How could it possibly be any other way?*

STILL, IN ALL, FANNY'S DICTATORSHIP OVER US USED TO BE AN essentially benevolent one. She never exercised her authority in obtrusive or oppressive ways—except, possibly, upon poor Laurence, who had to (and still has to) spend half his night tending to Fanny's scritching needs. For the most part, all Fanny ever seemed to want from any of us was on-demand affection and playtime when she was in the mood for it—and it probably goes without saying that we were always happy to comply without feeling the least bit put upon.

Then came the fateful day about six months ago when the helpful sales clerk at Fussy Friends, our local pet store, slipped a small sample bag of dry cat food in with my usual purchase of canned delicacies. And life as we knew it changed forever.

Dry food had been verboten in our home for quite some time. Scarlett was briefly diabetic during her last years, and it was only by cutting out dry food entirely that I'd been able to bring her condition under control and wean her off insulin shots. There was a minor flirtation with dry food once again during Homer's own final battle, with liver disease, when we were trying hard to keep him eating and Kitten Chow reliably made him so, *so* happy. Of course we let Clayton and Fanny partake of the Kitten Chow as well. It would have been impossible to keep them away from any food we'd left out for Homer, and I reasoned that—at a year and a half old—they were still young enough to outgrow any of the damaging long-term effects that dry food might have on their weight or blood sugar.

Perhaps I was right about the long-term effects, but I'd severely underestimated the short-term ones. Only a few weeks after Homer was gone, Clayton developed a urinary tract blockage—a condition that, while easily treated if caught in time, is still life threatening. Had I waited only a few hours longer to rush him to the 24-hour emergency animal hospital, we might have lost Clayton as well. It was a condition that some male cats were prone to, the doctor on call told me, before sternly warning that a diet of dry food could bring on another bout—one that, a second time around, might not end as happily as the first. I didn't need to be told twice. And, from that day in 2013, not so much as a single kibble had crossed our doorstep.

But then I unexpectedly found that small packet of (the packaging assured me) high-quality, grain-free dry food among my purchases, and I wavered. After all, I told myself, I typically gave Clayton and Fanny a handful of dry cat treats over the course of the day (they needed *some* crunch to clean their teeth with), and there hadn't been any adverse effects in all these years. Would it truly be catastrophic if I were to give them the *tiniest* smidgen of a sampling, just this *one* time, from this really *very* small sample bag I'd ended up with by accident?

Actually, it was Fanny—our self-appointed bag inspector, who carefully noses through each and every bag we bring into the house—who first discovered the dry food sample. Even through the sealed plastic, she could smell that it contained something intended for her. Dragging it carefully from its nest among the canned foods as I unpacked the shopping bag, Fanny ran one exploratory paw over the plastic and then—upon finding that nothing happened, positive or negative—began pawing at it in earnest. The plastic was sturdy enough that even when her claws came out, they didn't create more than superficial damage and certainly didn't succeed in ripping the thing open. Nevertheless, her intense desire to get at its contents was obvious.

Before that day, Fanny had been neither a poor eater nor an enthusiastic one. Even her abiding interest in the hunt seemed to be separated entirely from an interest in food; it always appeared to me that Fanny craved a kill purely for its own sake. As a general rule, she ate exactly the amount of food she needed—no more, no less—with an apparent indifference to the specifics of flavor or brand that was the exact opposite of Clayton's epicureanism.

Clayton was not only deeply concerned with getting sufficient food on a regular schedule, but he also demanded both abundance and constant variety. It was a fairly frequent occurrence in our home for Clayton to turn up his nose at a flavor of food that he'd wolfed down greedily only days before. *I'm bored with this! Bring me something new!* Clayton's vet had told me that the most important thing in keeping his urinary tract from blocking up again was to make sure he always had enough liquid moving through his system—and if the urinary-tract blockage *did* recur, the doctor said, they might have to perform an expensive and risky penectomy to widen the tract permanently. Since Clayton had next to no interest in drinking water—not even from the fancy cat fountain I'd bought specifically to make the quotidian act of water-drinking fun and exciting (*It's like a game!* I'd exhorted, to no avail)—the only way I could be confident he had enough fluid in his body was if he was eating all the moist food I gave him.

It was this ever-present fear of dehydration that kept me dancing to Clayton's tune when it came to his dietary preferences. It was like a weird inverse-Freudian thing, where Clayton held *his own* castration as a continual threat over *my* head (*Gimme the food I want or the penis gets it!*), whereas I as his "mom" was the one who was concerned with making sure his little *schmeckle* remained intact.

So, just to see Fanny, for once, excited about something food-related was enough of a novelty to immediately enlist my sympathies. We spent so much time and energy catering to Clayton's dining predilections, but what had Fanny ever asked for in the way of preferred fare?

Nothing, was the answer. Fanny was a veritable angel from heaven when it came to mealtimes. She demanded nothing and refused nothing. She'd never once awakened me earlier than I cared to get up, or made me run back to the cabinet—or even out to the store, as Clayton sometimes did, if the proverbial cupboard was otherwise bare of additional options—because she arbitrarily deemed unacceptable something I'd placed before her. She ate whatever I wanted her to eat—or, more accurately, whatever Clayton wanted the both of them to eat—while never asking a single thing for herself.

And now, at last, in the pleading yellow eyes she turned my way while that little bag of dry food dangled from her mouth, she was asking. It would have taken someone made of far sterner stuff than I am to say no.

After emptying the contents of one of the cans I'd just bought into their bowls, I used a pair of scissors to cut into the sample bag of dry food (which was surprisingly difficult to open) and carefully shook out a small portion—perhaps a baker's dozen of individual kibbles into each bowl—on top of the moist food. I took the additional precaution of pouring a spoonful of water over Clayton's serving, so that it wouldn't be *too* dry.

The addition of water had the automatic effect of making the dry food less interesting to Clayton, who took a few experimental bites before nosing his share aside so he could concentrate fully on the meaty temptation of the moist food beneath it.

For Fanny, however, crunching her kibbles was an entirely different experience—one of bliss, of ecstasy, an introduction to culinary pleasures previously undreamt of in the realm of her experience. The look on her face, as she slowly and carefully chewed one kernel of dry food at a time, was almost beatific, like the rapturous expressions of saints and martyrs in medieval paintings. *This is the very food of the gods themselves!*

I'd never seen such a look of intense pleasure on her face—not even when Laurence was giving her a particularly indulgent rubdown. And, happy as Fanny's happiness always made me, lurking just beneath it was a slight sinking feeling—the whisper of a foreboding that trouble of some kind was already winging its way in our direction.

I'M GUESSING YOU HAVE A SENSE BY NOW OF WHERE THIS STORY is going. There's a reason that a certain subset of feline nutrition experts refer to dry cat food as "kitty crack."

Most nights it was Clayton who began campaigning for his ten o'clock dinner as early as nine fifteen. Usually this campaign took the form of standing in front of me and uttering an increasingly anxious *"MEEEEEEE!"* every few minutes, while I sat on the couch and did my best to ignore him or else placate him with a few rounds of fetch. Eventually, when either impatience or hunger had hit its peak, he'd decide that the "subtle" approach wasn't working and station himself at the top of the stairs leading down from the living room to the kitchen. If I happened to walk by the entrance to the stairway without actually going down the stairs, he'd grab onto the bottom of my pants leg with all his front claws, forcing me to drag him along, sprawled on his side, while he clung to my ankle and continued to cry "*MEEEEEEE!*" until—having dragged him all the way from the staircase to my computer desk—I'd bend down to detach his chubby little body from my ankle with a sigh and say, "Clayton, do you not *see* how this demeans us both?" (His hopeful "*meeeeeee?*" of response would seem to indicate that, no, he did not.)

But on the night of the day when the Miracle of the Dry Food had revealed itself to Fanny, she preempted Clayton's nine fifteen campaign with her own efforts at eight thirty. At first—at the unexpected appearance of Fanny so early in the evening— Laurence and I greeted her with our customary enthusiasm ("It's FANNY!"), and even Clayton woke from his pre-dinner campaign nap with a slightly befuddled air, as if he would've checked his wristwatch had he worn one. *Is it dinnertime already?*

It quickly became apparent, however—as Fanny ran eagerly from the couch to the stairs, and then back, and then back and forth again and yet *again*—that her early arising from her own pre-meal snooze had nothing to do with any pleasure she took in our company and *everything* to do with the promise of another helping of the heavenly dry ambrosia she'd sampled that afternoon. Her sharp meows of annoyance (*Feed me now! Feed me NOW!*) rose in both pitch and frequency as she found her demands inexplicably ignored for perhaps the first time in living memory.

I did my best to hold firm until ten o'clock. But between Fanny's agitations, Clayton's clinging to my ankle with greater tenacity than he'd ever displayed before (his usual histrionics having been emboldened and intensified by Fanny's), and the increasingly loud cries coming from the both of them—so deafening that even the pretext of watching TV or having a conversation was laughably impossible—I'd had enough. "This is no way to live," Laurence informed me at nine thirty, as I made my way in defeat down the kitchen stairs, trailed closely by my two triumphant cats. And, as he always does when the cats are being particularly irritating (but never when they're being especially *adorable*, I should note), he added for good measure, "*You* did this to them."

I duly poured the remaining dry food over their moist food—Fanny helping me speed things along by jumping onto the countertop and slapping the bag a few times while it was still in my hand to make it empty faster. *And that's the end of that*, I thought. When Fanny awakened me at six o'clock the following morning—a full hour before the designated breakfast time that Clayton and I had long ago "agreed" upon between ourselves—I was able to tell her with a certain grim satisfaction, "I'll feed you now if you want, but there's no dry food left."

Except, all of a sudden, the cat who'd never cared all that much about food had become obsessed. The fact that the dry food was, indeed, gone didn't even seem to matter in Fanny's new conception of how feeding should work. As the next few weeks rolled by, she always showed up promptly—significantly ahead of schedule, actually—for feedings and ate as much as Clayton did. Sometimes, if he was a bit slower to arrive with his stumpy, three-legged run than she was, Fanny would even snatch a bit of the food from his bowl before starting on her own.

I was now called on to provide food at all hours of the day—an array of chicken, beef, turkey, tuna, salmon, liver, lamb, and even rabbit (Fanny, the ruthless carnivore, loved sinking her teeth into bunny meat more than anything else), which Fanny demanded in even greater rainbow varieties than Clayton ever had. It was as if, after all these years, a lightbulb had flipped on in Fanny's head—the startling new realization that, *Wait a minute . . . food can actually be ENJOYABLE!* And Clayton had lucked into an unexpected new ally in his as-yet-unrealized life-long dream of pushing his mealtimes so close together that his entire day would be one long and continuous grazing session, interrupted only by generous stretches of naps and frequent games of fetch.

You'd think that this sudden uptick in consumption would have begun to show on her slender frame, but Fanny remained as svelte as ever. It was an ongoing (and envy-inducing) mystery to me how a seven-pound cat could essentially double her food intake overnight, not engage in one minute more of additional activity on any given day, and yet not gain a single ounce. A trip to the vet confirmed her to be in perfect health, so there was nothing more sinister at work than a six-and-a-half-year-old cat's abrupt decision to make herself as well fed—and thoroughly annoying—as possible. And if Laurence's and my reaction to seeing her arrive in the living room during prime-time hours had diminished of late from, "It's FANNY!" to, "Oh . . . it's *Fanny*," she didn't seem to concern herself one bit about the change. *I'm a middle-aged woman with a teenager's metabolism*, I imagined her thinking. *Who do I have to worry about impressing?*

The downward "negotiation" of scheduled feeding times began in earnest. Over the course of a typical workday, I seemed to find myself in a near-constant state of exclaiming things like "No, Fanny! It is *NOT* your lunchtime yet!" or "Leave me alone, Fanny—dinner's not until ten!" until Laurence, rather sensibly, pointed out that I might as well save my breath—Fanny couldn't understand what I was saying, and it wouldn't have made any difference even if she could.

Eventually Fanny learned that active bullying had its limits, a lesson driven home the night when—unable to bear any longer the ragged caterwauling that drowned out a particularly interesting movie Laurence and I were watching—I locked her in the upstairs bedroom for half an hour. After that, she took a more measured approach. Rather than trouncing all over my computer keypad at eleven thirty in the morning—too early and overeager by far for her one o'clock lunchtime—she now restrained herself to stalking the kitchen counters impatiently, occasionally knocking things off them just to make sure I knew, one floor above, that she was waiting . . . and waiting . . . and *STILL WAITING!* If I went downstairs for a glass of water and paused to give her a friendly rub behind the ears, then headed back toward the stairs rather than toward the cupboard where the food was kept, she'd use her peremptory front paw to whack me in the face a few times as I started to turn away from her. *Get back here! You haven't fed me yet!*

The day when I came home from my weekly Fussy Friends food run to find that, once again, six—*six!*—little sample bags of dry food had been tucked in with my other purchases, I inwardly cursed the cheerful and well-meaning sales clerk. I knew there was no way I'd be able to slip six bags (or even one bag, for that matter) past Fanny's eagle-eyed watch over all the shopping bags I brought home. Her ceaseless vigilance was fueled by the certainty, not entirely without justification, that if she searched through those bags often and hard enough, eventually she'd hit pay dirt in one of them.

And I was right. Of course Fanny, already buried waist-deep in the shopping bag, had discovered this trove. Having been raised in part by my grandmother—who'd lived with us while I was growing up, and who'd drummed into my head that "it's a sin to waste food"—I couldn't quite bring myself to throw away the little bags of dry food. And, as irritating as Fanny had become of late when it came to her food, I wasn't heartless enough to entirely deny her something she loved so much, especially seeing as how the kibbled manna had been dropped so providentially, as it were, into our midst. So I put the six bags in the cabinet where I kept the canned food. "I'll let you have a little bit later with dinner," I assured Fanny, "*if* you're good." Fanny's round-eyed innocent gaze (*who . . . moi?*) didn't quite succeed in masking her frustration, and I knew that I hadn't heard the last of this.

Later that night, while I slept next to Laurence up on the third floor, I awoke to a commotion of slamming cabinet doors all the way downstairs in the kitchen—loud and repetitive enough to rouse me from a sound sleep. After a moment or two of disorientation, I was pretty sure that I knew what it was. Even so, that much noise coming from the kitchen at three in the morning warranted further investigation.

I saw no sign of either cat as I headed downstairs—which only supported my initial suspicions. When I turned on the light in the kitchen, the first thing I saw was Clayton on the ground, standing guard over three little bags of dry food that had been ripped open to spill their contents onto the tiled floor. Startled at the sudden brightness, Clayton whipped his head around in my direction.

The door to the cabinet where I kept the cats' food was closed but rattling violently, as if Jersey City was experiencing its first-ever earthquake. After a few unsuccessful head bonks from inside the cabinet, Fanny finally succeeded in pushing it open and emerged from its depths holding one of the bags of dry food in her mouth—caught red-pawed and four bags into a six-bag heist. Her gaze rapidly swept from Clayton on the floor over to where I stood; upon seeing me there with my arms crossed, her eyes flew open wide with alarm and she instantly dropped the little sack of pilfered kibble. *Busted!*

It wasn't hard to piece together what had happened. The agile and sure-footed Fanny was capable of climbing much higher than the three-legged Clayton could. Scaling the cabinet shelves—which, being of equal depths, didn't make for the greatest staircase—to reach the one at the very top would have stretched her climbing prowess to its limits. Nevertheless, she'd managed to pull it off and had successfully reached the prize at the top.

Getting the tightly sealed bags *opened*, however, was where Clayton's barrel-chested physique came in handy. His upper body, which bore the primary burden of carrying the weight displaced by his missing hind leg and hauling his bulk on and off beds and countertops, had become highly developed over the years. So Fanny was the second-story man (and almost certainly the brains behind this little caper), and Clayton was the

muscle. It was Fanny's job to retrieve the booty, and Clayton's to then mangle the bags open so the two of them could feast on the contents.

It was the *purr*fect crime. And they would have gotten away with it, too—if they hadn't been greedy and tried to go back for all six bags of food, rather than contenting themselves with one or two.

Those little stinkers! I thought—although I couldn't help feeling a grudging respect for Fanny's ingenuity.

I don't think Clayton even realized he'd done anything wrong. He'd only been following Fanny's "orders," which is pretty much what he always did. He squeak-mewed his delight upon seeing me awake and in the kitchen at the decidedly odd hour of three a.m., and immediately hippity-hopped over to rub his face against my shins and wrap his thick, vibrating club of a tail affectionately around my calf. *Whatcha doing up, Mom? Look—we're having a party!*

Fanny's longer, snakier tail was decidedly half-mast as she crept guiltily out of the cabinet to face my wrath. Try as I might, however, I couldn't do anything but laugh. "My two criminal masterminds," I told them. Fanny's ears perked up at hearing the amusement in my tone, and she leapt from the countertop to the floor at my feet, looking hopefully up into my face. "All right," I finally said. "I'll give you a *little* now. But only a *little*."

I shook a few kernels into their bowls, then swept up all the remaining kibble and tossed it and the unopened bags into the trash once and for all (the trash can safeguarded by a child-proof lock that even Fanny hasn't yet managed to crack). I shut off the kitchen light while the two of them crunched away happily, and as I headed back upstairs I called over my shoulder, "*Nobody* had better bother me for breakfast before seven."

PERHAPS, OVER THE COURSE OF THIS STORY, I'VE BEEN A BIT TOO hard on Fanny—who isn't a food-obsessed diva all, or even most, of the time. Mostly she's a gentle and affectionate little house panther, who scampers about adorably with her toys (when she isn't snoozing luxuriously in the back of my closet) and who—when she creeps into my lap and turns her large, luminous, love-studded eyes my way—is delectably impossible to resist. Even I wouldn't succumb so readily to the imperious whims of an occasionally irritating cat if there weren't some pretty hefty trade-offs—if my life, ultimately, weren't better with her in it than it would be without.

And I've even found that getting up at five a.m.—and having three or four glorious hours of quiet solitude before the rest of the world encroaches with its clamor of emails and texts and social media posts—is more conducive to my writing than otherwise. As I write these lines now, with the pink glow of imminent sunrise just beginning to cast its warmth over the little backyard garden I can see through the windows of my writing nook, I'm grateful for the serenity of this scene—punctuated by the gentle snoring of Clayton curled up beside me on the desk, and Fanny in my lap as she waits for Laurence to awaken and tell her, for the umpteenth time, what a pretty, pretty girl she is. Two cats enjoying all the bliss of being recently fed and continuously loved. What more could any cat writer ask for?

Still, these days I keep a sharp watch over the sales clerks at Fussy Friends. *"No sample bags of dry food,"* I admonish sternly as they pack up my purchases—although by now they've heard me say it often enough to know the drill.

But then I always end up adding, "You can throw in a couple of extra catnip toys, though."

I mean . . . I'm not a *monster*.

The Worm
Has Turned

Every so often you'll hear about a "breakout character" in a TV show—some minor foil who was originally intended to appear in an episode or two, but to whom viewers have such a strong and positive reaction that the show's writers expand her story line from one-off to recurring, or from recurring to series regular, or perhaps even to a spin-off show of her very own. Frasier Crane, originally of *Cheers,* is a great example. Another is Mork, a one-off *Happy Days* novelty before landing *Mork and Mindy. All in the Family* begat *Maude* and *Maude* begat *Good Times*, which centered on the family of Maude's housekeeper, Florida. Saul Goodman, for *Better Call Saul*'s sheer virtuosity, may be one of the strongest contenders in this category.

If an inanimate object can be considered a "character," then I inadvertently created just such a breakout character in *Homer's Odyssey*: a little stuffed worm made up of three fluffy balls of cotton yarn (one yellow, one orange, and one green) with a small bell attached to one end. I believe that, at one point, the opposite end featured two glued-on felt eyes to accompany its sewn-on smile. But memory is a chancy thing and tends to become blurrier the farther back you try to reach. If the worm ever did have eyes, they went missing so early that I can't be positive my memory of them is true.

The stuffed worm became a generational hand-me-down of sorts in my little cat family. I had first bought it for Scarlett, and of the many toys I attempted to bribe her affections with in our early days together, it was the only one she showed any consistent interest in. When we adopted Vashti a year later, she immediately laid claim to it herself. I don't know if it can be said that Scarlett relinquished the toy worm with good grace—her interest in it had waned as she'd gotten older, although once Vashti showed a liking for the toy, of course Scarlett decided she'd loved it all along. But, after a handful of tussles and a few token efforts at reclaiming it, eventually she left it for the new kitten.

The worm was already somewhat woebegone by the time Homer came to us a year after Vashti did, the cotton yarn that composed its torso having been teased out into loops, here and there, by playful feline claws. This didn't seem to bother Homer, however. Whether it was the worm's by-then eyelessness (which Homer couldn't really have known about) or the merrily ring-ing bell in its tail (which Homer most definitely *did* recognize and love), he was instantly charmed by the toy. He took it from Vashti—who parted with it far more benignly than Scarlett had—and cherished it for the next thirteen years.

Neither of Homer's big sisters was ever as rambunctious as Homer was, and there were only so many of Homer's high-spirited hijinks that that they'd voluntarily participate in. But the toy worm was always up for an adventure, a forever-willing playmate and co-conspirator. It became his constant companion, his partner in crime, the co-star in all the thrilling adventure stories that Homer loved to act out—the Sundance Kid to his Butch Cassidy, the Jimmy Olsen to his Superman, the Luca Brasi to his Don Corleone. (That last one, admittedly, may be a stretch; as far as I know, Homer and his stuffed worm never had any trouble with the Feds.)

Its stitched-on smile would beam as brightly the tenth time Homer used his mouth to toss it high in the air as it did the first, and the bell in its tail—which made an excellent homing device for a sightless cat—would tinkle just as cheerfully each and every time it hit the ground. It would patiently "hide" alongside Homer—who usually did so in plain sight, the nuances of hide-and-seek being somewhat fuzzy for a blind cat—whenever he tried to catch one of his sisters in a "surprise" attack. And if Homer decided to sneak up on the worm itself, the worm never once made Homer feel that there was anything fundamentally wrong with his directly-from-the-front assaults—unlike Scarlett, whose ever-ready instructional/retaliatory front paw let Homer know, in no uncertain terms, that hide-and-seek was a game at which he was utterly hopeless.

The worm never objected to filling the role of sidekick or second fiddle. When Homer wanted to play Mighty Big-Cat Hunter, it was perfectly content to be dangled by its neck from his mouth, dragging between his front paws, like some impressive beast that Homer had managed to overpower all by himself through sheer pluck and ingenuity. Or, if Homer was more inclined to play rescuer than hunter, the worm would remain unresisting in one spot until Homer leapt to its aid and carried it to safety, away from whatever dastardly menaces he'd dreamed up to fight off that day. And when the day's play was done, the worm would nestle happily—sticky with cat spittle and scruffy with love—beneath Homer's cheek for a long, companionable nap.

We moved six times over the course of Homer's life and, at each new home, the toy worm was always the first thing Homer sought out when I unpacked the bag or box in which cat supplies had been transported. When we moved to New York from Miami—and Homer flew on a plane with me for the first (and last) time—I bundled Homer and his little toy worm into his carrier together, feeling that having a soft and familiar "buddy" riding alongside him might help alleviate some of the inevitable anxiety a blind cat would feel under such unusual circumstances. Homer ended up being miserable the entire trip anyway (ears as sensitive as Homer's don't fare well on airplanes). Nevertheless, the first thing Homer did, upon being released from his carrier in his new northern home, was to pull the worm out behind him, holding it carefully aloft in his jaws as he methodically explored this unfamiliar space and sought out a safe repository for his most cherished possession.

Homer was nearly twelve years old by the time I sat down to write *Homer's Odyssey*, and I wrote this favored toy—such an integral component of Homer's day-to-day life—into the story. It was impossible not to. Trying to write Homer without his beloved inanimate companion would have been like trying to write Linus from *Peanuts* without his omnipresent security blanket.

Still, I was unprepared for how popular that little stuffed worm became among the book's readers. I received first dozens, then hundreds of emails wanting to know whether Homer still had the worm, whether I had pictures of the two of them together—or even just of the worm, by itself—that I could send to them. They wanted to know about the worm's "health," whether it seemed likely that it would "live" as long as Homer did, and what new adventures the two of them had gotten into together since *Homer's Odyssey* had been published.

One of the things you always have to remember as a writer is that your own opinions regarding your work really only matter up to the point when your book is published. Once it's given over to the public, it's up to them to decide what's good or bad, important or unimportant. Readers have a way of disliking characters you'd loved intensely while writing them, or of finding deep meaning in details that you'd thought of as little more than dashes of color, intended only to flesh out the background of a scene.

So while I, personally, had never thought of Homer's toy worm as being anything more than my main character's prop much less a breakout star in its own right—once the reading public got hold of him, that's exactly what he became. (And, having acknowledged as much, I now feel obligated to refer to "it" as "him.") The worm became so popular that I even briefly toyed with the idea of giving him his own "spin-off." Perhaps an illustrated children's book about the adventures of Homer and his toy worm—two buckaroos and best pals, side by side, going off on a series of glorious, Technicolor adventures together.

By then, though, the worm was a pitifully bedraggled thing. Only two of the original three cottony puffs were left—the smiling green head, in search of greener pastures, having detached itself from the rest of the body some two years back, never to be heard from again. The remaining orange and yellow puffs were encrusted with the kind of years-long accumulation of grime that not even a thorough laundering could remove entirely. The four metal prongs that closed the worm's bell and made his tail ring out so jauntily had somehow pried themselves open. Now the bell didn't ring so much as make a hollow clunking sound when it struck the ground. Even worse, these days the metal prongs faced outward instead of curling inward, and their sharp edges made for the occasional nasty surprise if I happened to step on the worm unawares while getting out of bed in the morning. It was only a matter of time, I knew, before those sharp, gaping prongs did real damage to a cat or a human, or both.

Intense loyalty was one of Homer's defining trademarks. Even as the worm grew, day by day, to be less like a plaything and more like a tiny four-pronged switchblade with a grungy yarn hilt, Homer clung to him tenaciously.

The inevitable time came, however—at more than fifteen years of age, having long outlived whatever life expectancy his manufacturer had intended him to have—when there was so little of him left that the worm had to go.

THERE PROBABLY NEVER WOULD HAVE BEEN A *GOOD* TIME FOR Homer to lose his favorite toy, treasured since his earliest kittenhood. Humans, I learned, aren't the only ones who attach intense emotional freight to inanimate objects, forcing them to bear the weight of cherished memories and younger days gone by. We're not alone in our tendency to love things deeply that will never have the capacity to love us back.

THE WORM HAS TURNED

Having to say goodbye to the worm, however, only a few weeks after we'd lost Vashti seemed like an especially cruel blow.

Vashti had always been something of a buffer between Homer and Scarlett, though Homer himself was probably unaware of this. Homer thought, until the very end, that he and Scarlett were the best of friends. To not only catch up to Scarlett, who always fled directly upon picking up Homer's unwitting visual cues that a pounce was imminent—the low crouch, the wiggling backside, the silent, stealthy approach made in full view of everyone—but to pin her down in play and definitively *best* her was the unfulfilled dream of Homer's life. But even without the advantages that sight gave Scarlett, this would have been a challenge. She was the largest of my three cats—at thirteen pounds, nearly three times Homer's size—and the force of her personality, aloof and unyielding as iron, cast an even longer shadow than her physical bulk. Once Scarlett had decreed that playtime was over, the other two cats knew from long and painful experience that no appeals would tempt her back into a game, and there was nothing to be done except find some way to entertain themselves without her.

For all his high energy and big-cat-predator pretensions, Homer didn't have an ounce of malice or genuine dislike in him. So foreign were those traits to his personality, he didn't even know how to recognize them in others. When Homer swatted at Scarlett, he did so in play—and he assumed that she was also playing when she swatted back at him, even if she had an uncomfortable tendency to unsheathe her claws. That's just how Scarlett was, Homer surely thought. That's just what their relationship was—two lifelong buddies in an endless game of tag that didn't need to be won by either in order to be great fun.

Scarlett herself did not share this opinion. Just about everything in life annoyed Scarlett at least a little—the very oxygen she breathed to stay alive only barely tolerated by virtue of its necessity—but the thing that annoyed her most of all was Homer.

All Homer ever wanted was to play with someone. All Scarlett ever wanted was to be left alone. Therefore the two of them were, to a certain extent, at perpetual cross-purposes. But the fact that Scarlett would flee and resist, would swipe at him with her claws and wrestle with him just long enough to show him who was boss, was what made her such an enticing playmate for Homer in the first place. He was always looking for a foe to triumph over, a challenge to overcome. Vashti was too gentle and patient, too apt to let Homer have his own way without putting up any kind of a fight. Where was the fun in that?

Still, Vashti was *there*, and her presence was a kind of safety valve that kept tensions from escalating to the point of no return. After Homer had chased Scarlett around for a while—until she'd whacked him in the face hard enough to indicate with finality: *The game is over*—he could come down off his not-quite-fulfilled high by taking a few swipes at Vashti. Vashti would submit patiently, offering a few affectionate licks to the cheek that Scarlett had just slapped so remorselessly. Homer could then maul his toy worm for a while and, his excess energy expended for the time being, curl up with the worm for a long snooze.

But now Vashti wasn't here anymore. The safety valve was gone. And with the toy worm gone as well, Homer found himself dangerously low on appropriate outlets for the full force of his playfulness. Suddenly, Scarlett was faced with bearing the entire brunt of it all on her own.

If I'd been paying closer attention, I might have seen the crisis that was brewing right underneath my nose. But I was dealing with my own grief. And while I'd had a sense ahead of time of how hard it would be to lose Vashti—something I'd been forced to think about almost daily during the nine long months that she and I had battled her chronic renal failure together—I still wasn't prepared for the full, body-blow force of it when it finally happened.

Laurence likes to say that if you live in New York long enough, you look around one day and realize that everyone on the subway is younger than you are. Clinging to a pole on the 6 train one afternoon about a week after we'd lost Vashti—at a moment when my iPod, set to "shuffle songs" and in a bit of unfortunate timing, presented me with "Landslide" by Fleetwood Mac—I felt a swift and awful gut punch of pain so intense that I doubled over, and a girl in her twenties who was seated nearby immediately jumped up to offer me her seat.

I was only a year shy of my fortieth birthday. I may not have been the oldest person in that subway car, but I was far from being the youngest—or even among the youngest. I had adopted Scarlett, Vashti, and Homer when they were wee kittens and I was still in my early twenties, barely out of college and only halfway launched into what would eventually be my adult life. Now I was nearly forty. I was nearly forty, and I'd just lost the first of my three cats—the cats of my youth—to old age. And the swift certainty that hit me in that moment on the train wasn't just that the four of us would never—not ever, not even one more time in all the time to come—all be together again.

It was that we would never all be young together again.

I won't put my thoughts into Homer's head and say that he felt the same way I did. But, acknowledged or not, the passage of years and the changes that come with it are both inevitable and inexorable for us all. At thirteen, Homer was far older in "cat years" than I was in human ones. Of the three beloved companions of his youth—Scarlett, Vashti, and that silly, tattered little toy worm—time had taken two of them already, one swiftly upon the heels of the other. Homer had never known—had never, in all his thirteen years, even suspected—that someone you loved with your whole heart could just up and leave you one day and never come back. The suddenness of the change must have been disorienting for him in ways that I could no more fully understand than he could fully understand my own feelings.

Grief has a way of making us selfish. I had tried to give my cats extra attention, in the form of treats and cuddles, after Vashti was gone, assuming they must have felt a general sadness that was similar to, if still less than, my own. But I didn't stop to think deeply about how painful and confusing it all must have been for Homer—for Homer and Scarlett both, and not just for me.

I didn't think about it until a few days after that subway ride, when I found my two remaining cats engaged in what gave every indication of being a knock-down, drag-out, and utterly serious battle to the death.

I
T WAS A W
EDNESDAY AFTERNOON IN EARLY S
EPTEMBER, AND I
 WAS home alone, sitting in the bedroom and going through my copy of *Homer's Odyssey* to make notes for an upcoming reading at

Blind Cat Rescue in North Carolina. I had just put down my pen and picked up a glass of water from the night table when I heard it. It was the sound of a cat screaming, and it was coming from the living room.

It was a piercing, gut-wrenching, terrifying sound—a sound that I'd never heard before in my life, and certainly not in my own home. Nevertheless, I instantly identified it as Scarlett. Dropping my book but still clutching my glass of water—for no reason other than not wanting to invest the extra second it would have taken to make sure the glass was far enough from the edge of the night table not to topple off it—I ran for the living room. The sight that greeted me was one that would have been, only moments earlier, unimaginable.

Homer and Scarlett were locked together in a ball of teeth, fur, and claws, rolling around and around the living room rug, their jaws at each other's ears and throats. Scattered all around them, and flying up into the air even as I watched, were little tufts of Scarlett's gray and Homer's black fur. Scarlett screamed again, and Homer growled with an anger I hadn't heard from him since that long-ago night in Miami when our apartment had been broken into.

"Hey!" I shouted. "*HEY! STOP IT!!!*" I yelled so loudly that my throat immediately flared up in pain. "*STOP IT RIGHT NOW!!!*" But I might as well have saved the strain on my vocal chords for all the good my shouting did. It was as if Homer and Scarlett hadn't heard me. (Although, as the descendant of a long line of barrel-chested Jewish yellers, I was pretty sure even our neighbors down the hall had heard me.)

Never before had I yelled like that at my cats without having them instantly stop whatever dangerous thing they were doing that had made me yell in the first place—and never before, until this moment, had I felt so utterly helpless where my cats were concerned.

As they continued to tumble over each other in a vicious, snarling embrace, I knew that something bad was about to happen—that something bad *was happening already*. At least one of them was about to get hurt, perhaps seriously. And even though I was standing *right there*, I couldn't stop it.

It took less than a second for my feeling of helplessness to become terror, and for terror to morph into a kind of hyper-adrenalized, clearheaded rage. Moving swiftly until I was nearly on top of them, I dumped the ice water from the glass I still held directly onto Scarlett and Homer. I'd never been one to discipline my cats with a spray bottle of water, and this might have been the first time that they'd ever been good and soaked. So I was expecting the cold water to have the immediate effect of causing them to spring apart from each other in alarm.

But it didn't. It didn't have any effect at all. And I realized then what I had to do.

As I later explained it to Laurence, if you're going to break up a fight between two drunks in a bar by actually getting into the middle of the brawl to separate them, you should go in prepared to catch a punch yourself. So when I decided to reach my arm into the crazed tangle of teeth and claws that had been— only minutes ago—my two beloved and thoroughly trusted cats, I knew that it wasn't a *great* idea while also acknowledging that it was the *only* idea likely to put an end to this before anything irreparable occurred. I was still the biggest one of the three of us, after all. Nobody was better equipped than I was to play the role of bouncer.

Bracing myself, I plunged my arm into the frenzied jumble of cats. My hand took an immediate and bloody blow from the full force of Scarlett's claws but, gritting my teeth rather than withdrawing my wounded hand, I wedged it farther into their struggle until I had Homer firmly by the scruff of his neck.

Truth be told, I was angrier at Homer in that moment than I was at Scarlett—angrier at him than I'd ever been at any point in all our life together. I knew to a certainty that this fight was mostly, if not entirely, Homer's doing. Scarlett—who religiously avoided close physical contact with Homer even on a good day—would have tried to get away from him long before things had escalated to this point. If she hadn't done so, it could only be because Homer hadn't let her. That her usual round of claws-out warning slaps hadn't deterred him, and her far-superior weight hadn't overpowered him and guaranteed her escape at the outset, was a testament to how riled Homer must have been before the actual, serious fight had even started.

So I was towering in my fury as I lifted Homer off Scarlett by the nape of his neck. (*How could you do this?! How could you do this NOW, when we're still mourning Vashti?!*) And Homer was furious at me right back. I still don't know how he managed it, with the fur of his neck clenched so tightly in my fist, but he turned his head around—pulling so hard against my grip that the skin of his face stretched back until his teeth were fully bared in a violent grimace—and sank those teeth deep into my hand. He bit me *hard*. His canines struck a nerve in the tender flesh of my palm, and a white-hot bolt of pain shot all the way up my arm.

I dropped Homer instantly and sank to the floor, clutching my injured hand and letting fly a high-volume string of obscenities in both English and Spanish that I won't embarrass myself by repeating here (although they must have given our neighbors quite a turn). Scarlett flew from the living room and down the bedroom hallway, into the guest room at the far end of the apartment—fleeing me, no doubt, as much as she was fleeing Homer.

Homer had rarely ever hurt me before, and had never done so intentionally. Usually, hearing me cry out in pain was enough to bring on instant contrition and a round of apologetic head-bonks.

Standing on the floor facing me now, the fur of his back and tail puffed out as far as it would go, Homer hesitated for a moment, as if wavering between his current rage and the force of habits built up over the previous thirteen years. Then, hissing wildly at me, at the retreating Scarlett, at the heavens themselves, he turned and ran for the master bedroom and burrowed deep under the bed—finally managing, after years of trying, to hide successfully. I was reminded of myself at thirteen, when—positive that I was the first and only teenager ever to be so thoroughly misunderstood by her parents—I'd storm down the hallway to my bedroom after an argument, slamming the door behind me.

Our apartment was almost preternaturally quiet over the next couple of hours. Scarlett and Homer made brief, tentative appearances in the living room eventually, as if testing the waters, studiously avoiding each other and me before heading once again for the solitude of their respective bedroom sanctuaries. Though I didn't see much of them, I saw enough to ascertain that neither cat was bleeding or limping, or swelling up in an ear or limb.

I, however, hadn't fared as well. By the time Laurence arrived home, my right hand had swollen to roughly the size of a catcher's mitt. Aghast, he immediately ferried me to the emergency room for a tetanus shot and antibiotics.

When you spend five or six hours in the emergency room (*My cat bit me*, in the realm of ER triage, not carrying quite the same urgency as *I'm having a heart attack* or *I've been shot*), you have plenty of time to think. I was long past being angry at Homer by then. After all, I had Laurence and my family—and the entirety of the cat-loving internet—to console me in my grief over Vashti. But who did Homer have?

I had made a half-hearted effort to be supportive, to help my cats through whatever grief they might be feeling. Clearly, however, I had drastically underestimated their needs. The intensity of Homer's pain and anger—because who among us is ever *not* angry when someone we love leaves us behind?—was proof. When you got right down to it, I had nobody to blame for that interminable wait in the ER—and the bruising tetanus shot that followed—but myself.

I HAD TAKEN VASHTI'S NAME FROM THE STORY OF THE JEWISH holiday known as Purim. The story begins when the proud and beautiful Queen Vashti, first among the wives of the king of Persia, is exiled from the land for refusing to dance naked at the command of her husband. The king then sends out an order to round up all the most beautiful young virgins in Persia so that he might choose a replacement queen. Among the lovely women paraded before the king's discriminating eye, the loveliest of all is a young Jewish girl named Esther, who is duly elevated to the exalted position of queen in a move that would eventually prove fateful for Persian Jews.

With *our* Vashti gone—along with Homer's happy-go-lucky toy worm—and in the wake of that ugly fight between Scarlett and Homer, I conducted my own beauty pageant of sorts. Instead of gathering a coterie of Persian virgins, however, I scoured the internet—and every pet supplies store within a reasonable traveling radius of our apartment—for cat toys, hoping that one among them might be sufficient to bring some joy back into Homer's heart.

My first thought was to try to find a brand-new version of the exact same worm, which had been one of dozens of identical toy worms on the shelf when I'd bought it in Miami more than fifteen years ago. I didn't remember it having cost much more than a dollar, and surely such an inexpensive and unremarkable plaything—just three little yarn balls with a bell at one end—must still exist.

So, it was with profound frustration and disappointment that, after searching high and low, I had to accept that I was searching in vain. I looked through page after page of cat toys online, browsing both large retailers like Amazon and Walmart and also small mom-and-pop shops with mail-order businesses in far-flung places like Idaho and New Mexico. I walked or took trains and buses to a full complement of Manhattan's pet supply retailers, hitting every single PetSmart in the city and also taking in my purview as many local stores as I could find: Litter and Leashes only three blocks from my home; Petopia, a legendary cornucopia of organic pet care options, in the East Village; Spoiled Brats in Hell's Kitchen; Happy Feet in

Midtown; Pet Central in Murray Hill; Petropolis way down in the Financial District. I even traveled to the Upper East Side to try Pet Town in Yorkville. Time after time, I drew amateurish sketches of the worm on the backs of receipts and other scraps of paper I found in my purse, trying to describe to a veritable army of happy-to-help sales clerks exactly what I was looking for.

In return I was shown just about every kind of toy worm imaginable—worms made from felt and plastic and rubber and gel and pipe cleaners; monochromatic worms and worms in vibrant rainbow hues; worms that were faceless and worms that bore ecstatic, manic-eyed grins; worms with neon stripes and wildly colored tufts of hair, like Troll dolls, atop their heads. I was also presented with anything that might, if you squinted, potentially be considered worm-*ish*, like toy snakes and centipedes. Sometimes a sales clerk would even haul out the *Yeowww!* brand of catnip-filled cloth cigars—which, while bearing an undeniably Freudian resemblance to the toy I sought, weren't quite the thing. Sometimes a cigar is just a cigar, but it's still almost never a worm.

It was probably just as well that I couldn't find what I was looking for—because even if I had, my quest was doomed from the outset. What difference would it have made if I'd found something that looked exactly like the playmate Homer had lost? Homer didn't know what things *looked* like. He knew only how things smelled, how they felt in his paws or against the fur of his face. A new toy worm would never come to him premanhandled by Scarlett and Vashti. Fresh from the pet store, it wouldn't carry the scent of the family he'd been adopted into,

the big sisters to whom he'd pledged his heart from his very first day with us—an aroma that told him *You are home* even when he was in some new house in a different city where everything but his family and his inanimate best friend was strange and unsettling.

I didn't want to come home from these forays empty-handed, however. From one shopping bag after another I pulled a seemingly endless array of brand-new toys featuring balls, bells, feathers, tails, and catnip. Trying to engage Homer's interest in them—to tempt him back into being his old, playful self—reminded me of my earliest days trying to win over Scarlett as a kitten. "What's *this*, Homer?" I'd say in that same playful, faux-astonished, talking-to-a-cat voice as I dangled one toy after another enticingly over his head. "What's *this*?"

Homer was far more willing to indulge me now than Scarlett had been then, giving each and every bauble I offered at least a few minutes of his attention. And while there was no specific toy that he seemed to take to more than the others, he showed a decided preference for anything stuffed with catnip. I had high hopes for one that was basically just a big round cloth ball, filled nearly to bursting with 'nip. Homer's undivided interest in the catnip ball lasted for two whole days, during which I thrilled with optimism as I watched him lovingly hug it to his chest with his front legs and kick "bunny feet" at it with his hind ones. But then, one morning, I came into the living room to find that he had systematically gnawed away at the cloth ball's stitching to spill the catnip it contained into an enormous mound on the floor—which he then proceeded to mush his whole face into. When he lifted his 'nip-covered snout to acknowledge my entrance, he looked not unlike Al Pacino in the final scenes of *Scarface.*

(A tip for cat parents: If you don't talk to your cats about 'nip, who will?)

Scarlett herself would often come out to investigate these proceedings. The expression on her face, as she found me doing my best to coax some enthusiasm from Homer with one toy after another, struck me as unmistakably amused. *I see we're doing this again . . .*

There had been no fresh outbreaks of violence since that one terrible afternoon, although Scarlett and Homer now regarded each other with a certain overly polite wariness. So I was more than a little surprised to find that, sometimes, it seemed almost as if Scarlett was allowing Homer to play with her—or, at least, tolerating his overtures toward play more indulgently than she'd ever done in the past. If, after batting a belled ball lazily a couple of times between her paws, she then took a few running steps after it as it rolled away and Homer ran after her, she didn't immediately turn on him with a snarl (*Stop crowding me!*) and walk off in a huff. Or if she was nuzzling a new catnip toy and Homer muscled his way in on the action, curious to know what she was so interested in, she stepped aside quietly without even whacking him in the face—although, once she'd allowed Homer a few exploratory sniffs, she'd use her shoulder to push him out of the way and reclaim the toy for herself.

Perhaps she'd been cowed by that thunderous and wholly unprecedented display of Homer's temper—one previously only hinted at during vet visits but never displayed in front of the other cats. But I don't think so. Her expression and posture didn't appear fearful. Rather, she seemed—dare I say it?—almost patient with Homer. Almost as if she had picked up some of Vashti's characteristic gentleness, after all these years. Or maybe it was just that, suddenly finding herself as short on friends as Homer was—and heading irreversibly toward old age herself—she'd come to appreciate the value of having a companion. Self-possessed in her crusty aloofness as Scarlett always was, it was difficult to tell what effect, if any, Vashti's loss had had on her. But perhaps she'd decided that wanting to be alone most of the time wasn't quite the same thing as *having* to be alone *all* of the time.

Then one evening, Laurence and I arrived home to a scene I'd never thought I'd live to see: In the middle of the living room rug—in the middle of a colorful clutter of new, barely used cat toys—Scarlett and Homer were curled up together, locked chest to chest and face to face, each with one leg slung over the other's back, holding each other in a full body embrace as they napped soundly and peacefully.

If I'd seen an actual miracle take place before my eyes—the Red Sea parting, manna raining from the heavens, my uncle Sasha picking up a check—I couldn't have been more flabbergasted.

I was torn between wanting to stand there and watch them, and wanting to beat a hasty retreat before one or both of them sensed my presence and the spell was broken. Silently waving Laurence into the living room behind me, with a warning finger raised to my lips, I bent down to slip off my shoes and tiptoed through the living room toward our bedroom. I motioned to Laurence that he should do the same.

"Did you put something in their water?" he whispered to me.

"Shhhh," I whispered back. "You'll ruin the moment."

I SUSPECT THAT, IN MY MAD HUNT FOR A NEW TOY THAT HOMER would love just as much as he'd loved the old one, I'd been engaging in a bit of magical thinking. Deep down, I had the wholly irrational idea that if I could get Homer to act young again, he would actually *be* young again. And if Homer were young again, maybe I would be too—maybe all of us would. Maybe we could turn back the clock far enough even to have my Vashti-girl—in some way, and against all reason—with us once more. Or, at the very least, maybe it would feel that way. Maybe our home would feel like it used to, falling into the same familiar rhythms we'd known so well and for so long that the routines of our days and our interactions with each other had relied almost more on muscle memory than actual thought.

But that was never in the cards. Clocks weren't going to turn back, Vashti would never return, and no new toy worm— or toy of any kind—was going to replace the one that Homer had loved. Just like the new cats who would eventually come into our lives were never going to replace Vashti. You can't replace something you've loved and lost—which isn't to say that you can't love again.

Homer and Scarlett never quite became the best and closest friends that Homer had always imagined—or wished—they were. Scarlett still preferred spending most of her time alone, or alone with me. But the two of them would now cuddle up together from time to time, which was a genuinely shocking breakthrough in the annals of Scarlett's personal history. And

Homer also got more comfortable spending time in rooms by himself if I wasn't around and Scarlett wouldn't let him get too close—which, after so many years of having his happiness in life solely invested in the physical presence of others, was probably a healthy development.

Life in a family is a series of ever-shifting connections, the complexity of which we tend to overlook because on the surface everything seems so simple and straightforward—everyone has their assigned role (parent, spouse, sibling) and tends to go through the everyday motions of that role without too much conscious thought. A family is like a body in that way, an amalgam of constituent parts (arms, legs, neck) that each work separately but still, together, create a whole. And when a wound opens, the body closes over the rupture. The resulting scar tissue may not look the same, but sometimes it ends up being even stronger.

So it was for us after Vashti was gone. It was time itself, and not some ersatz "replacement," that eventually mended the breach.

The day came, nearly two years later, when Homer was the only cat left—believing to the last that he and Scarlett had loved each other more than anyone ever had, except for him and me. And this, finally, was too much loneliness to expect a cat as social as Homer to simply work through and move past on his own—no matter how much time we might have given him. So we adopted a coal-black, roly-poly, "tripod" kitten we named Clayton, along with his littermate, a sleekly gorgeous black beauty we called Fanny.

If Scarlett had seemed, in the wake of Vashti's passing, to take on a little bit of Vashti's personality, it was amusing now

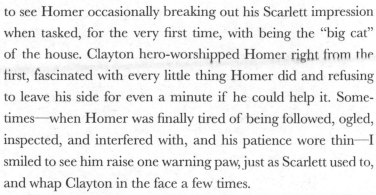

to see Homer occasionally breaking out his Scarlett impression when tasked, for the very first time, with being the "big cat" of the house. Clayton hero-worshipped Homer right from the first, fascinated with every little thing Homer did and refusing to leave his side for even a minute if he could help it. Sometimes—when Homer was finally tired of being followed, ogled, inspected, and interfered with, and his patience wore thin—I smiled to see him raise one warning paw, just as Scarlett used to, and whap Clayton in the face a few times.

Clayton never seemed to take this too personally, continuing to bounce excitedly after Homer as he walked from room to room or jumped on and off the bed or couch or countertops—forever uttering his trademark, *"MEEEEEEEEEE!"* In my head, I always saw them as Spike the Bulldog and Chester the Terrier from those old Looney Tunes cartoons—Homer striding impressively down the hallway while Clayton scampered eagerly around him in circles. *What are you doing, Homer? What are you doing today? Where are you going, Homer? Huh? Can I come with you, Homer? Can I?*—until finally Homer's paw would rise to backhand Clayton's snout with an impatient, *Ehhhhh . . . shut up.*

For all of Homer's newfound curmudgeonliness, it turned out that Clayton and Fanny made for better playmates than the fake worm ever had, and Homer soon warmed up to their naked adoration of him. His last years were as filled with playfulness, roughhousing, and adventure games as his first had been—maybe even more so.

What I learned is that while clocks will never run backward, and things that are lost may never return, the heart is a resilient organ that knows how to take care of itself—if you get out of its way and allow it to do so.

I also learned that, if you've just lost someone you loved dearly, and your world has flipped over into some Bizarro version of itself that makes you feel like a stranger in your own life, you should never—under any circumstances—in the freshness of your grief listen to "Landslide" by Fleetwood Mac.

Seriously. Don't do it.

CURL UP WITH A CAT TALE!

Thanks for reading these "tails," collected from the
Curl Up with a Cat Tale monthly series. If you'd like to enjoy
a new cat tale just like these each and every month, go to
www.gwencooper.com/cat-tales. Subscribing is
inexpensive, super simple, and will give you a fresh dose of
feline goodness to look forward to every four weeks!
www.gwencooper.com/cat-tales

**And for a <u>FREE</u> copy of an exclusive,
all-new Cat Tale by Gwen Cooper,
visit www.gwencooper.com.**

FOLLOW US ONLINE!

f homerblindcatfans

🅾 homerblindcat

🐦 homerblindcat

Homer, the world-renowned Blind Wonder Cat, returns this holiday season with an ins-*purr*-ational tale filled with holiday cheer!

FIFTEEN YEARS EARLIER, doctors had warned that Homer—a tiny, sightless kitten—was unlikely to survive and probably wouldn't have much of a life even if he did. Miraculously and against all the odds, however, Homer grew into a feline dynamo. Now, only two weeks before Christmas, with doctors once again decreeing that Homer didn't have much time, Homer showed everyone that he still had one more miracle left in him.

Acknowledgments

Heartfelt thanks to the following, without whose support this book wouldn't have been possible:

Literary agent Beth Davey, who saw potential in the Curl Up with a Cat Tale series—and this book—that even I didn't see.

The phenomenal team at BenBella Books: Leah Wilson, my sharp, insightful, and detail-oriented editor, who polished every single word in this book to its highest gloss; Karen Wise, the best copy editor I've ever worked with; Sarah Avinger, for her gorgeous cover designs of both this book and the monthly Curl Up with a Cat Tale stories; Monica Lowry in production, who smoothed over all the initial kinks in creating and distributing the monthly series; Heather Butterfield in marketing; and, of course, Glenn Yeffeth, without whose vision and faith none of this would ever have been written.

My family: My mother, Barbara Cooper; my sister, Dawn Cooper-Jackson; and my brother-in-law, Tyler Jackson. Also my mother-in-law, Saundra Lerman; my father-in-law, Ben Lerman (1936 – 2016); my sister-in-law, Hillary Cole; and my nephews, Alex and Zachary Cole.

My father, David Cooper (1943 – 2017), from whom I inherited a love of animals that still remains one of the great joys of my life.

Melanie Paradise—true friend, dedicated rescuer, and the greatest focus group of one that any cat writer could ask for.

Michele Rubin—former editor and forever friend, without whom I would never have published a single word.

My husband, Laurence Lerman—my best friend, my biggest hero, and still and always the first editor, collaborator, and idea lab for everything I write.

Most of all, I'd like to thank the subscribers to the Curl Up with a Cat Tale monthly series, whose faith in my ability to pull this off every month remains my biggest inspiration:

9th Life Hawaii, Lisa Abramowitz, Jen Acevedo, Rennie Ackerman, April Adams, Alicia Addeo, Pilar Albornoz, K Alex, Lori Alexander, Cori Allcock, Tara Allhands, Terrie Allison, Kevin Allred, Barb Alterman, Anna Amato, Cookie Ambler, Perry Ander, Hal Anderson, Jeanne Anderson, Sarah Anderson, Wendelyn Anderson, Laura Andrade, Kim Angle, Joyce Anthony, Barbara Antol, Christine Arbet, Ann Armijo, Amy Armour, April Arnold, Kristie Asel, Ariaal Ashlie, Lynn Athans, Wesley Atkinson, Dave Attell, Valerie Atwell, Jeanine Aubertin, Maria Auditor, Margaret Auld-Louie, Dave Avellone, Jayne Ayre, Charlene Bader, Barbara Bailes, Angie Bailey, Linda Balanesi, Joy Balla, Marcia Balonis, Kathy Banfield, BJ Bangs, Jennifer Bank, Joan Barlow, Tobin Barnecut, Carolyn Barnes, Lyl Barnes, Susan Barnes, Thomas Barr, Jamery Barry, Sandy Barstow, Karl Barsun, Holly Bartolotta, Anthony Charles, Russell Batten, Paul Battipaglia, Nancy Bauer, Mary Bauman-Stanhope, Gisele Baxter, Dawn Bean, Brenda Beasley, Elicia Beckerman, Beth Belew, Renee Bell, Isabelle Belman, Cheryl Bennett, Kathleen Bergeron, Geraldine Berggren, Zina Bergman, Joan Berkowitz, Monique Bernatchez, Adrienne Betar, Melissa Bethel, Marian Bickenbach, Julie Bickerstaff, Ginny Billodeau, Aldona Birmantas, Danielle Bissett, Debbie Blackburn, Patricia Blaho, Mark Blanchard, Mary Bledsoe, Gloria Blomberg, Wendy Bloomenrader, Janet Blume, Dawn Boarts, Melissa

ACKNOWLEDGMENTS

Boesch, Maria Bohager, Pam Bonanno, Melissa Bonnette, Jan Borgstadt, Ann Bosch, Risa Botvinick, Penny Boulis, Bonnie Bowles, Carey Boyce, Susan Bovett, Alyssa Bowker, Gloria Boyer, Kristy Brabon, Eva Bradshaw, Jennifer Bradshaw, Steve Brazeau, Jennifer Breedlove, Georgetta Brickey, Cynthia Brink, Robin Brock, Cathy Bromberg, Carolyn Brooks, Serena Brooks, Amanda Brooks-Kassak, Lisa Broshar, Emma Broun, Leona Brovitz, Dawn Brown, Catherine Brown, Dorothy Brown, Sarah Brown, Sheridan Brown, Susan Brown, Teresa Brown, Amy Brownmeier, Donna Brugger, Trish Bubenik, Patricia Bubenik, Jean Buckholz, P. Jo Anne Burgh, Sharon Burkett, Karen Burnette, Kate Burns, Len Burns, Jane Burrell, Catherine Burtch, Sandy Buzzelli, Lisa Byrd, Debbie Cabrera, Kim Cabrera, Michelle Cairol, Nalin Caldera, Staci Callahan, Sandra Calloway, Christa Campbell, Alexandra Camps, Kathy Canova, Deborah Cappa-Kotulski, Hillary Carlip, Joan Carlson, Lisa Carnley, Kris Carpenter, Kelly Carroll, Leslie Carter, Marie Carter, Joey Carvello, Georgia Carver, Maureen Casey, Ruth Castleberry, Staci Cate, Sharon Cathcart, Shellie Cavallaro, Sandra Cencelewski, Rennie Chamberlain, Mark Chambers, Steve Chang, Nancy Chapin, Linda Chase, Beth Cheadle, Patricia Chelton, Lisa Cheney, Cheryl Cheng, Pauline Chin, Maria Cisneros, Debra Clancy, Jamie Clapp, Michelle Clark, Samantha Clark, Lana Clayton, Debra Clear, Leslie Cobb, Sarah Coffin, Alexander Cole, Dawn Cole, Hillary Cole, Karen Cole, Maria Cole, Zachary Cole, Dana Colling, Britt Collins, Jane Collins, Merritt Scott Collins, Linda Conte, Veronique Guillemin Colomb, Deborah Conklin, Bonita Connolly, Barbara Cooper, Onan Cordova, Teresa Corner, Jean Cortes, Margarita Cortes, Roxanne Coryell, Cami Cottam, Jade Courville, Millie Covelli, Cindy Cowlishaw, April Crawford, Kelley Crawford, Kevin Crawford, Katherine Crispin, Lynda Criswell, Debbie Crnkovic, Christopher Crockett, Lori Croll, Marty Crome, Sheri Cromley, Susan Crosby, Jenna Cross, Denine Cruit, John Culp, Anna Curtis, Heather Curtis, Pete Cusack, Debbie Cuthbertson, Mary Ann Cwikla, Caroline Dahlstrom, Holly Dakos, Lauren Dale, Robert Dalton, Wayne & Micky Danieks, Arlene Davis, Sharon Stakofsky Davis, Marjorie Dawson, Marilyn Dawson, Alicia De Dios, Robin De Tota, Karen Deakins, Charlene Dean, Irene

Dean, Deanna Decko, Nancy Degenkolb, Nancy Delain, Carla DeLay, Kay DeMeritt, Victoria Denison, Paula DeNitto, Jane Dent, Mindy Defelice, Nancy DePaolo, Tyna Derhay, PL Derickson, Christina DeSalvo, Nicole Descoteaux, Cyndi Devlin, Katie DeYoung, Cathy Diaz, Patty Diaz, Rebecca Diaz, Charles Dickey, Judy Dillon, Maria DiMeglio, Sara Dinsmore, Denise Dixon, Margaret Domanski, Dianne Donadio, Melissa Donahue, Jenafor Donng, Chris Donohue, Sharyn Dooley, Dennis Doros, Judith Dorsey, Tonja Douge, Heather Dougherty-Gardner, Marilou Doughty, Jessica Dowling, Dennis Down, Debbie Driggers, AnnaMarie Dritto, Judith Duarte, Lu Ann Dumont, Suzanne Dunaway, Michael Dunkley, Alyssa Dunn, Danny Duran, Jane Dusek, Toni Eames, Cynthia Eardley, Brenda Eberst, Edith Eckert, Dicey Efantis, Lara Ehlers, Theresa Eilertsen, Peggy Eisenhauer, Irene Eldridge, Chloe Elkins, David Elliott, Leslie Ellis, Paul Engelberg, Peggy England, Bruce Erdman, Grayce Erickson, Judith Erickson, Carly Ervolino, Diana Essert, Tim Essert, Shelley Etherington, Sherri Eubanks, Annalie Evans, Patricia Everson, Birgit Eyrich, Robin Fales, John Falicki, Sam Faith, Maureen Farley, Vicki Faretta, Mari Fecarotta, Jodi Feinstein, Rachel Feinstein, Marlene Fennimore, Lydia Feole, Christine Ferguson, Fay Ferguson, Tom Ferguson, Giuliana Fernandez, Margaret Filanosky, James Finn, Judith Fiorot, Dena Fischer, Carole Fisher, Lisa Fisher, Sondra Fitch, Michael Flanary, Catherine Fleming, Lisa Flores, Marjorie Flowers, Shawn Flynn, Randy Fontana, Debbie Foresman, Jamie Forster, Carmel Forte, Diana Foster, David Frankel, Doreen Fraser, Connie Fraser, Carolyn Frederick, Becky Fredericks, Debra Free, Sharyn Fresia, Jana Fuentes, Gina Fulkerson, Adelaide Fullilove, Troy Fuss, Suzanne Gadelmeyer, Michelle Gahan, Kay Gale, Kelly Galloway, Denise Gamble, Shirley Gans, Melinda Garman, Danielle Garnier, Julia Garrett, Kathy Gasper, Nancy Gavin, Debi Geck, Nancy Gerstman, Lisa Gharebaghi, Cher Gibson, Kelly Giger, Ana Morales Gillard, Tim Gilmore, Tracy Ginnane, Christine Girty, Caren Gittleman, Sarah Glajch, Amy Glass, Rebecca Glen, Neil Glick, David Glicksman, Barbara Glover, David Gluckman, Sandra Godwin, Diane Gofferman, Elaine Goldberg, Michelle Goldberg, Nikki Goldberg, Denise Goll, Mandie Nickless Gonzales, Miriam Gonzalez, Chrystal Goodman, Kate

ACKNOWLEDGMENTS

Goodman, Sara Goodman, Breana Goodwin, Mary Anne Goodwin, Laurie Googasian, Laura Gould, Missy Grady, Christine Graham, Susan Graham, Ed Grant, Jacqui Grant, Joan Grasamkee, Beate Graves, Brenda Gray, Christine Gray, Jenny Gray, Marie Gray-Salas, Kathy Greathouse, Etty Green, Miriam Green, Samantha Green, Vickie Greenleaf, Robert Greenwald, Arin Greenwood, Lorraine Gregoire, Michele Gregoire, Vicki Greif, Janet Griebel, Kristi Grier, Staci Griesbach, C Griffin, Nancy Griffin, Alec Griffith, Diana Griffith, Ann Grismore, Brenda Gross, Brian Gross, Bonnie Grosshauer, Anna Gruber, Donna Guerrette, Andrea Guidebeck, April Gutierrez, Adriana Gwyn, Anita Hadley, Heather Hadley, Susan Haenicke, Dorian Hafen, Shellie Hagan, Liz Haggar, Sue Hains, Brenda Hake, Martha Halberstadt, Bobbi Hale, Carol Hall, Christina Hall, Diane Hall, Lisa Hallman, Judy Halls, Jessica Halverson, Rebecca Hammond, Barbara Hanc, Lynn Handley, Sue Ellen Hange, Kim Hankes, Susan Hansen, Dion Hanson, Elaine Harcourt, Nancy Hardesty, Marianne Harding, Athena Hardy, Kathryn Hardy, Laraine Harford, Kelly Hargraves, Nancy Harlan, Janice Harper, Carolyn Hart, Brian Hartig, Bunny Hartshorn, Miranda Harvey, Jan Havener, Donna Hayes, Patricia Hayes, Sam Hays, Cathy Heagy, Sherry Heatherly, Leilani Hedman, Andrew Heiden, Stephene Heiden-Cilley, Sandra Heilman, Valentine Heines, Margaret Heinz, Anne Heither, Amy Heller, Maria Heller, David Helt, Jan Henderson, Ida Henderson, Leslie Hendrex, Susan Henkelman, Sandy Hert, Greg Hesterberg, Ken Higgins, Mary Hill, Karen Hill, Walter Hill, Donna Hillman, Irma Hinkle, Michelle Hiseley, Laura Hite, Ann Hobbs, Darlene Hobson, Christi Hocking, Sandra Hodek, Barbara Hodsdon, Bonnie Hoffman, Pamela Hoffman, Elissa Hohler, Rocki Lu Holder, Vicki Holland, Julie Holley, Ronald Holmes, Cornelia Holodnik, Diane Holstrom, Catherine Horan, Marie Horowitz, Teresa Hough, Joni Howard, Jennifer Howell, Maggie Hrvol, Brandi Humphries, Bertha Hurst, Jerry Inwood, Dawn Cooper Jackson, Susan Jackson, Tyler Jackson, Lori Jacobs, Lynne Jaffe, Lynne Jamieson, Mary Janicki, Sarah Jefferson, Andrea Jeffery, Valerie Jeglum, Patti Jenkins, Joylinda Jenner, Kaitlin Jerric, Donna Didi Joao, Kristin Jonas, Ellen Jeffreys, Joylinda Jenner, Stephanie Jewett, Inez Johnson, Jennifer Johnson,

Joseph Johnson, Kelly Johnson, Michele Johnson, Stephanie Johnson, Tiffany Johnson, Mandy Johnston, Kristy Jolly, Becky Jones, Carol Jones, Pam Jones, Patricia Jones, Roseann Jones, Carol Jordan, Janet Jorgulesco, Kellyn Anne Judd, David Juskow, Susan K, Cynthia Kaan, Susan Anne Kadlec, Marc Kalfsbeek, Becky Kalinski, Maral Kaloustian, Andrew Kaplan, Grace Karish, Danielle Kaspaoff, Nancy Kaufman, Janette Kavanugh, Kathy Keim, Carol Kaye, Stephanie Kazmarski, Colleen Kearney, Roberta Kendall, Lori Kelley, Cynthia Kennedy, David Kennedy, Jennifer Kennedy, Julie Kennedy, Andrea Kenner, Gayle Keresey, Lisa Kerns, Naomi Kerstein, Rebecca Kesler, Madelynn Kessler, Jim Kiick, Kathleen Kimber, Ingrid King, Ken Kistner, Marci Kladnik, Lisa Klein, Andrea Kline, Steven Kline, Susan Kline, Libby Klos, Barbara Knicely, Terri Knopick, Gina Knox, Alyse Kobin, Susan Koch, Jodie Koenig, Elizabeth Koerber, Emily Kolatsky, Andrew Kole, Joan Kotenski, Laura Kraus, Michael Krauss, Francesa Kraut, Paulina Kraut, Patricia Krieger, Don Krim, Kathryn Krstulovich, Stephanie Krupla, Rebecca Krupla, Sandra Krutz, Elizabeth Krutzler, Jim Kurack, Cathy Kuziel, Lora Kyle, Wendy Kyle, Maggie Labouisse, Anise Labrum, Richard Laermer, Brian Laffin, Cindy LaForce, Joanne LaFreniere, Renee Lage, Laurie Lamb, John Lancaster, Dean Landmesser, Elizabeth Langford, Marianne Langlais, Kristy Langstraat-Bolte, Glenna Lansdown, Pamela Lanser, Melissa Lapierre, Kathleen Lapinski, Catherine Larklund, Linda Larson, Susan Larson, Mary Lash, Joanne Latko, Jennifer Lauer, Susan Lauzon, Christina Lednum, Louisa Lee, Vicki Lee, Marcy Leftridge, Diane Leibel, Digby Leibowitz, Luann Leonardi, David Leopold, Saundra Lerman, Kathleen Lessard, Rob Levin, Torey Levine, Julia Levy, Chloe Lewis, Jan Lewis, Alan Licht, Megan Liebenberg, Sarah Lifton, Kim Lightcap, Karen Lightheart, Chukyi Annie Lindsey, Christine Link, Cynthia Lockie, Carole Loftin, Mika Logan, Christie Lopez, Matthew Lorenzo, Sharon Loska, Lyliane Lounes, Mary Love, Laura Lovell, Michelle Lowe, Dawn Lublin, Maria Lucas, Renee Ludwig, Sara Ludwig, Sue Lund, Chip Luonuansuu, Donna Lusthoff, Patti Lynch, Wendi Lynch, Stuart Lyons, Dawn MacAllister, Linda MacDonald, Beverly MacKenzie, Georgie Maddams, David Mainwaring, Jaye Majors, Grace Maldonado, Cindy Malnasi,

ACKNOWLEDGMENTS

Kathleen Mancini, Howard Mandelbaum, Kelly Mantin, Marissa Manzino, Melinda Mara, Deborah Maria, Joann Mariani, Stephen Marks, Rowan Marques, Melinda Marshall, Jill Martin, Phyllis Martin, Carole Martine, Jennifer Martinez, Stephanie Mascharka, Alice Mashburn, Angela Mason, Diane Mason, Malou Mathys, Randolph Matice, Eva Matthews, Nicole Mattingly, Fran Mattucci, Carol Mauch, Jana Mauney, Kathryn Mayher, Judy McBeath, Alice McCauley, Buzz McClain, Josephine McClelland, Sandra McClelland, Beth McClinton, John McCloskey, Theresia Mccollom, Katherine McCrink, Stephanie McCurley, Tricia McFadden, Carol McFarlin, Helen McGawley, Jessica McGeary, Janine McGoldrick, Wendy McGrath, Melissa Mchale, Maurene McHenry, Cindy McIntosh, Karen McIntyre, Eileen McIver, Iwana McKay, Pam Mckenney, Sharleen McKinley, S McKinney, Trudy McMillan, Laura McMillon, Marie McMurrain, Mary McNeil, Heather McSweeney, Melinda McTaggart, Karen McVicar, Lora Medley, Amanda Mefford, Lea Melone, Debra Mendez, Jeannie Menor, Hanneke Mense, Lisa Merkel-Phillips, Charles Merrell, Denise Merritt, Sandy Mester, Jean Meyer, Jill Meyer, Bessie Michaels, Susan Michals, Amanda Micheels, Valerie Mignault, Ernetta Mikels, Katherine Miller, Linda Miller, Nancy Miller, Nancy Miller, Patty Miller, Rana Miller-Owen, SL Mills, Connie Minor, Jenny Mitchell, Monica Mitchell, Patsy Mitchell, Karen Moffett, Selena Moll, Kiera Montgomery, Vincent Mosso, Lee Morakis, Lisa Monet, Pam Montgomery, Fretta Mooney, Michele Moor, Julie Moore, Kim Moore, Raechel Moore, Erin Morey, Melanie Morningstar, Maryiane Morris, Debby Morrissette, Kathlyn Mossberg, Joanne Moulton, Katie Muhlbach, MaryEllen Muir, Constance Mullins, Martin Mulrenin, Mary Munoz, Elizabeth Murphy, Julia Murphy, Mary Murphy, Mary Murphy, Mary E. Murphy, TJ Murphy, Pat Murphy, Margaret Murray, Jen Myers, Caryn Nagler, Pebbles Campanella Napakh, Andrea Nalesso, Christy Nappi, Amy Narramore, Sherrie Narusis, Doris Nash, Lesley Nelson, Annete Nepomuceno, Gail Nettles, Jeannie Newman, Jo Anne Newman, Alexandra Nichols, Yvonne & Snickers Nicdermeyer, Yvette Niesel, Jane Nix, Donna Nixon, Karen Noell, Nathalie Noland, Anna Nordlinger, Stacey Nordquist, Amy Norris, Janice Nouis, Milo & Sugar Shack

Nugent, Catherine Nunez, Deneen Nunn, Jeanette Nunziata, Ashley Nutt, Heather Nutt, Mary Oakes, Anita Obrien, Chris O'Brien, Martina O Connor, Patrice OConnor, Stacy Odom, Larissa O'Donnell, Gloria Oest, Petie Ogg, Cindy Ohara, Monica Ollendorff, Ann Olsen, Ghita Olsen, Cheryl Olson, Marlen Olsson, Misty Omer, Jennifer ONeal, Lori Oostendorp, Karen Keser Onyshczak, Karen O'Quinn, Rebecca Orr, Kristine Oslund, Karen Ostermann, Camilla Owen, Dorothy Ownbey, Sarah Ozemko, Jenny Paap, Andrew Paek, Barbara Paine, Donna Painter, Leslie Palleria, Amy Palmer, Bruna Palmer, Medwiin Pang, Crystal Paone, Melanie Paradise, Sandra Parchow, Jenny Parke, Lisa Parker, Jackie Pasquini, Susanne Pass, Suzanne Paterno, Terry Patrickis, Leona Patterson, Stephanie Paul, Jennifer Peace, Cynthia Pearce, Karen Penhail, Donna Penzo, Cindy Pepper, Ruth Perkins, Teresa Pesce, Terri Petto, Linda Petsche, Carol Philpot, Meredith Pickering, Susan Pieper, Susan Pierce, Dora Pingel, Bonnie Pinkston, Beth Pitoniak, Lynne Pitts, Rosemary Placzkiewicz, Natalie Plummer, Susan Pollich, Janelle Pollock, Chris Poole, Monica Popov, Lois Porter, Rick Posten, Patricia Powell, Cynthia Prentice, Sue Procko, Ann Pryor, June Putt, April Quillen, Donna Rail, Holly Raines, Leslie Ramalho, Vanessa Ramirez, Heather Ramsey, Kenneth Ramsey Jr., Holly Randall, G.L. Ratafia, Mary Ann Ray, Cassie Raymond, Mindi Reid, Debbie Revock, Linda Reynertson, Amy Reynolds, Ed Reynolds, Kelly Reynolds, Teresa Rhodes, Debbie Rich, Joan Richter, Bruce Ricker, Susan Rieger, Lisa Riesmeyer, Kathryn Rigsby, Donna Riley, Rebecca Riley, Robert Riley, Elayne Riskin, Joanna Rives, Jan Rivers, Carrie & John Robare, Roxann Robbins, Andrea Robbs, Michelle Roberts, Susan Roberts, Marilyn Robinson, Steven Robinson, Debby Robles, Rodney Robles, Roseanna Robson, Deb Rodkey, P. L. Rodgers, Jessica Rodrigue, Amanda Rodriguez, Doris Rogers, Pat Roller, Teri Roofner, Aphrodite Rose, Shari Rose, Tonya Rosengren, Maureen Ross, Ronda Ross, Sherry Ross, Astrid Roterman, Lyni Rowan, Karen Rowe, Marianne Rowland, Kelly Rubalcava, Estra Rubin, Meredith Rubin, Michelle Rubin, Marilyn Rumschlag, Angela Rupp, Kristina Rus, Michelle Rushing, Emily Russo, Wanda Ryngwelski, Jeanne Ryun, Luke Sabala, Virginia Saccone, Andrea Sachs, Dayna Safranek, Vera-Julia Sakins, Memo Salazar, Heidi

ACKNOWLEDGMENTS

Salgado, Jennifer Sampson, Carl Samrock, Jeanne Sanders, Daniela Sapkar, Diane Sargent, Sabra Savers, Janay Sawdon, Marilyn Saxton, Terry Shepherd, Glen Schallman, Ruth Scharbach, Susan Scheck, Colleen Schelb, Thanna Schemmel, Sara Scherer, Esther Schiffman, Jeffrey Schiffman, Tyler Schirado, Kathy Schlichthernlein, Pat Schmidt, Sandra Schnaidt, Lisa Schoelles, Deborah Schonfeld, Gina Schramm, Ann Schroeder, Laureen Schulte, Jennifer Schusterman, Rosemary Schwartzseid, Joanne Scott, Laureen Schulte, Jennifer Schusterman, Rosemary Schwartzseid, Joanne Scott, Patti Sears, Catherine Seemayer, Donna Selati, Tamera Selhayer, Cindy Senecal, Susan Senko, Cindy Settle, Roree Severance, Scott Shadkam, Luise Shafritz, April Shalen, Nancy Shannon, Marilyn Sharpe, Mary Sharples, Robert Shaw, Kelly Shedlock, Maggi Shelbourn, Tina Shelby, Ellen Shippy, Tony Shillue, Kim Shoaf, Rachel Shubin, Krista Shull, Arlena Sidaris, Karen Sidwell, Harry Siegrist, Kris Simmons, Nancy Simon, Cheryl Simpson, Marcia Sinclair, Libertyhawk Singingwolf, Lisa Skidmore, Val Slamka, Irv Slifkin, Gail Sloane, Melissa Smalls, MJ Smeby, Alice Smith, Carole Smith, Craig Smith, Diane Smith, Heather Smith, Kavita Smith, Linda Smith, Patty Smith, Rebecca Smith, Sandra Smith, Sherry Smith, Susan Smith, Dorothy Smith-Davis, Leslie Smothers, Diane Smull, Joan Snow, Carolynn Snyder, Alan Sobol, Barbara Solis, Lisa Sommers, Timea Somogyi, Christine Sorenson, Tove-Lise Sorensen, Sally South, Lisa Spears, Verna Spier, Sharon Spinks, Jacqueline Splitt, Emily Stafford, Liz Stafford, Jeanne Stamm, Carol Stanninger, Karen Staples, Peri Stedman, Barbara Steele, Judith Steen, Steven Stefanski, Milos Stehlik, Susan Stein, Jill Steinberg, Jan Steiner, Maryann Steinmetz, Natalie Stephens, Carrie Aldrich Stephenson, Tracey Sternberg, Doreen Stevens, Melody Stevens, Tracee Stewart, Rita Strain, Cheryl Strait, Jennifer Strait, Beth Stratton, Lisa Striebel, Stephanie Suglian, Danielle Sullivan, Dorothy Sullivan, Kim Sullivan, Linda Susral, Rhonda Sussman, Caren Swart, Susan Szymcek, Mick Szydlowski, Linda Szymanski, Kristin Taggart, Janine Talbot, Jane Talbot, Glennis Tan, Sue Tanida, Beth Tapper, Abbie Taylor, Brandy Taylor, Charlene Taylor, Penny Taylor, Victoria Taylor, Anne Teghtmeyer, Mary Teichmann, Rebecca Teischman, Valerie Terusaki, Dorene Thomas, Eve

Thomas, Patricia Thomas, Sandra Thomas, Stacy Thomas, Teresa Thomas-Harris, Lisa Thompson, Lisa Thompson, Paul Thompson, Freyr Thor, Cathy Thornal, John Tierney, Kristin Tilert, Martha Tillinger, Jay Titerle, Patti Tobler, Tomi Tomek, Mary Tonks, Erin Toon, Maryanne Togerson, Rebecca Torres, Robin Trampe, Michael Tronn, Margaret Tucker, Yvette Tucker, Catherine Turner, Jeannie Turner, Katrina Turner, Mary Turzillo, Kristina Ulloa, Mary Umholtz, Melissa Underhill, Renee Unger, Anita Uotinen, Peggy Ushman, Matthew Vacek, Randal Vallee, Roberta Velez, Heather Vigue, Linden Vimislik, Kristyanna Virgona, Kerry Vistisen, Marg Vlielander, Alexandra Vogelbaum, Renee Vorbach, Nancy Voss, Judy Wadsworth, Jessica Wagner, Lenai Waite, Hilly Dean Waldman, Lisa Walker, Nancy Walker, Sylvia Walker, Allison Walls, Nancy Walsh, Jennifer Walters, Cindy Ward, Carrie Warkentin, Cynthia Warren, Shirley Washburn, Michelle Wayman, Pj Webb, Terri Webb, Ruby Weber, Gloria Weier-Linke, Clint Weiler, Lisa Weinberg, Stephen Weinberg, Heidi Weiner, Charissa Weiss, Dan Weiss, Helen Weisse, Stephanie Welch, Julia Wells, Marsha Wells, Patricia Wells, Sandi Wells, Sharon Wemple, Lynne Wendelstadt, Tanya Wersin, Dave Wessel, Faith Wheatley, Derval Whelan, Lola Whiteheaf, Sylvia Whitney, Becky Whittington, Marguerite Wickens, Adelle Wiesinger, Deb Wight, Layla Morgan Wilde, Jessica Wilden, Denise Wilds, April Wilk, Paul Wilkinson, Adelle Williams, Allyson Williams, Kathy Williams, Lisa Williams, Margaret Williams, Luis Willis, Susan Willis, Brent Wills, Cynthia Wilson, Tereasa Wilson, Terri Wilson, Wendy Wilson, Jane Winegardner, Kathleen Winger, Michelle Wiseman, Judy Witt, Claire Wolfington, Justine Wolk, Amy Wollenberg, Kim Womack, Bret Wood, Claudia Wood, Laura Wood, Randall Wood, Rachel Woodisse, Anne-Gaelle Wozniak, Melissa Wratschko, Jennifer Wright, Shawna Wright, Shanna Wynn, Cindi Yaeger, Rebecca Yager, Marilyn Yaksh, Tosha Yanich, Susan Yarnell, Ardyth Yetter, Kevin Yorn, Trisha Yost, Bonnie Young, Gypsy Young, Suzanne Young, Geralyn Yousuf, Cari Yuzzi, Stephanie Yuzzi, Carol Zahnow, Emily Zalenski, Ross Zapin, Michele Zarichny, Kathy Zavala, Cathy Zeider, Steven Zeller, Wilma Zeller, Anne Ziemann, Steve Zimmerman, Jan Zipfel, and Marianne Zoricak.

About the Author

GWEN COOPER is the *New York Times* best-selling author of the memoirs *Homer's Odyssey: A Fearless Feline Tale, or How I Learned About Love and Life with a Blind Wonder Cat; Homer: The Ninth Life of a Blind Wonder Cat;* and *My Life in a Cat House: True Tales of Love, Laughter, and Living with Five Felines*; as well as the novel *Love Saves the Day*, narrated from a cat's point of view. She also writes the Curl Up with a Cat Tale monthly short-story series about the ongoing adventures of her "fur kids." Her work has been published in nearly two dozen languages. She's a frequent speaker at shelter fund-raisers and donates 10 percent of her royalties from *Homer's Odyssey* to organizations that serve abused, abandoned, and disabled pets. Gwen lives in New Jersey with her husband, Laurence. She also lives with her two perfect cats—Clayton "the Tripod" and his littermate, Fanny—who aren't impressed with any of it.